**Winner National Outdoor Book Award for
Outdoor Literature (2008)**

"A painful, beautiful and truthful memoir. The denouement, though expected, almost startles: suddenly it is happening, and very hard to read, with anguishing yet affirmative background." —Alison Osius, *Rock and Ice*

"Honest memoir." —*Outside Magazine*

"Partly a women's memoir and partly an exotic travel adventure story." —*Publishers Weekly*

"Of all the memoirs published during 2008, *Forget Me Not* stands out for (at least) several reasons . . . But perhaps the most compelling reason *Forget Me Not* should move to the top of your book pile is Jennifer's skilled use of personal correspondence from her husband to entwine his international climbing career with her domestic pursuits of parenting and painting." —Chérie Newman, literary producer, Montana Public Radio

"I think people will be inspired by this book." —Ann Curry, *The Today Show*

"*Forget Me Not* will stay with you forever. It is a beautifully written story of great love, great daring, great loss, and great recovery. Most of all, it is a story of great courage." —Tom Brokaw

"In its convincing depiction of both exuberance and pain, *Forget Me Not* could be called 'the complete book' of mountaineering and adventure. A tribute not only to Jenni Lowe's famous husband but to his tribe—those people who sublimate themselves to the belief that heaven is here on earth—this book will remind you to step outside and look up at the stars." —Caroline Alexander, author of *The Endurance* and *The Bounty*

"We've been waiting to read the Alex Lowe story and who better to tell it than his wife and partner Jennifer, a strong climber in her own right. This is a tough tale, told in compelling style." —Yvon Chouinard

"This is a gentle, strong, complex, candid, and niftily written book about three extraordinary people—Alex Lowe, Jenni Lowe-Anker, and Conrad Anker. You'll be glad that you read it because they and their story are so deeply worth knowing." —David Quammen

Jennifer Lowe-Anker

FORGET ME
NOT

a memoir

FOREWORD BY JON KRAKAUER

THE MOUNTAINEERS BOOKS

THE MOUNTAINEERS BOOKS
is the nonprofit publishing arm of The Mountaineers, an organization founded in 1906 and dedicated to the exploration, preservation, and enjoyment of outdoor and wilderness areas.

1001 SW Klickitat Way, Suite 201, Seattle, WA 98134

Copy editor: Sherri Schultz
Design: Mayumi Thompson
Cover artwork: Jennifer Lowe-Anker
Author photograph on page 284: Devaki Ananda Murch

The Library of Congress has catalogued the hardcover edition as follows:
Lowe-Anker, Jennifer, 1955-
  Forget me not : a memoir / by Jennifer Lowe-Anker. — 1st ed.
     p. cm.
  ISBN-13: 978-1-59485-082-0 (alk. paper)
  ISBN-10: 1-59485-082-8 (alk. paper)
  1. Lowe, Alex, 1958-1999. 2. Mountaineers—United States—Biography. 3. Snow and ice climbing—United States. I. Title.
GV199.92.L67L69 2008
796.522092—dc22
[B]

                          2007047024

ISBN (hardcover): 978-1-59485-082-0
ISBN (paperback): 978-1-59485-274-9
ISBN (ebook): 978-1-59485-114-8

For Alex, Mother, and Jan

contents

foreword

IN 2005, A PREVIOUSLY NAMELESS 10,031-foot mountain in Montana's Gallatin Range was officially designated Alex Lowe Peak by the U.S. Board on Geographic Names. It was a hugely appropriate act. Not only was Alex Lowe one of the modern era's most extraordinary mountaineers, his life was intricately woven into the landscape of southwestern Montana.

Alex climbed and skied prodigiously throughout the Gallatin backcountry, but nowhere there is his presence more strongly felt than in Hyalite Canyon, a steep-walled valley immediately east of his namesake massif. Each November, the hundreds of waterfalls that spill down the canyon's flanks are transformed into finely wrought curtains of ice, attracting climbers from far and wide. Alex was the first person to ascend many of these routes, among them an ethereal frozen trickle he christened Winter Dance—an intermittent stripe of ghostly blue ice suspended two thousand feet above the valley, splattered down a cliff as black as onyx. Ascending it demands stamina, a sensitive touch, unwavering mind control, and utter mastery of technique. Only a handful of elite climbers have ever succeeded. Alex referred to Winter Dance as his favorite ice climb. Guidebook author Joe Josephson calls it one of the top ten winter routes of the world. The blow-by-blow of its first ascent is one of many "Alex stories" that are told and retold around campfires and in climbers' pubs across the planet.

Among the Alex stories, my personal favorite describes his attempt to climb a route named Airborne Ranger (for reasons that will shortly become apparent), which is also found in Hyalite Canyon, in this case just two miles from the summit of Alex Lowe Peak. In November 1994, during a routine visit to Hyalite, Alex noticed a stalactite of free-hanging ice suspended tenuously from an overhang halfway up a 300-foot cliff. He resolved to climb it, needless to say, and a raggedy band of acquaintances materialized to join the fun. After dispatching the initial hundred feet of frozen terrain, Alex and his longtime friend Jack Tackle arrived at a small ledge beneath the icicle, the slender tip of which hung twenty-five feet directly overhead like Damocles' sword. Tackle continued slightly above the ledge to place a bombproof anchor and put Alex on belay, and then Alex headed upward.

Between the ledge and the hanging ice lay a vertical wall of crumbly volcanic rock. Alex climbed this insecure terrain until he was high enough to lean out across the void and gently tap the pick of his ice ax into the fragile icicle. Although each peck of the tool caused the entire icicle to vibrate in an alarming fashion, after just a couple of pecks Alex determined that the pick had lodged solidly enough to hold his body weight. Hanging like a monkey from the lightly embedded tool, he cut his feet loose from the rock, swung his legs across to the icicle, then hooked his second tool beside the first and began shinnying upward.

Soon his head was level with the place where the icicle was attached to the overhanging rock face, by which point it had widened to a diameter of four or five feet. Convinced that the risk of the icicle breaking off was now minimal, he allowed himself a sigh of relief. Looking downward, however, he realized that another team of climbers had moved into the line of fire directly below; any chunks of ice his crampons or tools might knock loose could strike these other climbers. Out of concern for their safety, he decided to climb no higher until they had moved out of harm's way.

But gripping the shafts of ice tools hooked into a free-hanging icicle is exhausting, even for someone as strong as Alex. As his muscles began to burn with lactic acid, he calculated that he didn't have enough gas left in the tank to hang on until the climbers beneath him reached safe ground. So he decided to hammer a barbed steel hook called a Spectre into the ice, clip his rope through it, and let the Spectre take the weight off his fast-withering arms. Ever so gingerly he tapped in the hook, and for a second everything seemed fine. Then, without warning, the icicle snapped like a breadstick. Twelve inches below the embedded Spectre it fractured, breaking off cleanly just above the ice tools to which Alex was clinging.

The icicle, weighing many hundreds of pounds, dropped into space with Alex attached, like something from a Road Runner cartoon. A moment later, after plummeting approximately thirty-five feet, the frozen missile smashed into the ledge, shattering into hundreds of pieces that ricocheted in all directions before continuing their flight to the ground far below. Incredibly, as the icicle disintegrated beneath him, Alex landed squarely on the ledge feet-first, and somehow managed to maintain his balance and not topple over the side. No less incredibly, the climbers on the cliff below weren't hit by any of the falling ice. As shards cratered the snow slope at the base of the cliff, Alex yelled to Jack Tackle, "I'm OK! I'm OK!"

"No, you are definitely not OK!" replied Tackle, who was looking on in amazement from slightly above and a few yards to the side of where Alex had miraculously landed. "You're way fucked up. Sit down! Now!" What Alex didn't know, but Tackle could clearly see, was that a large flap of scalp had been peeled away from Alex's head, exposing a sickening expanse of skull. When his boots had struck the ledge, his face whipped downward and collided with the blade-like adze of his ice ax, which sliced an arc across his forehead that terminated just half an inch above his eye socket.

Maintaining their composure, Alex and Tackle rappelled to the ground, where friends stretched Alex's scalp back across his forehead and held it in place with several yards of athletic tape. Then the entire posse skied back to their cars and drove to the Bozeman emergency room—but not before first stopping at a local coffee shop for triple lattes, because, as Alex later told me, "we knew it was going to be a long evening in the ER." If his mangled head and blood-soaked clothing alarmed the barista, she didn't let on. When they finally arrived at the hospital, Dr. Fred Bahnson had to throw nearly fifty stitches to repair Alex's face. Early the next morning, despite the trauma to his head, Alex returned to Hyalite Canyon with his friend Doug Chabot, climbed all the way back up to the scene of the near-calamity, and plucked the Spectre from the broken stub of ice above the now-absent icicle. A Spectre cost more than $30, and Alex, being a frugal man, had been concerned that some other climber might claim it as booty if he didn't immediately retrieve it.

Alex hadn't bothered to inform his wife, Jennifer Lowe, of the incident described above until Dr. Bahnson had finished sewing up his head and he was waiting to be discharged from the hospital. When Alex finally called to let her know what had happened, Jenni took it in stride. An accomplished climber in her own right, by that time she had been Alex's life partner for more than thirteen years. Back in 1982, when he had taken a 170-foot leader fall high on the Rooster Comb in Alaska, Jenni had been present at base camp to nurse his broken hand and badly bruised body. A few weeks later she was again present when Alex emerged dripping wet from the Bitterroot River after an even closer brush with disaster. With his hand still in a cast from his Rooster Comb fall, and the Bitterroot roaring in full spring flood, Alex had impulsively launched a borrowed canoe down a stretch of big water. The small boat had capsized and was swept into a logjam. As the canoe was pulled beneath the tangle of roots, branches, and tree trunks by the torrent, Alex somehow managed—by means of his astounding athleticism and pure force of will—to hoist himself onto a slippery log and scramble to safety, escaping certain death by the skin of his teeth.

Jenni and Alex were married soon after his near-drowning in the Bitterroot. By the time he rode the falling icicle in Hyalite Canyon twelve years later, Jenni recently mused, "I was used to Alex having mishaps—he had totaled three cars since we had been together."

Jenni's forbearance and apparent unflappability made a lasting impression on Alex's climbing partners—especially those of us who were married ourselves and had firsthand experience with the intense strain that climbing tended to inject into marital relations. Alex's friends and family often asked him if he had any idea how lucky he was to have a wife who loved him for who he was and who didn't try to rein him in. "Yes," he would reply. "Yes I do." He referred to her at such moments as "Saint Jennifer."

Now Jenni Lowe has written *Forget Me Not*, the story of her late husband's life, and those who read it will discover that in fact there were limits to Saint Jennifer's forbearance. Although she loved Alex fiercely, being married to him was not always easy.

Jenni recounts their long, passionate partnership with remarkable candor. She tells it like it really was, describing the moments of conflict and worry as well as the periods of joy. To no small degree it is this disarming frankness that makes the book so engaging. As William Faulkner declared after winning the Nobel Prize for Literature in 1950, "the problems of the human heart in conflict with itself ... alone can make good writing because only that is worth writing about, worth the agony and the sweat." Faulkner went on to explain that conflicts of the heart are "the universal truths," and that any story that fails to examine such matters honestly "is ephemeral and doomed."

Forget Me Not is more than a biography of one of the world's most talented climbers. It is also a deeply felt meditation on love, and family, and perseverance, and the inevitability of loss, and the need to be true to one's nature for better or worse—despite the terrible collateral damage that might result from doing so. Above all, however, this book is about a fascinating, complicated man—Stewart Alexander Lowe—whose heart was frequently and most definitely in conflict with itself.

Alex was kind, loyal, outgoing, emotionally transparent. He possessed a curiosity that was insatiable and ranged across all subjects. His love for Jenni and his sons, Max, Sam, and Isaac, was unconditional.

His energy was nothing less than mind-boggling, his enthusiasm infectious. Much more than most of us, he tried to do the right thing. Although he was incredibly patient with climbers of lesser ability, especially beginners, he had a hair-trigger temper when it came to accepting his own shortcomings, both actual and imagined. His moods could be dark, and when the black dog was upon him it was painful to witness—yet, paradoxically, he was the most optimistic person I ever knew. Perhaps his defining trait, though, was his inability to remain at rest. Compelled by forces beyond his capacity to control or even understand, if he wasn't asleep he needed to be in near-constant motion.

He especially liked to be outside and on the move long before dawn, breathing deeply in the cold morning air, appraising the universe from some high vantage with a sweeping view. Alex never said so, exactly, but I got the feeling that he savored the sense of promise, the sense of limitless possibility, implicit in those fleeting minutes just before the sun came up.

Many of the things Alex did on steep rock and ice were so staggering and so far ahead of their time that they were terrifying to contemplate. I, for one, was sometimes frightened by the risks Alex took, and by the number of close calls he had. But he always emerged more or less unscathed. I came to appreciate that when you were as strong and talented as Alex, the odds that applied to ordinary mortals had to be recalculated. The old rules no longer seemed relevant. I convinced myself that he was indestructible.

Sadly, on October 5, 1999, I was proven wrong.

—Jonathan Krakauer

author's note

Sent: 7 July 1999 (9:26pm)
From: Alex Lowe (on the wall) Trango Tower

Dearest Jenni,

Mark, Jared and I are starting our third day on the wall. We're still just fixing rope up the world's largest slab to the base of the steep headwall. Everywhere I look the little Alpine forget-me-nots are blooming more profusely each day. Thus you are always with me as I work away. I know how much you love those delicate little flowers and I have pressed some and keep them with me, with my little stash of family photos. Do you think you could come up with an idea for a painting that ties together these flowers and our love for each other?

. . . It seems natural to converse with you via electrons. I can hear the marmots whistling far below. Occasional grumbles from the glacier emanate upwards. There's nary a cloud in the sky, the Karakoram is magnificent today and I love you! You remain in my heart always and I will do nothing that jeopardizes my safe return to my family.

Infinite Love, Alex

When my husband Alex Lowe's life ended and the events following his death began to unfold, I knew right away that someone should tell his story. In his forty years, Alex had achieved legendary status as a mountaineer. His résumé of climbs was impressive, but what I didn't realize until he died was that Alex, the person, had made an impact on a vast cross-section of humanity. It was his character, his pure magnetism that drew people to him. Alex was on fire for life. "There's not enough time in this life to do everything," he used to say. "If only there was more time."

Alex and I were together for eighteen years, but during that time we spent many months apart, adding up to years apart. The words we might have spoken to each other were, instead, routinely penned on paper or postcards and mailed. At times they were carried by porter, yak, or any willing hand to mail drops that were days or weeks away. In the last year of Alex's life, emails were added to our exchange. Thus we communicated and sustained our love, even when we were apart. The words remain to be reread, relived, and now shared.

I read my letters from Alex many times since his death, knowing that he often wrote to reassure me but also to reassure himself that he would come home. "I always come home," he once told me. "What if you die in the mountains?" I asked him, and his answer was "I won't, because to die would be to fail as a climber. Staying alive is the first rule. Besides, I have too much to live for."

"Right," I persisted, "but what if you do die in the mountains?"

"Just throw me into a crevasse!" he said and grinned.

We both knew that objective dangers were very real at the level that Alex pursued climbing. We had lost good friends and realized that alpinists face a myriad of risks. We faced it together in our impervious youth, climbing as partners with Alex leading the way. He shared his passion for climbing with me when we were newly in love and I was a willing participant, always confident in his judgment and ability. As years passed, our life together evolved. I carved out my niche as an artist and mother, but climbing remained Alex's great passion. Although he was a loving spouse and proud father, it was climbing that defined him. It was his gift, and he pursued it with measured care and persistent glee.

In sharing my picture of adventure, love, and sorrow, I have made every effort to provide an accurate account of the people, places, and events relating to Alex's life. I have relied on his many letters, my own memory, and the memories of friends, family, and fellow climbers. But *Forget Me Not* is my perspective on Alex and our life together. My story continues after his death. Any misrepresentation of facts is unintentional. I have attempted to confirm all details, but some inconsistencies may remain, for which I apologize.

Alex's request that I do a painting with alpine forget-me-nots has remained a poignant yet nagging thought at the back of my mind since his death. In fact, it's the only written request he ever made of me, transformed in my heart to be his dying wish. In this memoir, I hope to paint a picture of the life that I lived with Alex, touch on his many accomplishments, and remember him as the extraordinary, but very human, individual that he was.

Introduction

I love the upward ways
To the sun tipped crest of the mountains
High over the billowy world;
Where the wind sings hymns of praise,
And the snows break into fountains,
And life is a flag unfurled.
—HARRIET MONROE

IT HADN'T OCCURRED TO ME that we would see Shishapangma
from our plane as we flew toward Kathmandu. I had asked Conrad
if we might see it from our trek in the Khumbu, and he said no. And
so in my mind I had resolved that I would not lay eyes on the formidable mountain that had taken my husband Alex's life and, indeed,
still held his body prisoner beneath its snowy cloak.

It rose before me from a sea of clouds that were astounding in and
of themselves. Great chasms of grey canyons dropped between billowing mounds of white cumulus tinged in pink. Never had I seen such
clouds. Shishapangma's south face stood brazenly above this heaven,
brightly bathed in sunlight, staring at me as if to say, "What better place
could there be on this earth? What could possibly be more beautiful
than I?" My throat swelled and tears blurred my vision as I pressed my

nose to the window of the plane, riveted by the glacial skirt beneath the south face. Knowing that this place was where Alex spoke his last word, took his last step, and sucked in his last breath of air, I strained my eyes to see every feature. Knowing that was where the avalanche tore down from her summit at unfair speed and caught him.

In an instant she took him from us and changed our lives forever. I had hated her and yet, as I looked upon Shishapangma, I was stunned by her beauty. I stared until our plane began to descend and the clouds rose to conceal her. Conrad gently took my hand and whispered "You are strong" and "I am here for you." Unable to speak, I squeezed his hand in thanks. He understood that my heart still ached for Alex.

Conrad Anker, Alex's best friend and longtime climbing partner, had been at his side, along with high-altitude cameraman David Bridges, at the time of the avalanche. He had run straight across the slope, while Alex and Dave had run down. There was no time to think, only time to run. Instinct took over as the roaring cloud ripped toward them. "It was like being in a sleeping bag, being beaten with baseball bats and stones," Conrad had told me. Shishapangma had beaten him up and left him dazed and injured, but she had spared him. Dave and Alex belonged to her, but Conrad had walked away. He had come home and Alex had not.

When death was new to me and I awoke each day to the shock of its reality, I wanted nothing more than to claw my way back into sleep and my dreams, where there wasn't a pit of fear in my stomach and a heavy weight on my chest. I needed to breathe deeply, but it felt as though the air was rare and thin. I wanted only to stay in bed and cry, and when I looked around our bedroom and saw his things, ghostly images of Alex filled my mind, doing mundane things like pawing through a dresser drawer, looking for a sock.

And lying there looking at the dresser was terrifyingly lonely. "I'll never lay my head on his chest and hear his heart beat again," I thought. I pictured his chest, frozen and cold beneath the icy snows of Shishapangma. The finality of death gave "never" and "forever" a new and raw perspective.

"Tibet forever! Endlessly connected." That slogan is on a bumper sticker that graces the back of my minivan. It was meant to be a show of support for the International Campaign for Tibet, but since Alex's death, the sticker has taken on a more poignant and pointed meaning, an everyday reminder for me that Alex is there forever, on the 8,000-meter Shishapangma, which rises just across Nepal's Himalayan border in the mysterious kingdom of Tibet. I see it when I load the grocery bags into the back of the van, when I unload the dogs for a romp, or when I walk to the end of my driveway to water my flowers. I look at it and think, "Yes, we are connected, Alex; I know you are there." I remember the magnificence of Shishapangma, and oddly, it gives me comfort.

There is something fitting about Alex's remaining in Tibet, that most spiritual of mountain kingdoms. He was not a religious person, but of all religions, Buddhism piqued his interest the most. His library shelves were lined with books on the subject, including most of those written by the Dalai Lama. He was a staunch admirer of His Holiness and the fortitude of the Tibetan people. When Alex reached the summit of Mount Everest on his second ascent in 1993, he carried a Tibetan flag that had been blessed. Upon his return he and I, along with our young sons Max and Sam, were honored dinner guests of the Tibetan refugees who had settled in Salt Lake City, where we were living.

At the time Alex died, our youngest child, Isaac, was three; Sam was seven; and Max was about to turn eleven. Together, we strung Tibetan prayer flags all around our home, trying to celebrate Alex's life while facing his terminal absence. The gauzy multicolored prayer flags, which are commonly seen in the Buddhist Himalaya, have become synonymous with the mountaineers' base camps, a symbol of spiritual freedom. Alex had always brought them home to string across our porch and fly from flagpoles in the yard.

The boys were so young; facing death at their tender ages was frightening. But their need helped me to go on. I had to get up every morning, make their breakfast, get them to school, and be strong for them. The path before me was one I hadn't chosen. I'd lost my love of eighteen years and become a widow with three young children.

Family and friends, our community of Bozeman, and the outdoor community at large buoyed us through those first terrible months. Sadly, we would be faced with more heartbreak and challenge in the coming years. But new love arrived when least expected, and giving hope to others helped all of us to heal our hearts.

Love and Risk

There is a race of men that don't fit in,
A race that can't stay still;
So they break the hearts of kith and kin
And they roam the world at will.
They range the field and they rove the flood
And they climb the mountain's crest.
Theirs is the curse of gypsy blood
And they don't know how to rest.
—ROBERT SERVICE

I HAVE A VIVID MEMORY OF THE DAY I met Alex Lowe. I was young then, around twenty, but already tied to another. Barely out of high school, I had married my first boyfriend, Tom Ballard, a high-school crush who was a rock climber, skier, and the proprietor of a bicycle shop in Missoula, Montana, where I grew up. Alex was three years younger than I, perhaps still a senior in high school, and so I observed him with a distant curiosity that day. Still, I felt the magnetism of his presence.

He had come into the bike shop to get the beta, or inside scoop, on a local climb, and I happened to be there. He politely introduced himself with a confident grin: "I'm Alex," he said, emphasizing the X.

He was very boyish, tall and slim with wide shoulders and long limbs, truly gangly. I remember him with thick shaggy dark hair, tattered clothes, and the essence of climber, that hint that bathing wasn't high on his list of priorities. I was struck by his handsome features and his open enthusiasm, but most of all by his smile. He was a kid and could barely contain his excitement over climbing. The information he wanted that day was about the particulars of a route in the Bitterroot Mountains' Blodgett Canyon. Not long after, he came back to report on his success.

Alex ticked off the local climbers' test pieces, or most difficult routes, rather quickly. After a short go at college he was on to bigger places. He sporadically dropped in on Tom and me over the next few years with tales of his travels, the climbs he had done, and his grueling work stints in the oil fields of Wyoming. I recall seeing him huddled over a climbing magazine with a group of friends. A picture of Ray Jardine leading a desperate (very difficult) roof climb called Separate Reality in Yosemite Valley was featured, along with the new camming devices of the time, called Friends. Everyone else was incredulous at the difficult-looking route—except Alex, who exclaimed, "I can't wait to try that!" The other guys' response was "Right, dream on!" But within the next few years Alex went on to climb it, along with dozens of other routes that most Montana climbers only dreamed of.

Alex paid his last visit to Tom and me in the autumn of 1980. We were living near Boulder, Colorado, where Tom had taken a job after finishing his degree. That summer it had dawned on me that the age of twenty had been too young to get married. I knew I wanted children, and Tom knew he didn't. Love had waned. I had chased a ski bum with a bike shop, but now that he was an engineer with a mortgage, I had a bad case of remorse. I had attended art school but never finished my college degree, always needing to work at menial jobs to help pay the bills. Suddenly I felt trapped. I was miserable and panicky that my youth was slipping away. I wanted out of marriage to travel, to get a taste of adventure, to find passion and my own path while I was still young.

Alex arrived out of the blue, but his presence seemed seren-dipitous. He had come to hang out in Boulder for a while and get in as much climbing as possible in the local playgrounds of Eldorado Canyon, Boulder Canyon, and Rocky Mountain National Park. His lifestyle looked like freedom at its finest to me. Unencumbered with responsibilities and material possessions, Alex was like a migrating bird, able to take flight whenever the impulse struck and to alight in whatever green field beckoned. He got a job at Lowe Alpine Systems (no relation), where I was employed, and he rented the basement of our house as I made plans to return to Montana. To have found Tom a roommate lessened my guilt about leaving, but I didn't foresee fall-ing in love with that roommate.

I couldn't wait to leave my job, with its fluorescent lights and acrid fumes of hot-cut nylon. I gave notice and bolted for the freedom of the hills, taking every opportunity to head to the mountains around Boulder. Alex had introduced me to his good friends Alice Phinney and Eric Winkelman, whom I warmed to instantly. He'd met Eric in Yosemite the previous spring and they'd hitchhiked to the Canadian Rockies for a summer of rock, ice, and alpine climbing. While there, they'd made the fifth as-cent of Mount Kitchener's Grand Central Couloir, adding to an impressive sum of ascents. Alice had arrived later and joined Eric for some notable climbs of their own. They were a bright and fun young couple, and both were full of admiration for Alex, the "young gun" from Montana. With each passing day, my own admi-ration and fondness for Alex grew.

My first ice climbing experiences came early that winter, with Alice, who was excited to share the sport with me. A gifted athlete with a go-for-it attitude, Alice was a Boulder native whose parents had instilled in her a love of the outdoors and a passion for push-ing her limits. (Her brother Davis became an Olympic bike racer who rode in the Tour de France.) Although Alice channeled most of her energy into studying, first for a degree in biology and then for another in mechanical engineering, she was driven to climb for a few years of her life.

As we approached our first climb in Rocky Mountain National Park, crunching along through the ice and snow of a subalpine forest, I was candid with my new friend about my unhappiness, and she was empathetic. We walked in the fog of a grey cloud that had coated everything with a crystalline layer of fragile hoarfrost. Alice was certain that the cloud would burn off with the rising sun, and she was right. As we gained elevation, the sun shone through the ever brighter mist and lit the world around us in a dazzling burst of white. We peeled off layers of clothes and smeared on sunscreen while breathing in the cold pine-scented air. The gnarled and stunted trees of that high place were bent by harsh winds and deep snows of long winter months. Few and far between, they'd grown in one direction and then another, their seeds rooted in crevices of stone with barely a grain of soil. Their warped forms looked as if growth had been painful, yet they were beautiful and artful, like nature's bonsai among a scattering of talus.

We came upon a waterfall frozen in gentle tiers, a stairway of ice. There, Alice and I strapped on our crampons. Mine were newly acquired "foot fangs" that I had purchased at work. They had corrugated red plastic bottoms lined with shiny steel shark teeth biting downward and little sawlike front points. With ice ax in hand, I felt like a knight in armor bedecked in spikes. Alice taught me to plant my tools with the same wrist action used to swing a hammer. I watched her lead the clean blue ice, then followed, ascending with care as Alice coached me.

I had grown up skiing, biking, and hiking with girlfriends in Montana, but the climbing I had done was always with guys. The first day I went out with Alice was a day that I treasure. She was not taking me climbing but teaching me to climb ice, and on our next outing, I led a pitch myself. Our forays into Rocky Mountain National Park were both empowering and enchanting. They helped give me the impetus to strike out on my own. Alex, with his romantic life of adventure, would certainly have an influence on me too, but it was Alice who gave me the courage to try climbing some mountains of my own.

Eventually I returned to Montana and the remote comfort of my father's ranch near the Bob Marshall Wilderness, a good place to sort out my life. There I was able to find solace in the routine of feeding cattle and the daily chores of ranch life, watching over the place while Dad and his wife, Carol, enjoyed a visit to California, a hiatus from the long winter. With guilt and sadness, I reflected on my impending divorce. I thought of Tom's parents, whom I had grown to love, and thought of my own parents' divorce in my early teenage years, remembering my hurt and confusion. But things had turned out better in the end for each of my parents, it seemed.

As cattle began to drop their calves, I enjoyed the role of looking out for any that had trouble with the birthing process. I called on a neighboring ranch to help with one troubled young heifer I had brought to the barn. She was down and exhausted by labor, her bulging eyes rolled back with fear. When two brothers from the Copenhaver ranch arrived, we got her up, and one of them reached an arm dripping with iodine deep into her contracting body to get a rope around the calf's front feet. Once that was done, it took all of us to "pull the calf," but we managed to have it suckling in a couple of hours. The birth of that little bovine gave me a jolt of confidence. I stood before the frisky calf the next day and said, "Well, I managed to get you out into the world and on your feet. I ought to be able to do it for myself."

I was on the lookout for another job when my cousin called from Utah to say that a position was available on the seismic crew that employed him. Working outside was appealing, and the job would be lucrative. I assured his boss that I was tough enough, having done ranch work, tree thinning, and seasonal work for the Forest Service for many summers. I drove through the night to arrive at Heber City and sign on.

Alex left Boulder soon after I did. He returned to the Wyoming oil rigs, where he could make a higher wage and take double shifts, allowing for a shorter period of work between climbing adventures. He wrote to me at the ranch, and Dad forwarded his letters. I had become infatuated with the charismatic young climber who appeared to have life by the tail, and I wrote back to him:

> I *must thank you for inspiring me to take a risk and try a new lifestyle. My goal is to save enough money to go to Europe this summer. I want to visit some art museums and do some climbing. Seismic work is not bad at all. We "juggies" fly to work in helicopters that take us high up into the mountains. Once there, we lay out geophones and then set out charges of dynamite. After the shot, the geophones send a readout to the "box," where it is recorded; then a geologist somewhere can tell if there is oil in these hills.*

The next letter I got from Alex said he would be keen to get a job on my crew if an opening came up, and that he would be happy to accompany me to Europe.

In the meantime, we both had a few days off and planned to meet in the Tetons of Wyoming for some ice climbing. I drove into Jackson Hole with anticipation and there, by the antler arch in the sunny town square, stood Alex leaning against his old Volvo station wagon, arms folded across his chest, an enormous grin beneath his Vuarnet shades. It was still late winter, and he wore army-navy khakis and flip-flops with a wool sweater knit by his mom. His long arms were around me in an instant and it was pent-up love at first sight for both of us. We spent a steamy night in the back of his car, and the next day skied up Death Canyon to Prospector Falls.

It was a fresh winter day with sun sparkling on new snow as we approached the frozen waterfall. We found the vertical ice in perfect shape, and the day unfolded like a dream as we ascended. But about halfway up, an avalanche came roaring down upon us. Alex, who was above, yelled at me to plant my tools and hug the ice. Powdery spindrift poured over me as I held tightly to the shafts of my tools.

Then the snow was gone, the sun shone, and with a surge of adrenaline we quickly finished the climb. Only when we had rappelled and returned to the bottom did I realize the magnitude of the avalanche. The windblast had sent our packs more than fifty feet downslope, and there was stuff strewn everywhere: big chunks of frozen debris and bits of rock. "Whoa!" I said. "It was lucky we weren't standing here when that came down!" Alex looked a little spooked and answered sheepishly, "No kidding." The day was an auspicious start for the two of us, and fitting for the exhilaration of new love that felt somewhat illicit.

Soon after, Alex joined my crew. We adapted to seismic life and set a goal of working for three months. In that time, we figured we could save enough money to take a trip to Yosemite and then Europe, traveling for several months. As enamored of Alex as I was, I knew he was a vagabond so I didn't hold out hope for a long relationship. It didn't matter. He was twenty-two and I was twenty-five. Happy to live in the moment, we both agreed that we would travel to Europe together and see how it went.

As it turned out, we were glad for each other's daily companionship. Work on the seismic crew meant adopting a nomadic lifestyle with little chance for social interaction outside of our coworkers. Aside from a handful of frugal Mexicans, most of the crew approached life as a party and spent their fat paychecks quickly on drugs, booze, and expensive steak dinners. Alex and I did not fit the mold; we were lovers of nature and saw our jobs as a temporary means to an end. To save money, we bought food at the grocery store and ate in our hotel room.

When the weather got warm enough, we camped out to save even more of our precious paychecks. For a while we camped near Montpelier, Idaho, and Bear Lake, where the campground was mostly empty but for us. Alex did pull-ups in the outhouse doorway every evening to stay fit for climbing. I would watch his long arms pump up and down in slow rhythm as I cooked dinner on our camp stove, and then we'd sit by a fire reading. Alex played Neil Young, Cat Stevens, and John Prine songs on his guitar while I painted with watercolors or wrote letters, looking up now and then to watch his tongue curl over his lip in concentration. When tiredness overcame us, we'd crawl into the Volvo for the night.

Our salaries each amounted to two thousand dollars per month, which was great money at the time, and I remember getting paid in hundred-dollar bills. On a typical day we would be at the LZ, or landing zone, early. There were usually two helicopters, which would whisk us away at first light to the top of a ridge. As soon as the pilot gave a thumbs-up we were out the door, ducking beneath blades to scurry away with packs slung over a shoulder. The day would entail laying out equipment, setting up shots, or picking up equipment as the helicopters ferried loads of geophones from the back of the line to the front. Working outdoors and walking all day up and down hills was great, but it was a compromised existence knowing that we were looking for oil. Alex had worked on rigs for several years, taking advantage of the high-paying jobs provided by the oil boom, and he had seen firsthand the callous treatment of the environment. I dreaded the idea of roads and oil rigs invading the wild places where we walked each day. The terrain where we worked varied from steep and rocky with deep windblown snow, to timbered, to wide-open with wildflowers popping from the melting snowbanks as we followed a line left by surveyors.

For a while Alex and I "chained" for the survey crew, whose company we preferred. Far from the noise of shots, we traipsed through mountain groves of aspen, alone with red-tailed hawks, whitetail deer, and occasional cottontails, planting flags in the snowy ground. In the late afternoon or evening, our pilot would call on the radio saying, "Find an LZ," and we'd look for the flattest spot for a helicopter to land. On occasion we'd have a sketchy landing where the pilot would toe into a hillside, hovering while we carefully climbed into the floating chopper.

Although our pilots were usually skilled Vietnam vets or guys with military training who put us through regular safety drills and flew with sound judgment, we did have a couple of wild cards. I remember one guy nicknamed Captain Wa-wa who had a fondness for zooming along at what felt like inches above the water of Bear Lake. He loved to rocket up a ridge and then dive-bomb out of the sky, following the contours of the hills, while fellow "juggies" squealed with delight on this ultimate amusement ride.

When Alex and I gave our notice in the spring, most of the crew were amazed that we had amassed enough money for a trip to Europe. We smugly drove off toward Montana to make our plans, store our things, and meet each other's parents.

By this time I was completely in love with Alex, the skinny kid who surprised me with endless attributes. Aside from his climbing talent on rock and ice, and his proficiency at skiing and winter camping, Alex was knowledgeable about all things wild; he had hunted, fished, and become an Eagle Scout at the age of fourteen. He could identify insects and nearly every wildflower that we came across, and would rattle off their Latin names as well as the common. The alpine forget-me-not, or *Eritrichium aretioides*, with its tiny brilliant blue petals, was the flower that we both proclaimed as our favorite. Its habitat is exposed rocky or gravelly ridges or mountaintops, where the diminutive plant withstands harsh wind and blowing snow to show off its deep blue blossoms in early summer. We saw lots of them that first year together and would crouch head to head over the tiny palette of blue. In later years, whenever Alex came across them in his travels, he would press a few and bring them home to me from afar.

He loved wild birds as much as I, and he carried a field guide as we traveled, ticking off the various species we observed, the most delightful being the migrating sandhill cranes in Idaho. One evening after work we drove to a wetland field dotted with dozens of the elegant long-legged cranes, their spine-chilling prehistoric calls echoing off the hills. I was humbled by the presence of these ancient birds, their bright red heads bobbing like regal painted caps. They are the oldest bird species on earth, their ancestors' fossils dating back nine million years. It is daunting to think of all the history on this planet that has unfolded beneath their great migrating wings. We watched them gracefully strut and dance until the sun sank low and a white disk of moon rose from the east.

A complete romantic, Alex had lodged himself in my heart,

and I felt ever more content that our love was meant to be. He nicknamed me Bird, which endeared him to me no end. He played his guitar, singing soulfully and unabashedly while I watched, and loved telling a good joke or a funny story. Even when his jokes weren't funny, it was impossible not to join his infectious laughter.

Alex was a voracious reader and could recite entire poems, such as "The Cremation of Sam McGee" by Robert Service and "The Raven" by Edgar Allan Poe, and he often sang silly Tom Lehrer songs while cooking or driving. He left me poetic love notes and was lavish with his compliments, gifts, and surprises. I thought I had discovered my kindred spirit, my soul mate, and my knight in shining armor all wrapped in one. Indeed, some of his friends had dubbed him the White Knight.

I knew the saying "Love is blind" and tried to be objective, but aside from occasional moodiness and an inability to sit still, it was hard to find anything wrong with Alex. He didn't do drugs, rarely drank, and was concerned about eating healthy foods and staying fit. He seemed full of virtue, earnestness, and strong moral character.

Alex's parents had been somewhat horrified to hear that their son was shacking up with an older and previously married woman. I remember the phone call he made to them from a laundromat. I stood nearby as he told them, "I'm living with Jennifer here." There was a moment of silence on the other end, and Alex hung up with the knowledge of his parents' disapproval. "I'm corrupting you," I teased.

I wasn't exactly dying to knock on their door in Missoula, but I was certainly curious about the people who had raised Alex. My own mother and stepfather, Totsye and Lester Madsen, also lived in Missoula, and they too were less than thrilled with my pursuing a newfound bohemian lifestyle with "some kid" who appeared to have seduced me from my marriage. In the few conversations I'd had with them, I'd assured them that I was happy and making lots of money, but I knew they wanted a look for themselves, and I fully expected to get lectured. My mother was known for her directness, which could sometimes be rather uncomfortable, so I warned Alex, "Don't mind my mom. She's not shy about telling you what she thinks." We were both a bit nervous as we drove into our hometown of Missoula.

James and Dorothea Lowe had moved to Missoula around 1965, when Jim took a job at the University of Montana teaching in the school of forestry. He'd been in the PhD program at Yale specializing in entomology but was keen to find employment in Montana, where he had worked as a seasonal smoke jumper. Alex was seven at the time, the second of three brothers. Andy was two years older, and baby Ted was seven years younger. Jim and Dottie both came from Tennessee; Jim spent a good deal of his youth in the Great Smoky Mountains, while Dottie spent years canoeing, swimming, and boating on the lakes near her home of Chattanooga. The Lowe family life was outdoor-oriented, and Alex took to the wilderness activities with vigor.

Alex described his parents as sweet but strict, and said he'd been poised like a rock in a slingshot to get out of the nest. He felt he'd had far too much discipline and too few freedoms in his childhood, although I thought that I would have loved growing up in a family who backpacked together. My family had car-camped, fished, skied, and occasionally horse-packed. I had ventured out backpacking with friends in high school and felt that I had a late start in gaining true wilderness experience.

When I met the Lowes, I could see that Alex took after his mom in his looks with a square jaw, wide smile, and expressive wide-set eyes beneath dark brows. Dottie was beautiful, polite, and reserved. We grew to love each other, but I know that her first impression of me was not favorable. Jim, however, seemed completely accepting, jovial and friendly. He was full of fun, and I saw right away where Alex had gotten his charismatic personality. As night fell, we were given separate bedrooms; I wasn't surprised by the matter-of-fact disapproval of our lifestyle, but it did make me a bit uncomfortable. (Alex snuck into my room soon after I'd drifted off to sleep, in blatant defiance.) We stayed at my parents' after that, as they saw no point in providing us with more than one bed.

In my family, I was the second of four sisters and the tomboy of the group. Jan, Paula, and I were close in age, with Camilla seven years behind, but from a very early age I was always the one who wanted to tag along with my dad on any of his outdoor forays. My father, Paul Daly, had also grown up in Montana and was an avid horseman, hunter, and fisherman. He served in the navy during World War II, where he flew fighters from the deck of a carrier in the Pacific. After the war he was stationed in Pensacola, where he met my mother. His grandparents had homesteaded and run cattle on a ranch in the Grasshopper Valley, near Dillon; Dad spent the summers of his youth working the ranch and loved it.

When we were small and living in Missoula, Dad bought a couple of horses. He kept them at a friend's ranch nearby in exchange for labor, and I fell in love with riding. We spent summer vacations at Grandmother's cabin on Grasshopper Creek, a tiny log homestead with no electricity or running water. To my mother it was no vacation at all, but a reminder of earlier hardship. She was the daughter of a humble Alabama farmer with a large family, and both of her parents had died when she was young. She had worked hard to help her younger siblings and to escape the stigma of being poor in the South. I was too young to appreciate this, though, and could not understand Mother's aversion to the place I loved most of all.

In our family, Mom had sewn clothes, gardened, canned food, cooked, and cleaned. Later, when my parents were divorced and Mother remarried, she took up golf and excelled at it, indulging herself in the pleasure of a hobby for the first time in her life. I was proud of her but never tried the sport, preferring to bike, hike, or ride my horse. I loved to join her in the garden, helping to care for the flowers and vegetables that always adorned our yard. In later years I often accompanied my stepdad to fly-fish the banks of the many rivers and streams surrounding the Missoula valley. "Papa," the son of a dairyman, had also grown up in that valley, where young boys and fishing went hand in hand. He did his best to teach me the fine art of casting a fly, and with our forays came a closeness and an acceptance, on my part, of my parents' changing course.

Alex and I drove along the winding Blackfoot River to the ranch in Ovando to meet Dad and Carol. To my delight, they welcomed Alex and were impressed when he spent several hours chopping wood to double the size of their woodpile, then hopped up to do dishes after dinner. On another visit to the ranch, Dad was incredulous at Alex's strength and work ethic. "You make a good ranch hand!" he said, giving him the ultimate compliment.

Back in Missoula, Mother was not too warm toward Alex, but Papa was more accepting. Mom softened a little when I told her that Alex had received a scholarship in chemical engineering and was just taking a break from school. She did find him good-looking and very charming, but worried that he might not have my best interests in mind. Perhaps both of our mothers sensed that the two of us made for a dangerous duo, and now that I am a mother too, I can understand their fears and hesitation to condone our alliance. I know now that mothers are programmed to worry about their children.

My mother is gone now, and Dottie and Jim live far away in North Carolina. Dad and Carol sold their ranch in Ovando long ago. Only my stepfather, Papa, remains in Missoula with those memories, and so much life has been lived since then. One recent summer, Conrad, the boys, and I shared a picnic with Papa on the banks of Rock Creek. He helped the boys to rig and cast their lines on the same stretch of water that he and I had fished alongside my mom and sisters years before, when our family was newly pieced together. The river tossed the flies over waves and around rocks, sucking them into swirling holes and spitting them out until they were lifted skyward and flung back upriver for another ride.

I awoke in the early hours of dawn one spring morning in the year following Alex's death. The exuberant song of a robin wafting on cool air drifted through my window. The dim grey of first light told me the hour was before six and I closed my eyes to listen to the robin's chorus, his voice crisply cutting the still air with continuous song for perhaps ten minutes. In a half sleep, I drifted with the song to another spring morning long ago in Yosemite Valley. There I had lain in Alex's arms in the tent that was our home in Camp 4, the climbers' campground, and listened to a cacophony of robins' voices, all competing loudly like an orchestra tuning their instruments before performing. In Camp 4 the granite walls soar to create a natural amphitheater for a sound made ever grander. For the robins, it was their performance, a daily ritual to announce the coming dawn.

Abruptly the song ended and I awoke fully to the present, a sharp elbow against my back. I turned to look at Isaac in the growing light and watched his little chest rise and fall with that miraculous involuntary motion. "He is alive and Alex is not," I thought, but Alex does live in his face, the thick dark hair, the wide grin and square jaw. And Isaac has a similarly endless amount of energy and drive for perfection that sometimes leads him to frustration and tears. The way he sleeps flat on his back, with his hands behind his head and his elbows straight out, is also a gift from his father, oddly enough. I had no idea that genetics could dish out something as unique as a sleeping position. But there it is. Isaac seems to have gotten nothing from me except a mole on his left ankle and a stubborn streak. He is a daily reminder that life with Alex was not a dream, and though Alex is gone from us, he is still here in many ways.

Yosemite

The mountains are calling and I must go.
—JOHN MUIR

HAVING MET EACH OTHER'S PARENTS, Alex and I joyously embarked on the first leg of our journey. By the time we arrived in Yosemite Valley, he was beside himself to share the cherished place with me. We drove along the winding road past El Portal, the tiny settlement at the western entrance, with Alex whooping in excitement. "Psyched, I'm psyched, welcome to heaven!" he sang out. As we neared his favorite meadow view of the 3,000-foot El Capitan, he made me close my eyes. "Don't open them until I say!" he commanded. We pulled into the parking lot and "Not yet, wait," he said, leading me from the car to the meadow. "Now, feast your eyes on the Captain, Bird!" Alex had climbed El Cap many times by various routes and he revered the mighty rock, which stands out among lesser sentinels of the valley with its imposing vertical face.

I had been to Yosemite once before, but it didn't matter to Alex. From his perspective, I was seeing it for the first time. And it felt that way to me. With great celebration he showed me his beloved "Valley"—all of his favorite routes, hangouts, and hideaways. He was smooth and graceful on the rock, and although he climbed at a much higher grade than I, he was an adept guide, instilling the confidence necessary for the sometimes unnerving sport. He taught me the art of crack climbing—how to jam fingers, hands, and fists into vertical crevices, and how best to use one's feet. He taught me how to use the tiny chocks and cams to protect a climb and lead it. Alex was full of enthusiasm and encouragement, always joking and cackling with glee. "Go for it Jen, you animal!" he'd yell, coaching me as I strained to pull through some difficult move. "Right hand up to that little ledge and left foot in the crack! You can do it!"

To get from place to place in the valley we rode the open-air double-decker shuttle buses, fondly dubbed the Scuttles. One day Alex leapt from the top of one into the Merced River as it crossed a bridge, while I sat shrinking into my seat in surprised laughter. Our car was left in the parking lot and served as a sort of home base where we cooked and kept our gear. When we tired of peanut butter, ramen, and refried beans, a splurge was in order at the cafeteria, deli, or the sweet shop at the elegant Ahwahnee Hotel.

Alex versed me in the art of "scarfing," an Artful Dodger sort of grabbing of untouched or partly eaten food from abandoned cafeteria trays. Though I didn't have the guts to scarf, I was intrigued by this sneaky survival tactic of young climbers who took great pride in their ability to live off society's excess while climbing to their heart's content. The practice exemplified the bohemian subculture of "dirtbag" climbers. For the more flush among us, the Ahwahnee offered an all-you-can-eat Sunday brunch served up on silver platters. Every couple of weeks we'd splurge, gorging ourselves to the point of discomfort; then we'd lie around the rest of the day like well-fed wolves after a kill.

On rainy days we'd visit the Ahwahnee and find a cozy corner in the palatial lodge to read while fires crackled. Early on one of those first mornings in the valley, Alex took me to the pond in front of the hotel, and we walked gingerly along its boggy edge to sit on a log. "You're in for a treat," he said. "Just watch and listen." The voices of bullfrogs filled the air around us, and one by one he pointed them out among the reeds and lily pads in the dark, still water.

Though they were a nonnative species in the park and have now been removed, I found the enormous amphibians delightful. It's a fine memory, sitting there among ferns with the blinking eyes, ballooning throats, and vibrating voices of frogs. As the years followed, I took each of the boys to the pond to witness the melancholy music of bellowing bullfrogs.

A highlight of the trip for me was climbing the East Buttress of El Capitan. We started early that day, climbing thirteen pitches (rope lengths) all together, with Alex leading the difficult ones to arrive at the top in late afternoon. The wind sent ropes flying wildly as we rappelled down the East Ledges, and Alex cursed and screamed over a stuck rope. "Alex was the worst cusser at Meadow Hill school!" his brother Andy once told me. I was growing accustomed to Alex's habit of losing his temper when things didn't go right; my father had exhibited an "Irish temper" throughout my childhood, so yelling and swearing didn't faze me as long as it wasn't directed my way. When it was, I could hold my own, but Alex and I rarely argued. Occasionally he succumbed to quiet moodiness, and I always confronted him to find out the cause. I often had to pry his thoughts from deep within his soul during our first years together, so conditioned was he to avoid confrontation. I on the other hand would readily burst forth with anger, laughter, or tears.

One pitch on the East Buttress entailed a leftward traverse, which Alex led with little in the way of protection to direct the rope. He was far above me when I followed, and he couldn't hear me yelling for slack to get over to the route. I had my own temper tantrum when the tight rope forced me to climb a section of difficult face. As I fell repeatedly, I screamed and pounded the rock. "Did the rope get stuck?" he asked meekly when I reached the belay. "No, I did, and that was a lousy lead," I shot back.

Though it's not considered a part of El Capitan proper, the East Buttress was the first route climbed on the expanse of granite in 1952, by climbing pioneers Allen Steck, Willi Unsoeld, Bill Long, and Will Siri. Eleven years later it was free-climbed (without the use of aid, such as pitons and hooks), and at thirteen pitches it remains a long and popular classic. I was proud to have climbed something on the golden monolith, official or not. It's exhilarating to pull yourself up two thousand feet of sheer rock and look down, knowing that you made all the right decisions to get there, avoiding the obvious risks. On top, Alex and I sat thigh to thigh watching peregrine falcons, at home in the vertical world, ride breezes while we shared the satisfaction of a summit and a chocolate bar.

My sister Jan arrived in the valley that spring, driving from Seattle for what I promised her would be a grand adventure in Yosemite. I wanted to share the fun and beauty of that newly discovered world with her in my company. Alex and I took her camping and climbing in the Tuolumne backcountry, where we ascended the beautiful spire of Cathedral Peak. She loved it, as I had guessed she would, and she loved Alex too. When he and his buddies Perry Beckham and Tom Gibson went up on Half Dome to climb a route called Zenith, Jan and I decided to hike to Mirror Lake, which would afford a perfect view of their progress. While the three of them hung beneath the Space Flake, trying to muster the courage to climb past the immense loose rock, Jan and I sat on the sandy, sunny beaches of the Merced River looking up at the beautiful granite face and the tiny spidery figures.

"I have an idea," I said out of the blue. "Let's write a message for them with toilet paper!" We debated over what to write, not wanting to incriminate ourselves for littering or to embarrass the guys, so decided that it had to be a secret code. "Cool Wheels! Then they'll know it's us," I said, referring to the ice-cream sandwich that Alex and I both had a weakness for. We wrote out the message quickly and left it visible for fifteen minutes before picking it up.

From high on Half Dome, the white words appeared in the green meadow, and Alex knew immediately that they were from Jan and me. They howled with laughter, but unfortunately lost their momentum to finish the climb. With the Space Flake looming above and Cool Wheels beckoning from below, they rappelled off Zenith, shouldered their mammoth haul bags, and hiked down from Half Dome in defeat. But Jan and Perry got acquainted that evening, and thus began a courtship that eventually resulted in their marriage.

I was never lonely when Alex went off on long wall climbs, as there were always interesting people around to climb and hang out with. We met a young man named Hugh Herr, there with his brother Hans. A veritable babe at the age of sixteen, Hugh was a gymnast and already a strong and gifted climber. He joined Alex on some difficult free climbs, and he and I climbed the Central Pillar of Frenzy on Middle Cathedral Spire. "This is the first climb I've done with a girl," he shyly admitted at the top.

"Really? Congratulations," I said, planting a kiss on his blushing cheek.

The following winter, Hugh and a friend became lost in a storm on Mount Washington and, tragically, they both suffered frostbite. Alex and I were shocked by the accident, which resulted in Hugh losing his feet. But with prosthetic feet, he continued to climb and never lost his drive.

My independence strengthened my young relationship with Alex, who was happy that I didn't sit waiting for him at the bottom of crags. Whenever we would meet after several days apart, we had both lived our own adventures. Alex often wrote to me from his wall climbs; the following was penned on a route called Mescalito, high on El Capitan:

Here we sit on the Bismark Ledge. I led the off-width pitch [very wide crack]—I should say the lie-back pitch because I certainly didn't off-width it! Thank goodness we fixed the feared thing. I was completely terrified of it. It wasn't so bad though. We will spend one more night on the wall, then top out on Thursday. I love the summit of El Cap. It's so wonderful to lie back in the grass and pine needles up there. How I enjoy the falcons. They do the most amazing power dives. It sounds like a falling rock, then you spot its wings tucked back falling free like a stone. Finally it pulls out its wings screaming as it does. There is an amazing array of life clinging to this wall. We've seen all kinds of flowers, *purple gentian, lovely orange stonecrop, little white forget-me-nots and of course dozens of swallows diving, swooping, twisting and always screeching. Also there are the little frogs who inhabit the cracks up here and, of course, people. So cumbersome, noisy and destructive we are up here. This rock wasn't made with us in mind; we don't really belong here. But just as men are drawn to the moon or the bottom of the sea, something about an unknown and hostile environment is compelling. Perhaps that's the challenge. Plus, it's good fun and ledges like these are great places to sit and think. Mostly I think about you. I love you immensely!*

One night in Camp 4, Alex gently shook me. "Jenni, wake up, you've got to come see this," he whispered. I stumbled along behind him through a night filled with the song of crickets and frogs to arrive at the bathrooms. We entered a black cinderblock chamber echoing with high-pitched sound and Alex turned on his headlamp to reveal dozens of tiny tree frogs suddenly silent, clinging to the walls. Then he turned off the light and we stood holding hands until their sweet serenade resumed. The intense beauty and excitement of life was amplified by the wonder of new love that first spring in Yosemite, giving the valley a special place in my heart forever.

Rocky Road

The only people for me are the mad ones, the ones who are mad to live,
mad to talk, mad to be saved, desirous of everything at the same time, the
ones who never yawn or say a commonplace thing, but burn, burn, burn,
like fabulous yellow roman candles exploding like spiders across the stars.

—JACK KEROUAC

IN EARLY JULY WE SAT KNEE TO KNEE in the back seat of a hot
car with warm air blasting through open windows. Alex's shaggy
shoulder-length hair was whipping about. His parents' station
wagon was en route to Butte, Montana. I was sandwiched between
Alex and his younger brother, Ted.

Ted had spent part of the summer working on a Boy Scout
project. He built nest boxes for wood ducks and placed them along
the banks of a nearby river to restore riparian health. Wood ducks
nest high in hollowed-out trees to stay out of harm's way, and their
fledglings leap from their nests to water or land some ten feet or
more below. I thought of Ted as the last nestling, eager to fledge,
watching us anxiously and with awe.

We had purchased cheap round-trip tickets from New York to
London months before but determined to hitchhike from Butte to
New York, saving our precious cash so we could afford the maximum

number of vacation days. Our belongings were stored in Missoula, our cars were parked, and Alex and I were poised for flight. Jim and Dottie volunteered to take us as far as Butte in the safety of their car, postponing their worry and sharing a bit more time as they sent us off on our journey to Europe.

They asked tentative questions about the practice of hitchhiking as the mile markers passed, and Alex assured them we'd be careful.

"How do you know if it's a good ride before you get in?" Dottie asked.

"We look for the gun rack and the Playboy Bunny mud flaps!" Alex joked. "Then we look inside and take note of how many beer bottles there are."

"And whether there are any full ones left," Jim chimed in.

We all laughed, but I knew they were nervous, as were my own parents. Alex had been hitchhiking regularly for several years but I had never tried it, other than to the ski hill in my small, safe community. I was caught up in the whole daring adventure, however, and convinced by Alex that we'd be fine.

After a picnic complete with watermelon and chocolate chip cookies, we stood roadside in running shorts, T-shirts, and flip-flops with a cardboard sign reading "New York" scrawled in Magic Marker next to our bulging backpacks. Dottie has since told me that this is one of her most vivid memories of Alex and me, standing there like twins with our long skinny legs. "I'll pray for you," she told us as Alex gave her a hug. Then they all waved goodbye and drove home.

At first we tried hitching as a duo, side by side like a vaudeville act, thumbs out eagerly to every car. A few hours of sparse traffic with drivers staring stone faced or straight ahead dampened our spirit, though. I sat against my pack in the gravel, reading, while Alex threw out his thumb for the travelers and juggled rocks during traffic lulls.

"Is it always this bad?" I asked.

"Naw . . . we'll get there," he answered. Finally a semi pulled over and took us to Billings, where a summer thundershower was in full force. It was nearly evening, and we had made it only a few hundred miles toward New York. The prospect of standing in the pouring rain at night was more than we could bear, so we walked to the local Greyhound station and bought tickets to New York City. When we called to tell our parents they were greatly relieved, and once on board we collapsed against each other in the back of the bus for a long diesel-fumed ride across the northern reaches of the United States. I turned twenty-six on that Greyhound somewhere in Pennsylvania, and Alex gave me a card that he had made, some climbing chocks, and a single red rose.

When our bus rolled into Penn Station in the middle of the night and dumped us off, it was the first time I'd laid eyes on New York City. Alex and I walked through the littered, echoing corridors, full of musicians, panhandlers, and the crumpled forms of homeless people on benches and bare floors. Out on the streets I trailed along, zombielike, as Alex gleefully pointed out the sights of the largest city I had ever seen. It was a blur of taxis, sirens, graffiti, tall buildings, and garbage heaped on curbs, with people sleeping here and there in doorways. A bus took us to the airport, where we found public showers and then fell asleep on the floor to wait for our flight. It had been days since we'd slept in a bed or even a comfortable position, and though Alex had the ability to drop off anywhere, contorting his long legs and arms into whatever space was available for a few hours' rest, I was exhausted by the time we landed in London.

We took a train to the modest city of Redditch to meet up with an old friend of Alex's. We jostled through the crowded station to find our platform, and childhood memories came flooding back to me, of a ride from Montana to Florida with my mom and sisters when I was four. It was the first time I realized how big the world actually was, but my most vivid memory is of sleeping berths that folded away during the day and magically appeared at night. My sisters and I fell asleep and awoke in a different world: trees hung with moss, beaches and swamps, alligators and steaming pots of bright red crabs. The newness of everything was what I loved.

"My mother used to put rum in our Coke to get us to fall

asleep when we traveled!" Alex told me. "As young boys, we were a real handful."

"I can imagine," I answered, but I really couldn't. I grew up with only sisters, and we were never wild enough for my mom to consider such a thing. But I tried to imagine a small Alex. Dottie had told me that he never sat still for a minute.

Some years later, I thought of that train ride to Redditch with Alex and our conversation. With three boys in tow, ages one, four, and seven, I was flying from Montana to Switzerland, where Alex had been guiding. We had long looked forward to this trip to Europe as the first with our children, and we planned to tour Italy, spending most of our time trekking in the Dolomites. Isaac threw up on me in the first hour of the flight, and I didn't have any clothes to change into. I tried to cover up the sour smell with cologne from the bathroom, which gave me a horrendous headache. The boys were so excited that sitting still in the airplane for the long flight was nearly impossible. Max and Sam squabbled over toys. Isaac ran laps up and down the aisles whenever he could squirm away. Each time we changed planes there were jackets, books, crayons, and toys to gather into day packs. By the time we got to Europe, I was thinking that rum in Coke might be worth trying, at least for me.

When Alex and I arrived in Redditch, his climbing buddy was to meet us at the station. Ian Parsons had hooked up with Alex in Yosemite a few years before to climb The Shield, a classic nail-up, or aid climb, on the southwest face of El Capitan. With his dry sense of humor, Ian had kept Alex laughing in the face of danger when they were both neophyte wall climbers. In the crowded station, Alex made me guess who Ian was. I noticed a mop of black hair, dark eyes, and a shadow of beard on a shy-looking young fellow with a well-worn fleece jacket. "That's got to be him."

I was right. Ian shuffled toward us in shoes with no laces, grinning at Alex. We piled into his little car and drove out into the countryside, past verdant hills zigzagged with ivy-covered stone fences and dotted with dairy farms, to the White House on Callow Hill, where Ian resided with his parents. From the moment we ducked out of the car and stood in the barnyard, I felt as though I had arrived in a Beatrix Potter story where everything was charming and old, from the towering trees and the stone-fenced pasture below to the tall, sturdy white house, its contrasting thick frame timbers black with four hundred years of age. Chickens and ducks scattered as we walked toward the door, and an orange tabby cat sat snug in a window framed by red geraniums and white lace curtains.

I was drawn in by the warmth and welcome of that wonderful historic house: the smooth worn wood of the floors and thresholds, the large open hearth with iron hooks for holding the cook pots of past residents, and the kitchen where there was always a pot of tea and a beautiful cast-iron stove radiating heat. Mike and Paddy presided over their home with the quiet, comforting grace of two kindly librarians. I was ushered to an upstairs bedroom with pink satin bedcovers, and after a hot bath I fell blissfully asleep until dinner was announced.

I hated leaving the White House, but Ian and Alex were keen to get to the crags so the next day we were off to Wales, where we spent a week climbing between rainstorms at Tremadog. Actually, they weren't storms at all, more like drizzles that crept up on you until you realized that it wasn't just cold and damp but actually raining. It was great fun pronouncing the local place names, such as Craig Bwlch y Moch, which translates to "Crag of the Pass of the Pigs."

Vector was one of the climbs we did on that cliff, a classic hard route that was put up, or first climbed, by the legendary Joe Brown in 1960. I followed Alex and remember falling out of the overhanging crack and dangling on the rope, to the delight of onlookers below. We stayed in a climbers' hut there and brewed copious amounts of tea. Alex consumed guidebooks and, with Ian's advice, charted out all of the climbing areas we needed to visit in Britain. For the next month and a half we traveled about from one crag to another, hitching or catching rides with other climbers. We hooked up with an Australian friend of Alex's, Kim Carrigan, and a bevy of talented young Brits.

One of the more driven climbers I've known aside from Alex,

Kim made rock climbing his complete focus. He had a list of difficult climbs that he doggedly ticked off as he did them, and he was very serious about his diet and exercise regime. Alex looked up to Kim as an athlete, striving to match his pace and level of fitness. Kim teased Alex about being too skinny and Alex took it to heart, doubling workouts for his arms and upper body over the next year. Each day we caught a bus to a different crag, where they would methodically climb the most difficult three-star routes. I usually belayed and followed the few I could manage, then climbed less difficult pitches. In the gritstone quarries of the Peak District, Alex got a taste for bold leads with long run-outs (unprotected sections with no place to put a nut or piton), climbing routes such as Edge Lane, Great Arête, and Green Death at Millstone Edge.

My favorite climbing area was Bosigran, a group of sea-cliffs near Lands End in Cornwall. There we stayed in another hut, called the Count House. Wandering through fields of heather, taking care not to step on the abundant large slugs, we made our way to the cliffs each day to climb beneath the cry of gulls. Alex perfected an imitation of the gulls' escalating screams and the ever present foghorns to provide amusement for his partners, usually when they were right in the middle of a desperate lead. We climbed hard on the beautiful granite until our arms and fingers were spent, then sat atop sea-cliffs watching sailboats, giant freighters, and fishermen as an orange sun sank into the ocean.

In the Great Zawn, a chasm that drops to the sea, I did a climb with Alex and Kim called the Green Cormorant Face. We had to rappel down to a ledge at the base of the cliff at low tide where, once the ropes were pulled down, we were truly committed, as crashing surf began to rise with the tide toward us. A wild leap across a yawn of sea to a sloping ledge was the most difficult move. It really added to the excitement of climbing, as did the bird's nest halfway up the route. Kim was leading and had to pass the nest first. Parent birds swooped and dive-bombed, screaming their concern as Kim neared the chicks, but the most excitement occurred when the nestlings began to projectile-vomit as he came within range. Alex and I roared with laughter while Kim dodged the puking fuzz balls, but we each got our chance to live dangerously as we had to pass by the downy chicks ourselves.

While climbing in Cornwall, a favorite indulgence was to visit local cafes for Cornish cream teas. Feathery warm scones are served with fresh strawberry jam and clotted cream, a rich thick spread. We got rather addicted to the fattening fare, but climbing every day made it easy to burn off calories.

Another sport for burning calories was skinny-dipping in the ocean, a frigid pursuit that I succumbed to only because of peer pressure. Getting naked in front of a bunch of guys was bad enough, but the salty sea was like an ice bath. On the day of Prince Charles and Diana's wedding, we dined in Penzance after a dip in the ocean, then joined the entire country in celebrating through the night at various pubs. Cutouts of Charles and Diana peered from the back of every car window, with cardboard hands on springs that waved from side to side. In years following, our time in Cornwall has come to feel quite like my own fairytale.

We drifted north to Sheffield, where Kim shared a flat with some locals and Alex and I crashed on the floor for a couple of weeks. A charismatic and entertaining character, Kim sported a punk look on a jock body. He wore the tiniest wired climbing nuts, called RPs, as earrings and convinced Alex to pierce his ear, offering to do it for him with a rather primitive method involving an ice cube, a hot sewing needle, and a potato behind the earlobe. Alex nearly passed out, as the ice cube didn't quite numb his ear and the needle didn't quite make a big enough hole for the earring to pass through. (When we arrived back in Montana, his parents were horrified, much to his delight. He wore the earring for the next year or so, until his earlobe got infected and he tired of swabbing it with alcohol.) On the day of the piercing, Kim decided to dye his hair with blue spots. His roommate did the honors by cutting holes in a pink shower cap and pulling bits of Kim's black hair through to bleach with peroxide and then dye blue. But the blue ended up being dark enough that the finished effect wasn't as dramatic as Kim had hoped.

Hanging out with the tribe of climbers was fun, but I began to tire of the pace and routine. Although I was becoming quite fit, I still felt out of my league and missed the more cultural side of travel, so I began lobbying to take in some museums and historic sites. We did make a trip to Liverpool to see the stomping ground of the Beatles and visit the spectacular Liverpool Cathedral, but when Alex decided to spend our last week in Great Britain climbing in Wales, I chose to return to the White House to have some downtime with Ian and his family. Ian had a job, which prevented him from going climbing with Alex, but on his days off he and his mother were nice enough to take me sightseeing to the Cotswolds and to a nearby heritage museum where there was a working windmill. We also spent a day at Warwick Castle, where we toured the palatial home of Henry VIII, complete with dungeon and torture chamber. I walked through the great halls and corridors, slipping into the past to imagine knights in armor, women imprisoned in heavy gowns, and splendid feasts laid out on endless tables.

I felt like a queen at the White House, where a local dairy delivered milk to the back step each morning in glass bottles with a thick layer of cream beneath the caps. At breakfast, Paddy always provided me with a fresh bottle so I could pour the top cream over my cereal; perhaps she was trying to fatten me up. Relaxing at the farm, reading, sketching, and getting to know the Parson family, gave me a much-needed breather from the intense, driven climbing agenda of the previous five weeks.

When Alex returned, we were off to Chamonix with an Aussie climber named Ben. He drove a car that was barely running; it had been given to him by Kim, who just wanted to be rid of it. It had expired license plates, a gaping hole in the front fender, bald tires that we changed several times along the way, no brakes aside from the handbrake, and only one working headlight. Our first challenge was getting it on the ferry, which cost more than any of us were willing to give up. Alex and I walked on board and paid our fare, leaving Ben to his dilemma, but soon he appeared. We assumed he had ditched the car, but no: "I swiped a ferry pass off another vehicle that was sitting in line and rolled right on board! It's my criminal background," he quipped. Alex hooted with laughter but I was nervous that we would be arrested as accomplices to the wild young Australian. Then my mother would really think I had dropped off the deep end.

Once in France, en route to Chamonix, we were stopped several times by gendarmes, but Ben somehow talked his way out of a ticket each time by promising to fix the headlight and showing his title. Each day we drove until dusk, stopping at bakeries and fruit stands for snacks, then threw our sleeping bags in fields beside the road. Our first night in France, the moon rose full, enormous, and spectacularly yellow over the vineyard where we had camped between rows of grapevines, thick with foliage and heavy clumps of dark grapes that cast a shadow on our bivy site. It was romantic lying on the soft, fragrant dirt of a foreign land. My great-grandfather had come from France, and though I never knew him, I'd heard enough about him from my grandmother and father to feel that I was connecting with a bit of my past. Alex too was swept up with the excitement of visiting the Alps. The night was one of the loveliest we ever had together beneath the moon.

Chamonix was all that Alex had dreamed of, a quaint mountain village with dramatic snow-covered peaks rising above glaciers and into clouds. The town was steeped in the history of mountaineering; it was where European gentry had first ventured to climb for sport, hiring local shepherds as porters and guides. Over the years, it became a climbing mecca, and Alex was ecstatic to be there in the fold of this brotherhood. We rode the Téléphérique out of the valley to the Aiguilles right off, and climbed for a couple of days on long rock and mixed (rock and ice) routes.

At first we stayed in the traditional climbers' campground, Snells Field, but a few days of rain rendered it a virtual mud pit and theft was rampant, so we rented a rustic barn a few miles down the road from Chamonix. It offered an incredible view of the Argentière Glacier out the swinging doors of a hay-filled loft, while at night we could peer out at the stars. The barn was also home to docile dairy cows, and its walls were adorned with beautiful wooden rakes with hand-carved tines. The hay was gathered into vertical bunches that reminded me of a van Gogh painting.

One day we went to the Argentière Glacier to practice some ice climbing on the jumbled seracs. While walking over the aged, dirty ice, I happened on what I first believed to be a glove. Closer inspection revealed fingernails and a bone protruding from the wrist, where it had been severed or, more likely, ripped from the arm. I yelled for Alex, and together we bent over the leathery appendage, wondering about its former owner. I was quite disturbed by the whole event, as it brought to the forefront of my mind the idea that climbing could result in death.

When we reported it to authorities, however, we learned a plane had crashed on the glacier thirty years before. I was somewhat relieved to know that the casualty wasn't a climber, but I sometimes think of that hand as the first dark forecast of what lay ahead for Alex on another glacier in another mountain range, where he too would become a prisoner in the ice.

Alex led me into the alpine world with a climb on the north face of Les Courtes, the Swiss Route, which rose elegantly to a lofty summit several thousand feet above the glacier. We rode a train to the high glacial valley and walked up the frozen river of ancient snow, picking our way around and over crevasses to the alpine hut that was perched on a moraine. Across from it was the imposing face of Les Courtes with our intended climb. We arose very early in a cold, black night after fitfully few hours of sleep and started across the glacier with headlamps. Fear gripped my stomach as we came closer to the steep face, looking up at several thousand feet of ghostly grey ice and rock. But once we crossed the deep bergschrund at the base, I began to relax. Alex was ever the exuberant cheerleader, spouting off about how easy it looked, how perfect the weather was, and how burly I was.

"This will be a cakewalk! You're gonna cruise this thing, Jen."

"Right," I'd answer, a little dubious but trying to be brave. It didn't look as steep as the water ice I was used to climbing, and since it was dark, I couldn't really see how big and scary it was.

Alex led out by headlamp, and by the time it was light we had already climbed many pitches on solid névé, moving quickly on the steep Styrofoam-like snow and passing a couple of French climbers to our left. As the sun crept up and I became acutely aware of my exposure a thousand feet above the glacier, adrenaline heightened my senses, but the sick feeling returned to my stomach in the form of a cramp.

"I've really got to go!" I told Alex.

"No problem," he said cheerfully, and belayed me as I traversed off route to pursue the unpleasant but urgent release of my cramping bowel.

"I hope no one's watching," I mumbled, thinking of the French team.

"Just the ravens," laughed Alex.

There is nothing quite like baring your butt with a thousand feet of cold air beneath you. We climbed on without incident, moving together over mixed ground and belaying a section of water ice. Summiting around noon on a clear day afforded fantastic views of the entire range and sweeping glacial valleys.

On descent, we down-climbed into the next valley and stopped to rope up and have a snack before crossing the glacier. The French team passed us, and Alex pointed out that they were traveling across the glacier unroped. "Not a good idea!" he said to them, gesturing toward the rope on one fellow's shoulder. Whether or not they understood, they continued on as before, until suddenly, the man with the rope dropped out of sight into a crevasse. His partner came running back toward us, screaming. We hurried along, trying to assure him that we would help, and were a little shocked by his attempt to grab our extra rope away from Alex the moment he was within reach.

Alex remained calm, however, and hung on to his rope while holding the fellow by the arm and looking him in the eye. Neither of us could speak much French, but Alex said something to the poor guy that made him calm down. I sat down to belay Alex toward the crevasse opening, where he in turn set up a belay for the climber, who was thirty feet below on a ledge but uninjured. After dropping him the end of our rope, Alex took the weight of the climber and literally hauled him out within a few moments, while his partner watched.

Tearful hugs and handshakes went around, but that evening in the hut, I watched indignantly as they indulged in a hot meal while Alex and I shared a candy bar and tea at the next table. Our pack had been rifled at the other hut, so we were missing food, clothing, and money. Even so, we were giddy from our climb and our spirits could not be dampened.

Alex was keen to try some more difficult routes, such as the Walker Spur on the Grand Jorasses, but the weather turned bad again, and so did his mood. Suddenly he was regretting having climbed the Swiss Route with me and perhaps using up his only window of good weather on a relatively easy ascent. He was irritable and full of pent-up energy, looking to the socked-in mountains above us each day with longing. After his partner backed out of another planned climb he became even more hostile and withdrawn, fiendishly doing pull-ups and push-ups in the loft of the barn. He drank espresso out of boredom and became ever more exasperated. "I'm better off alone, where I can focus on my own goals, Jenni. I'm a selfish person," he said when I called him on his mood. So I decided to take a short trip to Paris to enjoy some culture.

We had met another young couple from Colorado on our trip, Deedee and Joe Lladick. Joe was a strong, willing partner for Alex, and they were determined to climb together as soon as weather allowed. Deedee was a stained-glass artist who, like me, was keen to see Paris and the Louvre. She was easygoing but game for an adventure, so we decided to hitchhike to Paris together, then go to the coast and travel back to Chamonix through the Bordeaux country.

After a chilly goodbye to Alex, I walked down the road at Deedee's side, feeling uncertain whether Alex and I would be able to work out our differences. It had been an intense trip, and we needed time apart; that much was clear. I had known from the beginning that Alex was a rambler and a free spirit, I reminded myself. And I had learned that when he was satiated with continued success on hard climbs, he was an extraordinary companion, full of fun, kindness, and love; but if he felt that he was not meeting his goals or climbing up to his expectations, he became distracted and distant.

Hitchhiking was a breeze with Deedee. Youth hostels provided cheap refuge in Geneva and Paris, where we spent several days wandering through every gallery and cathedral we could find while indulging in fabulous cuisine. We could hardly walk past a patisserie without being lured in by the glistening confections. Almond croissants became my weakness. We sipped espressos at bistros in the shadow of the Eiffel Tower and splurged on dinners in fancy restaurants, enjoying new delicacies such as truffles, escargot, and goose liver pâté with an ever present bottle of red wine and a crusty baguette.

The Louvre was more magnificent than I had dreamed, with its vast and hallowed halls of paintings and sculpture. I delighted in the familiarity of many pieces that I had studied in art history. The Mona Lisa seemed to preside over the entire museum, so important was she in my mind. I was surprised to find the canvas with her form quite small compared with what I had imagined. Still, she held my gaze for over an hour as I tried to envision da Vinci himself laboring to give her eternal life with a fistful of brushes smelling of turpentine. It is said that Leonardo loved the painting so much himself that he carried it around with him for years. I wondered about her life, about his. She was much younger than he and married to another, but maybe he loved her. In the background of her image is a landscape of crags and mountains. I thought of Alex and wondered whether he was climbing the mountains he dreamed of, then wondered whether he still loved me. "What do you think, Mona Lisa?" She smiled.

From Paris we traveled to Chartres, where the youth hostel afforded a breathtaking view of the town's famous cathedral at night, lit by floodlights and ethereal from its hilltop vantage. I loved that little village, with its narrow cobbled streets. The cathedral was exquisite from within, stained-glass windows glowing in hues of deep cobalt blue. I could have stayed there longer, reading, painting, and writing letters to my grandmother, who held a special place in my heart. She was always there for me in times of duress and she wrote to me religiously, even to post office boxes and general delivery—wherever

I happened to be. The pastoral setting reminded me of her and the countryside that she loved in Montana.

But we traveled on, down the coast, rolling through golden hills of wheat, sunflowers, and corn and then heading back through Bordeaux, visiting wonderful diminutive villages surrounded by orchards and vineyards. I was at peace and feeling content with this rambling life, but I wondered about Alex and me.

A young doctor pulled over to offer us a lift one morning, and we clambered into his black Mercedes for the luxurious ride. He spoke perfect English, was incredibly courteous and handsome, and offered an exemplary tour of the country we passed through. He insisted on treating us to an incredible six-course meal at a country château, which we at first protested but ultimately couldn't resist. We wondered if he might be expecting some "payback," but decided not to worry about it. Between the three of us, we drank two bottles of wine and indulged in exquisite desserts.

After our meal we parted ways amicably, as he was en route to a conference in Geneva and we were returning to Chamonix. He offered us money for a train and lectured about the dangers of hitchhiking as we said goodbye. Deedee and I slept in a pear orchard that night, and I dreamed about running away with the doctor to live here forever in the romantic hillsides of France, creating art and dining on rich cuisine and bottles of wine. We arose at dawn to pick ripe pears from the closest tree before making our way back to the road. I had never tasted a pear so sweet.

Once back in Chamonix, Alex and I reunited, but there was still a distance between us. He and Joe had done some climbing in the Alps and then gone to the Mediterranean to rock climb in a beautiful cove with a nude beach. (And to think I had wondered if he was missing me!) I determined to climb one more significant route before we left the Alps and was planning to do it solo, but Alex wouldn't have it. "You don't have enough experience, Jen!" he argued, and so we did the Gervasutti Couloir on Mont Blanc du Tacul together. We climbed fast and were cordial, but we hardly shared the joy that we had experienced on the Swiss Route. I figured it would be our last ascent together, as I wasn't keen to be with Alex when he was keeping me at arm's length. It felt too painful to have had such passionate love simply evaporate after six months.

When we returned to the barn, I told Alex that I wanted to go home and get a job. I was running low on money and suddenly felt terribly insecure and homesick for familiar comforts and people. I had decided I would leave right away, expecting Alex to be relieved. Surprisingly, he wasn't. "We planned this trip together, and I want to finish it together," he said. "Besides, I feel responsible for making sure you get home OK."

"I'll be fine!" I bristled. "I don't need your help. I have enough money for a bus ride from New York. I'm twenty-six years old."

Perhaps it was my defiance and independence that appealed to him, but suddenly Alex again became the caring guy I had fallen in love with, and put all his heart into wooing me back. He appeared the next morning with flowers and a loving written apology.

Before long we were off to the train station, traveling back to Britain to board our plane for New York. As the miles flew by, Alex talked me into spending a week or two at the Shawangunks in upstate New York. He had spent the last fall there and had wonderful memories of the people, the place, and a perfect autumn. With some hesitation I agreed to go, but worried about our dwindling funds. "We can camp for nothing," argued Alex. "I know a great little hideaway, and you're going to love this place, Jen. We can't miss the Gunks! It will be the perfect ending to our trip, and we can hitch home before it gets too cold."

"Then what?" I thought, but said nothing. "OK, I'll go."

From New York City, we traveled north to New Paltz by train. The rhythmic cadence of steel rolling on steel lulled me into solace, reminding me of the bumpy tracks I'd traveled so far and leaving me to wonder about the road ahead. I stared out the window, watching New York go by in all of its unfamiliar forms. As we picked up speed, I looked at Alex sitting next to me, engrossed in a James Michener novel. His handsome features were framed against the window, with everything beyond him in a blur. I felt like a water-skier behind his boat with an enormous wake tossing me about, and wondered if I would be able to hang on. But the farther north we went, the more at home I felt, with countryside expanding between cities and towns. The trees had begun to turn color with the sun sitting low, casting its long crisp shadows. Weaned from photosynthesis, they were resplendent in red, orange, and brilliant yellow.

In New Paltz we were welcomed by Alex's friends from past trips. Young Hugh Herr was there too, and since we'd last seen him had put up routes that Alex was keen to try. Delicious pizza and calzones at local restaurants tempted us to spend the last of our money on dinners out, although we survived mostly on crisp tart apples, pumpkin bread, and cider from local orchards.

We climbed on the spectacular overhangs that comprise the cliffs of the Shawangunk Preserve just north of New Paltz. The quartz conglomerate cliffs rise two to three hundred feet with horizontal fractures that provide great jugs and ledges, not obvious from below, enabling even novice climbers to ascend overhangs with relative ease. The outcrops snake above old carriage roads that provide a scenic stroll along their base and above the pastoral valley. We walked these roads and picked our routes each day beneath the falling leaves of hardwoods, mingling with other migrating climbers who also had come for the loveliness of autumn.

At first Alex did not feel he was climbing up to his standards, but he managed to "on-sight," or climb without falling the first time he tried, some very difficult routes before we left: Hugh's routes, called Sticky Bun Power and Position, and other coveted climbs such as Gravity's Rainbow, Project X, and the King of Swing, which Alex declared the best route in the Gunks. Those names strike a whimsical chord in my heart today, conjuring up that time of carefree challenge with an unknown tomorrow; lean fit bodies, grimy with dirt and sweat; and double ropes leading to the sky, falling from overhangs to swing out in space. It was glorious, but I wasn't quite as carefree as Alex or as passionate about climbing, and I began to fret about getting back to work. I asked him what he envisioned as our future.

"I'm not ready to be tied down," he said bluntly.

"Neither am I. Been there, done that," I countered, "but I do feel like maybe I should be thinking about getting a job and putting a roof over my head before winter!"

My fretting served to push Alex away. Weary, I decided to lose myself in a book and forgo strenuous climbs for a few days to clear my head. But as I sat reading, I became depressed by my quandary. I had the life I had dreamt of with Alex, but I felt ready to take flight. Alex had talked of getting a job here—fixing squirrel guards on telephone wires, which he had done the previous year—but I was none too keen about staying. Nor was I excited to hitch across the country alone, but I was too proud to call my folks and ask them to wire money. I felt the need to get home before winter, but where was home?

One night as we lay in our now well-ripened sleeping bags on the hard floor of the hut, I tossed and turned to find comfort for my bony hips. I missed having Alex's firm arm around me, felt defiant at his indifference, and told him I was leaving. "It seems to be over between us. I'm hitching out of here tomorrow," I said.

"OK, I'll come with you," he replied, resigned.

"You don't need to, Alex. I hitched across France without you, and I'll have no problem getting home. I'm a Montana girl." Despite my tough words, I was daunted by the prospect. When morning came, my resolve melted with his insistence that we leave together.

We were picked up by a trucker and made a long haul with him, driving into the night across the northeastern United States. He welcomed our company to help pass the time and keep him alert by sharing tales of our summer travels. His rig had a berth in the cab and, exhausted, I crawled up into it for a nap while Alex slurped truck-stop coffee and told oil rig stories to keep the driver entertained. In no time we had gone hundreds of miles. Near the end of his line, our driver called the next truck stop on his CB radio to ask if anyone wanted riders. Thanks to Alex's storytelling charm, our next ride was waiting when we reached the stop. Thus we made incredibly good time, and within a couple of days we were in North Dakota.

There we had a frightening experience. The driver was from

Texas and told us all about his gun collection, which was reportedly vast, and his wife collection, which was nearly as vast. "I've had six wives and five divorces," he bragged.

"Well, how's it going with your current wife?" Alex asked politely.

"Oh, she's dead," he said, and then proceeded to tell a grisly story about finding her in bed with a boyfriend after a long haul. "I just lost it and killed her. Killed 'em both!" he said in a matter-of-fact way.

My heart leapt to my throat and I was gripped with fear as my mind raced along with my heart. Alex replied, "Really?" as if the guy had just said he liked the color blue.

I sat in silence while my head was in complete riot. "Is he for real? No way! He's just trying to scare the shit out of us—and it's working. What if he pulls out a gun and shoots us right now?" Then I heard Alex talking as though nothing was amiss, changing the subject. "I used to hunt . . . had some great times hunting with my dad and brother . . . " The minutes seemed like hours as snow began to fall thickly, obscuring everything and making it seem even more as though we were trapped with this strange and possibly homicidal man. But Alex kept talking, and eventually talked him into pulling over to let us out at the next stop. I was filled with relief as he drove away, but worried about his story.

"My God, do you think he was telling the truth?" I asked Alex.

"Naw, he was just bullshitting," Alex said. "But I figured we'd better get out."

"Thanks! You were great!" I said, and he gave me a hug, apologizing, "I'm sorry I got you into this."

The last ride was another big rig, and he was heading right through Missoula to Spokane, which made us greatly relieved: we had found a ticket home! The driver was a very nice fellow, young and friendly. He showed us pictures of his wife and kids, spoke of them lovingly, and played Janis Joplin, which we all sang along with when it came to "Me and Bobby Magee." The last pass that the big truck geared down to climb was Pipestone, near Butte, Montana, and there we saw the northern lights dancing across the sky. I had seen them only a few times in my life, so it was a grand homecoming. I felt happy yet sad that Alex and I would soon be in Missoula, our journey together over.

I went to my mom's house, and Alex went to his parents'. There wasn't much discussion about breaking up, but it seemed understood. I called my cousin right away to see if he knew of any seismic work. Within a day or two he called back to say that there was an opening. "There are two openings if Alex is around," he said. I told him I wasn't sure, but I would definitely come down right away. Then I called Alex to say I would be leaving for Colorado.

"Is there a job for me?" he asked.

I hesitated. "Yes, there is . . . but I found this job, and I don't feel like hanging out if we're not together. It's too hard for me. I'm leaving tomorrow if you want to drop by." When I hung up I began to cry, thinking of all we had been through together and the love we had shared.

My mom was sympathetic. "You'll be fine," she said, hugging me. "I've had plenty of heartache in my life. You'll get past it."

Later that evening, Alex came to the door and asked if I'd go for a walk. We strolled to the Dairy Queen, and he handed me a letter to read as we walked. "Dear Jennifer," it began, "Just a little note letting you know how dear you are to me . . . "

I took his hands, and he made his plea. "It's been a great year, Jenni," he said. "You know, I can find another job, but I know I'll never find another woman like you." I remember thinking he'd make a great used car salesman, but I put my arms around him, laughing, and we left together the next morning.

Working-Class Blues

> To be alive is to love.
> Those who live dangerously,
> Creatively
> And wonderfully
> Are the great lovers in the world.
> —FATHER WILLIAM MCNAMARA

GLENWOOD SPRINGS, COLORADO, rests in a narrow, scenic canyon with its namesake, an inviting natural hot spring, sending forth steam from the center of town. Alex and I waded into the hot outdoor pool within an hour of our arrival and sat enveloped in a thick, dreamy cloud. We liked the town with its cozy coffee shops, good local restaurants, and community of outdoor enthusiasts. But our life there was work, and within a week it was as if we had never left the unique subculture of the seismic world, where the only days off were weather days, few and far between, and the only community was that of our coworkers and each other at the end of an arduous workday.

There was the same plethora of drugs, rednecks with hangovers, and the disheartening routine of leaving for work in the dark and returning in the dark, breathing secondhand smoke while droning along in a dual-wheeled pickup to and from the landing zone and waiting for choppers to fly. I steeled myself for the constant barrage of profane language. We'd been given little yellow foam marshmallow earplugs for helicopter flights, but I stuffed them into my ears to dull the boom of heavy metal music for the long ride in the truck as well.

We battled through thick scrub oak on steep hillsides where mule deer hid from hunters, and wrestled with geophones while clad in neon orange vests so that our movement would not be mistaken by the scope of a hunter's rifle. In mid-November, we switched crews and moved north to the aspen groves near Steamboat Springs. Alex and I volunteered to stay in a little trailer in the woods near the landing zone so we could guard the "mag site," where a store of dynamite for shots could not be left unattended.

Our first Thanksgiving together was spent there in the tiny trailer among aspen, with snow falling silently while two Cornish game hens roasted to a nutty brown. We prepared a resplendent feast on our precious day off, cooking with the added challenge and humor of a miniature oven, sparse utensils, and a cramped kitchen. Outside, mountain chickadees and juncos flitted about in feathery snow while inside, Vivaldi on our tape deck provided a soundtrack for their movement. We dined by candlelight in the intimate space.

At Alex's urging, we skied up a mountain beneath a full moon amid glades of ghostly aspen and open meadows of deep powder, then made swooping telemark turns back down. From quiet cold came the warmth of exertion and the gleeful joy of speeding through the chill night air until our hair and hats were thick with frost and our lungs burned.

Because we were always moving from one small town to another, most of the crew stayed in motels, but Alex and I hoarded our money by scamming places to camp or bivy. One night we were offered the use of a bedroom in a coworker's apartment, and we accepted without really knowing him. We retired early, crawling into sleeping bags on a squeaky bed. But a loud party revved into gear in the next room, and soon we heard the sounds of a drunken brawl. We froze with fear as a gunshot exploded from the living room. With hearts pounding, we slithered beneath the bed until Alex was certain no bullets would fly. "Assholes!" Alex hissed. Then we pulled on our clothes, wadded our sleeping bags into a pack, and crawled out the window, sprinting to the car. After a few hours of restless sleep in the frosty Volvo, we reported to work.

By Christmas our crew had drifted to Cody, Wyoming, and worked near Meeteetse, where a colony of endangered black-footed ferrets lived. In the 1970s biologists had thought they were extinct, but around a hundred of the small predators were discovered there during the 1980s. I was intrigued by the little animals, but our boss warned everyone to stay clear. I think he worried that some on our crew might wipe them out altogether. Gopher hunting was great sport among juggies.

Unlike our coworkers, Alex and I kept appreciative track of the wildlife as we rambled across the western landscape and walked miles of open space. Whitetail, mule deer, and antelope dotted the hills and valleys. Elk exploded from their beds, crashing through timber. Rabbits, squirrels, and many small rodents were constant reminders of the minutiae of life, along with hundreds of species of birds and other wild things. Bobcats and bear were rarely seen but left their tracks for us to find. Once we caught sight of a pine martin, which is a truly rare thing. The shy animals have a catlike face and a weasel-like body but are much larger.

As we put in long days of work, we dreamed of a world apart, planning another climbing expedition to the Ruth Glacier in Alaska with friends Eric and Alice. Around Christmas they hired on to our crew, leaving their jobs in Boulder behind for the promise of more lucrative pay as we all saved our pennies for Alaska. Having them join us felt like being back in touch with a familiar world. That Christmas we cut our own tree and baked gingerbread cookies to hang on it, then draped it with strung popcorn and cranberries and pinecones and ribbons. It was a wonderful holiday, as Alex related in a whimsical letter to my grandmother:

*Dear Grandest, Thanks for all the goodies. We've been eating
them with relish. . . . We had a very merry Christmas and a
couple of friends to celebrate with. Jenni created a most exorbitant
feast including a turkey with stuffing, sweet potatoes, green
beans, cranberry sauce and apple pie, apple pie with extra apple
pie. Your box of Russell Stover candies lasted an amazingly long
time—about eight and a half minutes. So after all was said and
done, not much was said or done but a lot of food was consumed!*

My grandmother's acceptance of Alex had been immediate and
unquestioning when I had brought him to meet her the previous
spring. Nothing made her happier than cooking for appreciative
guests, and Alex was a hearty eater and expert dishwasher; also, he
had a physique that appeared to need feeding. Plus she knew I loved
him. "How is that beau of yours?" she would ask me. "Has he gained
a pound or two?"

Soon after Christmas, our entire crew was laid off as the oil boom
began a decline. We drifted to Bozeman, where Alex surprised me
one evening at dinner out. Adhering to ritual, he presented me with
a small velveteen box, and in it I was completely astonished to find
a ring with a tiny blue stone like a bright forget-me-not on a gold
rope band. "It's a Montana sapphire," he said, "so you can always
have a little bit of Montana with you wherever you journey to. We
don't have to get married right away, Jen," he added with charming
awkwardness, "but I wanted you to know how I feel." "It's beautiful,"
I whispered as my eyes filled with tears and Alex knelt before me to
slip the ring on my finger. The few other restaurant customers could
not help but notice, and clapped as we both stood up to embrace
before resuming our meal.

February found us in Ovando at Dad and Carol's ranch. They
were kind enough to provide work for us, which gave me an opportunity to share my knowledge of the ranch with Alex as we dove
into chores together. We shoveled snow and threw bales to bawling

cows, and I saddled up horses for us to ride. "I'm terrified of these things," he admitted after our first ride, and was duly impressed with my skills. My father stared with raised eyebrows when Alex, charged with keeping the creek open so the cows could drink, made an enormous hole in the dense ice on the creek in an hour's time. "My God," Dad said, laughing. "That would have taken me half the day."

Alex shared the experience with my grandmother:

What a beautiful place this is. The mountains behind us are absolutely heavenly—especially in the evening. They look so soft and clean with so much new snow around. . . . We'll be leaving for Missoula in a few days but I've enjoyed this opportunity to get away from fast lifestyles and get to know Jenni's father (and your son!). I find him a bit intimidating although we've gotten to be good friends now. I almost passed out asking him for Jenni's hand. Jenni thought I'd never do it!

By mid-April, we'd saved enough money and were ready to depart for Alaska. Alex and I planned to elope in the tiny village of Talkeetna after our climbing expedition, escaping from the trappings of a ritualized wedding and reinforcing our commitment to adventure. Talkeetna is where climbers gather to board their chartered bush planes and fly into the distant glaciated mountains. The light planes are equipped with skis as well as wheels for landing on the snow-covered glaciers, where they drop their passengers among the sirens of their calling. Talkeetna sits on the banks of the Susitna River, with a breathtaking view of the Alaska Range, and at that time consisted of an airstrip, a ranger station, a handful of buildings, and a muddy main street.

We flew to Anchorage and then traveled by train to Talkeetna, joining a sizable group of Japanese climbers. Our plan was to fly into the Ruth Glacier, where Alice and I hoped to climb one of its finer sculpted forms, a beautiful 10,000-foot peak called the Moose's Tooth, and Alex and Eric planned to climb Mount Huntington's dramatic north face. We also planned to traverse over a pass to the Kahiltna and do an ascent of Denali (Mount McKinley) to wrap things up. It was ambitious, to say the least, for four young climbers on their first trip to Alaska, but it's amazing how plausible things look when one is poring over a map and peering at eight-by-ten-inch photos. We had dubbed our team Alice and the Aggressors.

Our plan was met with skepticism by the park rangers, who review all climbing permits. They recognized an abundance of youthful enthusiasm but a little less common sense. They encouraged us to consider taking a flight from the Ruth to the Kahiltna, explaining kindly that the heavily crevassed pass was a rather serious undertaking. But our experience in the Canadian Rockies and the Alps passed muster for a permit, and they sent us on our way with good wishes for success.

With enough gear and food for a month stuffed into the plane, we flew into the Ruth. The reality of our situation, and a few doubts, began to register only as we watched the bright red Cessna roar back down the glacier and rise into the Ruth Amphitheater, where it became like a toy in the immense white landscape. There we stood, surrounded by massive snow-covered peaks for hundreds of miles, like formidable sleeping giants. Within minutes, an enormous avalanche roared from the slopes of one great monolith, tearing across miles of glacier and up the flank of another in a billowing cloud of white that left us feeling awestruck, minute, and vulnerable.

From the landing strip, Alice and I had a good vantage to look at our proposed route up the Moose's Tooth. We eyed it with fear and trepidation for a few days until we summoned enough nerve to give it a go. We set out across the glacier on skis, roped together and watching for crevasses that could easily be hidden beneath a blanket of snow, ready to swallow us up.

In retrospect, we were completely naive and unprepared. Had one of us fallen into a crevasse, the consequences could have been grave. We had never practiced prusiking (ascending the rope by sliding smaller knotted ropes up and weighting them alternately) while dangling on a rope or holding a fall with a self-arrest. I recall peering into one yawning canyon, its ice layers in varying hues of blue dropping hundreds of feet into darkness.

But we were lucky. We managed to make our way around and through an ever increasing maze of deep chasms as we neared the base of the peak and found refuge beneath a large rock buttress. There we made our first camp. Enormous ravens circled above us, with their gravelly cries echoing off granite walls.

It was both thrilling and frightening to be there by ourselves that first night. I felt completely aware that my every move could have dire consequences, that my survival rested completely on my own ability and judgment combined with Alice's. We were thoroughly tuned into each other's emotions and thoughts with a constant exchange of communication as we progressed. "What do you think about this snow bridge?" "Let's avoid that serac." "Does this look good to you?" "Shall we belay here?" We both agreed that if either of us felt uncomfortable in any situation, we would stop and evaluate or turn around. The route we followed had been established in the 1960s on the first ascent of the beautiful mountain, by a team of Germans.

Two days later we reached our high point. We had camped in a snow cave dug by other climbers on the buttress shoulder, then traversed across a dicey section of rock slab to a steep snow couloir, which led to the top of the ridge. As we looked down the couloir, we saw a sea of clouds hugging the base of the mountain and the glacier far below. Small clouds drifted about me, there one moment, gone the next, sending crystalline snow flakes dancing through sunlight and giving me a surreal feeling of being in heaven.

Punching my ice axs into stiff snow, methodically climbing ever higher, I heard the cry of geese and turned to see them below, a wavering formation flying south. At the point where the couloir met the ridge, we could see an enormous cornice to our left, which made us leery of going farther. Meanwhile, a cloud spewing thick flakes of snow fogged in around us, making it difficult to see. Neither of us were keen to travel on the long corniced ridge in a thick fog to find the west summit or any summit. We had made it to the ridge and Alice was nervous about frostbite, as her boots were tight and her feet had gone numb. We had climbed what we set out to climb, and our thoughts turned to getting down to our last camp before dark.

As Alice and I had made our way up the Moose's Tooth, Eric and Alex had been struggling across the valley to advance our base camp up the glacier closer to the objective they hoped to climb. It was slow-going over the glacier, with heavy sleds to drag containing all of the gear and food. The two decided to try a warm-up climb on a lower peak but found hip-deep snow that made it dangerous. Their disappointment and loss of confidence led to squabbling. In frustration, Alex quietly led on, breaking trail, pushing harder with determined effort and practically dragging Eric, adding insult to strife.

When Alice and I arrived back at the scenic camp, happy with our perceived success, we found a brooding duo with bruised egos who were barely speaking to each other. After watching Huntington shed one avalanche after another, they had realized it would be foolhardy to climb. It took a day or two for them to regroup and choose a new target: a steep mixed route on the north buttress of the Rooster's Comb.

On the route, they once again found their comfortable rhythm and humor as seasoned partners, joking and laughing between leads. They had done several pitches and were making fast time when Alex led out on a near-vertical chimney of ice. Feeling confident, he had placed only one screw halfway up the pitch and then had run it out to the belay. There, with a solid stance, he beat a screw into the ice and fumbled to clip the carabiner, but suddenly found himself airborne as his crampon front points popped from their purchase.

Eric had already removed the belay and was ready to climb when he heard a piercing scream and looked skyward to see Alex's falling form well out from the wall. His thoughts were matter-of-fact: "We're going to die." But he grabbed the loop of rope and braced for the impact of the fall, and in those critical seconds saved both of their lives. The rope sang through his hands, melting several layers of nylon in the palms of his mitts, before that single screw took the final force and the weight of both men as Eric was pulled upward. It was a long fall, 170 feet, with a bounce against a rock section that left Alex with a severely damaged helmet and torn pack, but physically almost unscathed.

Meanwhile, Alice and I were in camp brewing tea, happy that our men were back on good terms. We had just enjoyed a grandstand view of them cruising the route across the glacier through our binoculars when Alice noticed that something was wrong. "It looks like they're coming down," she said. We strained to see, but even with the binoculars, they were mere specks against the ice. They must have had another fight, we concluded sadly, and watched as they slowly made their way back across the glacier toward us. Only when they arrived in camp did we realize they'd had an accident.

"We were so lucky," Eric said gravely. "We should be dead."

It turned out that Alex's crampons were prototypes, and the front-point design had not yet been finalized. The metal had fatigued and bent, sending him into space as his ax pulled out with the sudden force of all his weight. He had suffered a deep puncture wound and broken bone in his hand from the pick of his ice ax, and was seriously bruised, beat up, and shaken. But outwardly, Alex was jazzed. He apologized, thanked Eric over and over, and hugged me as though he would never let go.

At first he was not in any pain, but it hit him shortly, and we gave him medication for the long night. Eric and Alice decided to stay on the glacier, take a ski tour, and climb another small peak, but they helped Alex and me to pack up, make our way to the landing strip, and stamp an SOS into the snow to alert a pilot. One pilot or another circled through the valley on an almost daily basis if weather allowed, and it wasn't long before we were picked up and winging our way out of the Ruth.

Our wedding plans were dashed as Alex was flown on to the Anchorage hospital for treatment while I remained in Talkeetna to report the accident, gather our gear, and catch the train to join him. Once there, I took the longest, most welcome shower of my life, filled with relief by the steamy warmth, as I processed the events of the last two weeks. On our flight home, Alex was despondent, his hand in a cast. The euphoria of having survived the tremendous fall had evaporated, with a sense of embarrassment and failure taking its place.

In Missoula, we rescheduled our wedding to include immediate family and a few friends, giving Alex time to heal and Eric and Alice time to join us. Our parents seemed happy to be included in the event and hopeful that we would settle down after getting married. Eric and Alice had swayed us toward moving to Boulder, where rock and ice climbing sites were plentiful, but we knew we would need money in order to settle in the pricey college town, which meant more seismic work.

Montana had record rains that spring, which didn't help Alex's already depressed mood after the epic trip. We sat reading day after day beneath a grey ceiling of storm while another storm brewed inside of Alex. One morning he loaded his brother's canoe onto the car and told me to bundle up in rain gear for an outing to the Metcalf Bird Refuge near the Bitterroot River. With a plastic bag protecting his cast, we paddled about on the quiet ponds, green with fresh life, spooking up herons and young families of mallards and listening to the trill of red-winged blackbirds defending their territories as they clung to cattail spikes.

It was a peaceful and pleasant time. But one flooded section of wetland took us near the swollen and raging Bitterroot, where Alex had the sudden desire to go on the river. "Let's just take it down to the bridge," he pleaded.

"No way. I'm not a paddler, Alex. Let's get out of here." He pulled the canoe up to the bank and I clambered out, but then he pushed off into the current. "What are you doing?" "Meet me at the bridge!" he yelled, laughing, while I stood dumbfounded, watching him sweep away down the brown torrent.

I slogged to the car, then drove the few miles to the bridge with wipers slapping and the heater roaring at the fogged windows. I peered upriver nervously, trying to get a glimpse of Alex's yellow jacket on the wide swath of deep runoff. The river was a hundred feet wide and easily fifty feet deep at some points with logs, debris, and entire uprooted trees floating in its mad rush. "My God, he is crazy!" I thought. But then he appeared up over the bank, and relief washed over me as I watched him strolling through the woods, waving.

I hopped out, expecting to go with him to fetch the canoe, but noticed that he was soaked with more than rainwater and wearing a funny expression. "I lost the canoe," he said. The swift current had turned it sideways and it had flipped as torrid water carried it around a bend toward a massive rumbling logjam. He had pushed the canoe out in front of him and lunged for one of the logs, kicking his legs, as the boat was sucked beneath the twisted mass of trees. It had taken all of his strength to pull himself up onto the logjam and gingerly crawl across the slippery wood toward the bank. I stared at him in disbelief. "Are you trying to kill yourself to get out of our marriage? Because it isn't necessary. I'm having serious doubts about your sanity and whether I want to spend my life like this!"

"If you had come with me, the canoe never would have flipped," he argued quietly.

"If I had come with you, I would be at the bottom of the river, but thank God I'm not that stupid!"

We sat fuming in wet silence on our drive back to Missoula. I looked out across the river at the ranchland where my father had kept his horses when I was growing up. I thought of the time my sister Jan and I had ridden beneath the cottonwoods along a sandy shoal of the river in summer, when I suddenly found my horse thrashing beneath me in quicksand. It happened so fast, I somehow leapt from his back to the shallow water and made it to the bank, still holding his rein and pulling with all my might as he lunged his way out of the sandy muck. Both the horse and I stood shaking with adrenaline while my wide-eyed sister asked, "Are you OK?"

I looked at Alex and asked, "Are you OK?"

"I'm OK," he said. "I'm sorry, Jen. You're right—it was stupid. Do you still want to marry me?" he asked, offering his hand.

"I'll think about it," I answered, rolling my eyes and looking out at the passing landscape.

A few days before our wedding, the weather cleared and Alex, just out of his cast, was off for a run in the mountains. He had wanted to go climbing, but the doctor had warned against it, as his hand was still in a brace. "Good," I thought. "He can't get hurt running." I knew that he would lope up the trail to snow line and perhaps scramble up a peak, expending his pent-up energy and wrestling with the demons of his failed expedition, which were still weighing heavily on his mind.

I was somewhat shocked to see him back from running sooner than expected, with a bloody knee and a scraped-up hip.

"I fell on the trail," he said sheepishly.

I looked into his eyes. "You fell on the trail," I echoed. "No you didn't. You went climbing, didn't you?"

He had gone up the trail where all of his favorite rock climbs were and could not resist trying a few moves on a route called No Sweat Arête. The climb was relatively easy for his skill level, one that he had done many times. Everything felt great for him, so he just kept moving up until he happened to pull on a loose block of granite. The television-sized block teetered against him, and he knew for a few seconds that it would push him off the climb. He levered away from the block and landed on a small ledge that saved him from a possibly fatal fall to the ground.

I was incredulous as he told me the story with nervous laughter. "My God, Alex, I'm willing to take risks in our life, but this is getting ridiculous!"

"It was completely reasonable for me to solo that climb!" he countered. "It was a fluke that the block came loose!"

I didn't tell my own parents about Alex's mishap, but Jim and Dottie certainly knew. Perhaps they thought of it as Alex's way of having a bachelor party and hoped that, once married, he would become more responsible and settled.

I hoped our decision to marry wasn't as reckless as my betrothed appeared to be, and made Alex promise to be more careful. I knew our future was uncertain, but somehow I found that attractive. It made me more keenly aware of everything that was good about his energy and what we shared. Thomas Moore wrote in *Soul Mates*, "All endings are potential beginnings and all beginnings carry the potential seeds of ending. The willful approach to life feels ending as a contradiction, but the soulful imagination, constructed out of many little initiations, looks from a different sense of time, recognizing that beginnings and endings enfold into one another in a mysterious way." At the moment, Alex was very much alive, and the thought of life without him was unbearable. Although his antics made me crazy, I also found them inexplicably intoxicating. Perhaps I carried a gene for risk myself. After all, my father had been a fighter pilot.

We married on May 28, 1982, among our immediate family and a few friends in a quiet home ceremony in Missoula. A colorful cluster of wildflowers picked by Alex on an early morning walk served as my bouquet. It was made of balsamroot, Indian paintbrush, shooting stars, old man's beard, and forget-me-nots, sounding like a metaphor for a good long life and serving to remind us of all the fields of wildflowers that awaited our steps. Mother decorated her home with the spring blossoms of honeysuckle and forsythia cut from bushes that lined her yard. Our cake was baked by Dottie and decorated by young Ted with two Canada geese flying against a blue sky. Geese mate for life and, though they migrate thousands of miles in their lifetimes, they always return to their nesting ground.

Alex had landed a job with seismic surveyors that began in Dillon, Montana, where we rented a tiny cabin. At first I was hopeful of getting hired on his crew, but I grew impatient after a few weeks of waiting. Alex's wage was plenty for us to live on but not enough to save much, and although I had taken a waitressing job, my paycheck was dismal next to the wage I could earn on a seismic crew. When I located a job in Blanding, Utah, we agreed to part ways for its duration, perhaps two months, after which we would meet again in Boulder.

Blanding was a tiny community in the southeast corner of Utah, located amid the ancient ruins of the Anasazi. Alex and I had climbed nearby the year before, and I was eager to spend time among its rugged bluffs and mesas, where the ancestral Puebloans had built sophisticated apartment dwellings nestled against cliff walls. It was astounding to realize that they had been there seven hundred years before, and their culture had endured for twelve hundred years before that.

Upon arrival I checked in with my crew boss at the KOA campground, but the weather was quite hot—blistering, in fact, with temperatures in the 90s and 100s. The campground was crowded, so I set about looking for a place to live where I could have my own shower, shade, and peace and quiet. I decided to go door to door and ask local folks whether they knew of anyone with a room to rent by the week.

The center of town was largely Mormon, with quaint well-kept houses in tidy neighborhoods. The people I approached at their doorsteps did not seem taken aback at my boldness; in fact, at the third house whose sidewalk I strolled up, I was invited in for tea by a friendly looking couple. They were a little younger than my parents and invited me to stay in their spare bedroom for a few nights, until a friend of theirs had her cottage ready to rent. Their kindness was unprecedented. Perhaps they thought of me as out on my own mission of sorts, just as their children had taken, in the Mormon tradition. Within the week I had a tiny studio apartment where I could cook and have my own shower and refrigerator. There, I wrote letters to Grandmother, my mother, and Alex each night. Soon I was receiving his letters back.

It was so good to hear from you, I reread the letters several times. Glad to hear you're working, you have a place to live and sound reasonably happy. You're the kind of person who will be happy anywhere and in any situation. I only wish I could be with you. How typical of you to come up with an apartment the way you did.

I told him of the desert where we walked each day, with hundreds of tiny bits of pot shards from the Anasazi and hidden cliff dwellings. I felt guilty, searching for oil in this archaeologist's paradise, and I felt like a trespasser walking over the land where that ancient culture once thrived. The heat took some getting used to, but after a few days I fell in love with the desert itself. Tracks left in the red soil showed the abundance of wild things that lived there, and we regularly scared up cottontails and big jackrabbits that leapt from their shade, racing off through the yucca and giant sagebrush. One evening, I took a drive and happened on a bobcat as the road curved through a draw. The sun was glowing pink and the moment magic.

The shy animal stood at the edge of the road, watching me with wide golden eyes as I slowed to a stop; then he bounded into the brush.

Alex and his survey crew had moved to Ephraim, Utah, and he wrote to me of a great horned owl that he had discovered in the local cemetery on a starlight stroll.

> *Dearest, the other night I went over to see the owl and he was sitting on a tombstone about three feet from a big pine tree. I positioned myself so as to keep the tree between us and sneaked up on him. I slowly peeked around the tree and got to see him so close. He didn't even notice me for a minute or so and it was so exciting watching his huge yellow eyes. Finally he saw me and must have had a real shock as he just froze for a few seconds then flapped away. He's a fine big chap!*

We spent one weekend together before Alex left for Europe. He had been invited to participate in a climbing exchange to the United Kingdom, sponsored by the American Alpine Club and the British Mountaineering Club. American and British rock climbers would join together on a tour of select climbing areas throughout Britain for three weeks in September. It was just the boost he needed to restore his confidence, and I was only marginally disappointed that I would not get to go with him. I was on my way north to a jobsite in Wyoming, so I traveled to Ephraim for an impassioned but brief reunion. Two weeks later, Alex left Ephraim by hitchhiking east through Boulder and on to New York, but not before making a plea for me to join him in Europe.

> *Jenni, I've been missing you so badly since you left, worse than ever before. I just don't want to be away from you for two months. I'm realizing more and more that you give me peace and happiness not to be found in self-serving adventures and actions. I need you more than I let on to you and more than I realize when I'm with you. . . . What would you think of flying from Seattle to London around Sept 22—right after my exchange? We could meet there and spend one or two months in Europe.*

I was touched and very tempted, but ultimately didn't go. My sister Jan and Perry Beckham were about to marry, and I couldn't miss my sister's day. So I was desperately missing Alex by the time we found each other again in Boulder in the fall of 1982. We rented an apartment in a renovated stone carriage house in Eldorado Canyon and settled in. Our home was nestled against the hill, with the river running close by and excellent climbing in the canyon just a stroll up the road. Alex took a job as a waiter and I found work at the Bagel Bakery downtown. We planned to gain residency, then return to school at the University of Colorado (CU). Together once more, Alex and Eric climbed avidly on the abundant local rock and, when winter came, they traveled to Telluride, Vail, and Rocky Mountain National Park to do all of the ice climbs they could find.

Another frequent partner of Alex's was Jeff Lowe (no relation), who had established himself as one of the best ice climbers of the day. Sometime that winter, Alex and Jeff hatched the idea of going on an expedition to Peru. A friend who had visited the Cordillera Blanca gave us a breathtaking slideshow of climbing and scenic villages. Alex consumed history, mountaineering, and travel books to prepare, and we both worked extra night jobs to make enough money for the trip.

In spring of 1983 we gave up our apartment and moved everything into storage. Alex and I rode a Greyhound bus to Miami, being too broke to take that leg of the trip by air. It rained all across Texas and Oklahoma and I saw my first opossum—lots of them, actually, smashed on the road and viewed from my blurry rain-streaked window. In Miami, Alex and I hitched south to a littered beach lined with coconut palms for a day of combing and a night of camping before returning to meet Jeff and his wife, Janie, for the flight to Lima.

The ancient capital intoxicated Alex and me with its beauty, history, and culture, but we were saddened by Peru's poverty. Barrios of cardboard and plywood shacks housed bedraggled families who scavenged from nearby heaps of garbage. It was the first time either of us had witnessed such scenes, and we felt a mix of shame, guilt, and helplessness.

We took an excursion flight south to Cuzco for a trek to the beautiful hidden Inca city of Machu Picchu. From Cuzco, we traveled on the train that switchbacks its way up a hillside, then rambles up the Urubamba River valley to kilometer marker 88, dumping off trekkers for the Inca Trail. At the trailhead where we shouldered our packs a striking young Quechua woman walked briskly by us, her baby peering from the brightly colored blanket across her chest, and an enormous bundle of sticks on her back. Her black eyes shot from beneath the flat brim of her straw hat to survey and dismiss us in one proud glance.

Beginning in dense subtropical forest and climbing up to open grassland, we spent three days on the extraordinary trail, which wound its way over passes reaching 4,000 meters (about 13,000 feet). Our son Max recently made the same trek with a group of teenagers, half of whom were blind; he helped guide them on the precipitous trail. "It was cool to think of you and Dad having been there," he told me.

It was a perfect way to acclimatize for the peaks that Alex and I planned to climb later. We camped near ruins along the way, old outposts for the couriers who traveled these roads five hundred years before us. Alex had no trouble with the altitude; I recall laboring up one steep hill to find him doing push-ups atop the stone wall of an old ruin. Sitting together on the wall, we surveyed the rugged hills around us and were startled when an enormous hummingbird came near, hovering noisily for a moment before disappearing into the brush. The stonework of the Inca highway was an incredible feat of engineering and a preview of what lay ahead at Machu Picchu.

There, an island in the sky had been carved over thousands of years by the forces of water far below in the Urubamba River gorge. Atop the brilliant green island, the remarkable terraced city perched beneath the peak of Huayna Picchu. We arrived early in the morning, before the tourist train, to stroll through the perfect stone walls and stairways of the city by ourselves, quietly awed by the achievement of ancient people. Like pieces of a great puzzle, the massive stones weighing many tons fit together without the use of mortar so tightly that a thin knife blade cannot penetrate the space between them. It was inspiring to think of the sophisticated and tenacious character of people who had built such a marvelous place, and I had a flash of understanding the young woman whose glance had burned itself into my memory. Many months later, I drew her portrait in bright pastels, and it hangs in my bedroom today. "Who is that lady?" Isaac asked recently. "She's a mom I saw a long time ago," I tell him. "A strong, proud mom."

Traveling north to Huaraz in the Cordillera Blanca, Jeff and Alex prepared to climb the beautiful Taulliraju, or "flower of ice," which was named for the spiked flower of the *taulli*, a species of lupine growing in the valleys below. We made our way into the mountains from the tiny village of Cashapampa with burros carrying our gear to the base camp, accompanied by Alejandro, who served as burro driver and cook. Quiet and soft-spoken, he surprised us by taking a slingshot from his pocket, grabbing a rock, and taking aim at a group of wild ducks and Andean geese on a lake we passed by. Though close to the shore, the birds were quite a distance away. We assumed he was just having fun, but he nailed a duck square in the head, fetched it up, and prepared it as part of our delicious meal that night. Only later did I learn that the geese were a protected species, and thus fully appreciate the precision of his aim.

Jeff and Alex made the second ascent of the Italian Route, a sheer buttress of rock and ice on the southwest face. Janie and I waited in base camp with Alejandro, watching through binoculars as they progressed up the face. On the third day, we spied one person waving from the summit. The person disappeared and returned, waving again.

"They must be in trouble," we thought. "One of them must be hurt!"

Alejandro stayed to guard the camp while we took his burros and raced up the switchbacks of the adjacent pass to get a better view of where they were to descend. "I hate climbing," Janie blurted out as we hiked the steep trail, frantic with worry.

It turned out they had taken precautions on the rotten, corniced snow, belaying one person at a time to the summit. With enormous relief we met them at the top of the pass as they descended from the east face, happy to let the burros carry their packs back to base camp.

Alex and I then embarked on our own objective, the renowned Alpamayo, often referred to as the most beautiful mountain in the world for its perfect snow-covered pyramid. We climbed to the col between Alpamayo and neighboring Kitaraju for a high bivy; then, as dawn approached, we ascended the steep snow and ice of the classic southwest face. About halfway up the fluted runnel of ice, we came upon the frozen corpse of a climber—a discovery that was both shocking and unnerving for me, even though we had been told by other climbers that the body was there.

"I didn't realize how close we would be," I told Alex as I reached the belay with a knot in my stomach and tears stinging my eyes. "I'm not sure I want to go on." We had climbed within twenty feet of his body, which held my gaze in a surreal vision. His torso was mostly buried in the ice but his legs were exposed, still clothed in knickers, harness, and boots, and I couldn't help but think of his young life ended and a grieving family far away. I had never seen a dead person aside from a distant aunt in a funeral home when I was about five. This man had died in a fall from the summit a few years before, and his partner at the other end of the rope was somewhere above us beneath the snow. He had died doing the very thing that I was doing. He remained there, a testimonial to the risk he had taken, and I felt akin to him in some odd way.

"It's your choice, Jen, but we'll be fine," Alex said, putting an arm around me. "I'll make safe belays all the way to the top, and then we'll belay coming down. The conditions are perfectly safe. We're making really good time, and you're climbing well."

"OK," I decided, looking up at the corniced ridge above and then at Alex.

"We'll be fine," he said once more, and we climbed on to the summit.

Once there, we took only a few moments to survey the heights. The sky was deep blue, and brilliant white peaks marched across the horizon to the north, south, and east, where we had a fine view of Taulliraju. To the west was the patchwork of villages and fields, the wide river valley of civilization, more arid mountains, and then the Pacific. I strained my eyes trying to see the ocean. I looked to the glacier below and the col that we had crossed to reach it, to the valley leading back to Cashapampa. I had seen it all in detail, but now it became a different place, a sum of parts, all connected by the steps we had taken. High overhead we heard the dull roar of engines and looked to see the glint of a jet leaving its thread of white against the blue. At 19,000 feet, Alpamayo was the highest mountain either of us had stood on, and we were giddy with shared success as we carefully descended past the frozen climber.

That evening, camped beneath a starry sky, I spoke to Alex about the possibility of dying in the mountains. "It's so sad that they are still up there, frozen like that," I said.

"It is sad, but it would be difficult to bring them down and expensive to ship them home, and what for?" he answered. "Frankly, I'd rather be left on the most beautiful mountain in the world if it was me."

"I don't want it to be you," I mused, wondering how each of us would end our lives.

"We've all got to go somehow," he said. "I'd rather die on a mountain than in a car wreck."

As a child, traveling through Montana in my parents' car, I'd asked about the white crosses that appeared now and then along the side of the road. "That's where people died in a car wreck," Mom explained. For a long time, I thought the person was buried right where they had died, as some of the crosses had little flower wreaths adorning them. Only later did I learn that the crosses were not graves, just reminders or warnings to other drivers that death can be around a corner.

"I don't want to be frozen on a mountain, and I don't want to have a little white cross," I said to Alex, as if I had a choice. "I want to be an old lady like my grandmother, with lots of wonderful memories of every place I've been, and I want to share them with my grandchildren."

"You will," said Alex . "I'm sure you will."

Troubled Dreams

I awoke with a sense of wonder that I was in the very heart of Central Asia,
In a dream world of mountains and deserts and measureless distance . . .
an antique land, unaltered since the days of Marco Polo.
—ERIC SHIPTON

WORKING RETAIL AND WAITING TABLES to pay our rent during the winter of 1983, Alex and I realized that it would be impossible for us to ever earn enough in Boulder to attend CU. The following spring we migrated back to Bozeman, Montana, and settled in the upstairs apartment of a lovely old house on the south side of town. In summer, the walkway garden was rife with fat yellow and orange Iceland poppies, and a lush vine of deep purple clematis laced the porch trellis. In winter we awoke often to the scrape of a snow shovel before dawn as our retired landlord, who lived next to us, eagerly cleared the walks. We had been so transient that our residency was still intact for Montana State University, where we both enrolled in the fall of 1984. We were just a few hours' drive from our parents and full of anticipation for school, life, and our future.

Alex had all but flunked out during his last stint at MSU, on a chemical engineering scholarship out of high school. He'd become infatuated with rock climbing and spent too many days studying the crags instead of the chemistry books. He ashamedly admitted to me that there were some bad grades on his transcripts. "I got a couple of frogs," he said. An F was such an embarrassment that he couldn't even bring himself to say it.

Alex was his own harshest critic, failure his greatest fear. Driven to perfection in whatever he pursued, he had obviously pursued climbing instead of academia and had simply quit going to class. But that was all in the past. Alex returned to school wanting nothing less than a 4.0, studying like crazy and obsessing over grades. Every time he took a test he was completely neurotic, certain he'd bombed until scores were posted and he found his name next to an A.

Alex decided on a major in applied math, which he truly loved. "Math has a simple beauty like that found in nature," he told me. He sometimes hauled math books along on his expeditions, years after he graduated, to solve problems just for fun. The photojournalist and adventurer Gordon Wiltsie tells of Alex poring over differential equations on the face of Great Sail Peak on Baffin Island, which they climbed together in 1997.

"What are you going to be when you grow up?" We've all heard that question. "An artist," was the answer I had given since I was six. I kept drawing, painting, and taking art lessons, with encouragement from my parents, but they worried that I needed something to fall back on. I enrolled in art education courses as a nod to their concerns, but Alex's spirit awakened my own determination, and privately I set my sights on becoming an artist. At MSU I was fortunate to have an outstanding art history professor, Tony Benvin, whose animated lectures immersed me in the creations of past cultures. They stirred in me the desire to create, and I never left his class without a feeling of excitement and eagerness to make art of my own.

An advanced drawing class had an accidental influence on my entire future. A fellow student brought in some fat, brightly colored paint sticks to draw with one day. They were livestock markers, generally used by ranchers to mark the hides of sheep and cattle, but they made a perfect art medium. The vivid, greasy crayons, owning a consistency of paint when applied thickly, had the added attraction of being cheap. At the local ranch supply store, I bought up all the colors they had available. Before long I was drawing and painting exclusively with the bright fat markers to create simple forms of wild animals, birds, horses, and cowgirls, giving the familiar images a whimsical touch. I developed techniques of blending with my fingers, using brushes for detail, and scribbling with the markers directly on paper for a coarse, painterly quality.

Alex had no trouble finding partners for climbing when school allowed, and I accompanied him less and less. Whenever we drove down the Gallatin or near any rock outcrop, his eyes would peel the cliffs for possible new lines and the car would veer wildly. "I'll drive, Alex," I'd offer pointedly.

He made his share of first ascents on local rock, and whenever someone else put up a test piece, he was eager to give it a go— occasionally too eager. Letting impatience and excitement get the best of him, he intruded a few times on other climbers' projects, which did not endear him to all. Climbers have an unwritten rule that when someone has spotted and cleaned a new route—knocking off loose rock and dirt, and sometimes scrubbing holds with a brush—that climber gets a chance to lead the first ascent before the route is fair game for others to try. That could take days, weeks, or months depending on the difficulty of the route and the talent of the climber. "I started climbing it and I just couldn't quit," Alex told me sheepishly when I asked him about the fuss over one such route that he had snatched from the climber who had found it.

Many climbers in those days, including Alex, claimed not to be competitive, but I saw through that line. They all coveted first ascents. "You guys are a bit like dogs marking your territories," I'd joke, but I understood the desire to distinguish oneself as a pioneer with vision and creativity, to see possibilities where others had not.

But Alex inspired many others with his cheerful spirit, unbridled enthusiasm for climbing, and pure joy of being in the mountains. Mixed rock and ice climbing is where he found a new frontier, with Bozeman's abundance of frozen water. Having cut his teeth in Colorado on the most difficult test pieces there, Alex came back to Bozeman eyeing Hyalite Canyon with a new perspective on what was possible. He found it to be the perfect blend of rock and ice climbing moves.

In the winter of 1986, I accompanied Alex and Pat Callis on an early morning outing in Hyalite Canyon. A hero of Alex's, Pat is lean and fit with a soft-spoken, modest nature. He's a chemistry professor at MSU, a teacher and researcher, and a husband, father, and now grandfather. Back then he had a cat named Crampon and a wild look in his eye, both of which hinted at his other passion. Pat had forged new routes in California and Yosemite with the late Warren Harding before coming to Bozeman to teach in the late sixties. In Alex's view, Pat had done it all with style and grace.

We drove as far as the Palisade Falls turnoff in deep snow and continued on skis along the road at the boggy end of frozen Hyalite Lake. The last stars had faded from grey skies when a great horned owl perched on an old snag called out and silently swooped away. We stopped to watch his elegant slow-motion wing beats take the big bird to a distant pine, then continued pushing our skis single-file through the snow. "A good omen!" Alex said, and I thought of his parents' childhood nickname for him, Owlex. His mother had wallpapered his room with a pattern of owls swooping and peering from tree branches.

We skied to a smear of ice that Alex had spotted on the lower west side of the canyon. A section of black rock with a corner crack led to the ice covering the upper half of the route. Alex led the climb, gleefully whooping and exclaiming about how much fun it was, while Pat belayed with a bemused smile and occasional chuckles, making quiet comments such as "I'm glad you're leading."

I snapped pictures as Alex gracefully dry-tooled, placing the picks of his axs delicately on rock, then ascended the ice curtain. Pat and I followed. We chose the name Black Magic for the black rock that comprised the first seventy feet of climbing up a dihedral. The magic happened as you moved left and gingerly switched from climbing rock to hooking axes in the thin curtain of ice that led to the top. Pat looks a bit like a magician with his dark expressive eyes and his swooping stride, so in my mind the name was perfect.

Alex worked as a waiter at the elegantly restored Gallatin Gateway Inn, fifteen miles outside of Bozeman en route to the Gallatin Canyon and West Yellowstone. The inn was built in the early part of the century by the Milwaukee Railroad for tourists on their way to the park. Alex enjoyed the history, ambiance, and fast pace of working with a polished professional staff, and he made great tips. He had an old VW bus that he bought from a classmate. It was white with spray-painted zebra stripes, and he drove the thing like a madman to and from work, careening around the corners on Gooch Hill Road. I worried about him driving home late at night, especially on winter roads, and especially after he and his coworkers got into a habit of finishing off the leftover wine at closing time to wind down.

Occasionally we ventured to the inn for a romantic date. We sat in front of the massive fireplace sipping wine and talking before dining on rich gourmet meals that Alex usually served to others. He'd joke with his fellow waiters as they gave us the red-carpet treatment. "This butter has gone flaccid," he would quip with an English accent. "Excuse me, waiter . . . " He spoiled me with flowers, a card, or some small gift at our table, and often planned dates to coincide with a full moon.

In Montana's early winter, there are a few weeks near Thanksgiving when water turns to ice in the mountains and the snow depth is reasonably scant, making for an easy approach for climbers. One such fall Alex and I went out together and put up a new route on the north face of the Sphinx in the Madison Range. When the alarm erupted at 3:30 AM, Alex shot out of bed while I hunkered in, convinced we didn't need to get up so early. "God, my husband is nuts," I thought, listening to the rattle of pans in the kitchen as he prepared biscuits and coffee. "Who else would make biscuits at this hour?"

"Come on, dear!" he squawked, delivering coffee in bed. "We're goin' climbin'!" Alex set the record for "early to rise."

We had packed our ice gear the night before to expedite an early start. The streets were empty and traffic lights flashing yellow as Alex steered our little Subaru down Main and out of Bozeman toward the snaking canyon of the Madison River. By the time we reached the Ennis Valley, we had passed maybe one car and I was whining, "Even the hunters are still in bed." But Alex just snorted, "This is the best time of the day, Bird. Have some coffee!" and shoved the thermos in my direction, urging me to refill his own mug.

In the dark at the trailhead, we strapped on gaiters, shouldered packs, and grabbed ski poles. Even with Alex breaking trail through six to nine inches of snow that varied in consistency, I didn't have a prayer of matching his pace. He would stride out for thirty minutes, then wait and walk with me awhile before stretching his legs to race ahead. It was a comfortable pattern of hiking that we had adopted in our first years together, and it mimicked our life in a way. Time together to talk and share the experience alternated with time apart to go at our own comfortable paces and get lost in our thoughts. Alex was familiar with the trail, having hunted deer there recently; that was when he had discovered the smears of ice that fell from the north face of the Sphinx.

The snow became deeper and Alex took my pack to speed our approach. It was daylight long before we reached the base of the climb, since we had to scramble up a steep cliffy section through powdery snow. We realized too late that we could have taken a faster route up the next drainage, cutting over a high ridge to access our climb, which would have saved several hours of laborious slogging. The crack of a rifle broke the winter silence, sending ravens cawing across the valley and a shiver of fear through me. I hoped the hunters weren't near. I was more frightened of a rogue bullet than the icy face before us, and was glad for my red anorak and the orange vests that Alex and I wore. I thought of the beautiful bighorn sheep I had seen on the mountain, hoping they were well hidden.

The climbing was interesting but not terribly difficult: several serious pitches, one thin mixed one with red fractured rock and tiers of ice. Belay stances were cold on the northern exposure. Alex pulled big down mittens from his pack and surprised me with a thermos of hot cocoa with a dash of schnapps. My hands had gone numb after climbing one pitch, and he stuffed them beneath his fleece into his armpits. "I love having frozen hands in my armpits," he gasped. "That's true love!" I answered, sucking in my breath as the pain of blood returning to my icy fingers brought tears to my eyes: "chilblains," my grandmother used to call it.

"Damn, couldn't you have found someone else to do this with you?" I whined beneath the last roped pitch. There, tied to that quixotic man with a length of ice-covered rope in the middle of a windblown north face in winter, I wondered about my sanity. Alex swiped my dripping nose with his mitten and kissed me before leading the pitch. "Sorry dear, but I never get to do that with my other partners," he quipped with a grin.

Near the solstice, daylight hours are few and we topped out after the final easy scramble in late afternoon with temperatures plummeting. A full ghostly moon was rising in a pink sky over the blue-white landscape, but a storm was sending dark fingers of clouds from the north. As we walked off the summit, a small herd of wild sheep ran across the rocky slope. They stopped to stare from beneath curled horns at a safe distance, blowing puffs of steam from their nostrils. "Don't worry," I whispered to them, "we're not the hunters."

We made a rapid descent on the west slope, where wind had scoured away the snowy talus. Running down, glissading where we could, in no time we reached the forest as snow began to fall. It was dark and I followed Alex's bobbing headlight through quiet woods, plodding in silence while frost grew thick on my hair and eyelashes. At the car, we clambered in exhausted and soaked but happy to have stood atop that wild mountain together in winter. At a diner in Ennis, we ordered burgers just before they closed the kitchen. The room was empty except for a couple of cowboys who sat at the bar watching TV. Our cheeks burned red in the warmth and our bodies reeked with sweat as we slid into a corner booth. "Now this is a hot date!" Alex grinned, and we clinked beer glasses to toast our ascent.

Joanne Dornan was one of my best friends. She had moved to Bozeman from Jackson Hole, Wyoming, with her two young sons and her partner, Jack Tackle, who was a climbing chum of Alex's. We shared many dinners, evenings, and outings with Jack and Joanne, and I often stopped by their house on my way back and forth from MSU. I'd flop down in an overstuffed chair and we'd sip coffee, talking about our classes, our lives, and the challenges and rewards of sharing them with climbers. Though she was taking premed classes, her home was always a cozy refuge, with the children in and out and something delicious in the oven. Joanne had an artistic, playful sense of style. When I showed her my paintings, she was quite taken with them. "Jenni, these are wonderful!" she said, and proceeded to tell everyone she knew.

One day Joanne dropped by our apartment with Yvon and Malinda Chouinard, whom I had never met. Though I knew that Joanne and Malinda had raised their babies together among the wildflower meadows and sandy lakeshores of the Teton basin, I was surprised and a little starstruck. To me the petite couple was larger than life. Yvon Chouinard is a legend among climbers, having made his reputation as a visionary wall climber in Yosemite and then as a successful businessman at the helm of Chouinard Equipment and the well-known clothing company Patagonia. Malinda is his business partner, an art graduate and teacher. I knew that they had collected some fine works of art as they grew their company. They are also staunch champions of the environment and sustainable business ethics, and are not afraid to wear their colors boldly within the business world.

Without preamble that day, Joanne said, "I want to show Yvon and Malinda your art." I turned some shade of pink at the thought. It seemed premature, having just met this famous duo, to be pulling out a piece of my soul to show them two minutes later. But Joanne was insistent. I apologized as I brought out the paintings, explaining that Joanne was a loyal friend. Then I stood like a kid at show-and-tell, staring at the colorful images with stick figures dancing precariously across mountaintops, white rabbits, and rainbow trout leaping across the paper.

It was Yvon who broke the silence. "These are great! If they're for sale, we'd like to buy them."

"You're kidding," I said, stupefied. But they weren't kidding, and that day they bought several pieces, which still hang at Patagonia headquarters in Ventura, California. Over the years they collected more, and their support helped me acquire a number of other patrons in the Ventura area.

I picked up the phone as soon as they left. "Alex—Yvon and Malinda Chouinard bought three of my paintings!" I blurted. That evening Alex brought home roses, and we dined out to celebrate.

Alex went to the gym religiously and cranked pull-ups in any handy doorway. Our kitchen doorjamb was white with chalk. When we fixed meals together, he'd hang from one arm between tasks of chopping veggies or washing dishes. If he had an hour, he'd go for a quick run on a nearby trail or a session on the Nordic ski tracks that were set in the park, and at least one day a week he'd go for an all-day run, climb, or ski in the mountains. If he didn't do something physical, he wasn't pleasant to be with, so I always encouraged him to go.

But ultimately, being a weekend warrior wasn't proving to be enough for Alex. Even with academic success, he was not truly fulfilled by life as a student. Moody and depressed, working doggedly and silently at his desk for hours, he would drink too much coffee and too much beer in turn. He never felt he had put in enough hours of study or done well enough on any assignment, paper, or test. His perfectionism invoked an emotional turmoil that few knew of. His colleagues and professors saw only the exemplary student, as Alex was always composed, polite, and engaging in public.

I began to realize that climbing gave Alex an inner calm that he was unable to find elsewhere in his life. I remember him exploding into angry tirades about how he needed to feel the sun on his face and the wind in his hair, that life had no meaning sitting in front of a computer. "Go," I would command. "Get out of here and go! Go climbing, Alex." And he went. Canada, the Tetons, and Yosemite provided a greater challenge than local crags for holiday road trips. For a while these forays satisfied Alex's climbing appetite as he honed his skills on rock, ice, and alpine terrain, becoming ever more respected among his peers. He would come home calm and happy, but he had a growing desire to be part of an even bigger adventure. When he was invited to join an expedition to climb K2, the world's second-highest mountain, in the spring of 1986 with a strong American team, he was ecstatic.

The trip, organized and led by Lance Owens, was to be partially funded by the revenue from the team's guiding a group of trekkers across the Taklimakan Desert to base camp on the north side of K2 in China. Actually, there were two groups of trekkers; one was composed of load carriers, who were donating their labor as partial payment for the privilege of being on the expedition. At first I thought perhaps I would qualify, but when I found out I would still need to pay four thousand dollars, I gave up on the idea. I also sensed that Alex was not keen to have me come along. That was painful, since we had done all of our major adventuring together until that point, and this would be a very long expedition. Alex would be sent ahead with Choc Quinn from Calgary to oversee the load carriers and advance as much of their food and gear as possible up the long glacier beneath K2 before the remaining team members arrived. I would not see him for three months or more.

There was no question in either of our minds that he would go. The team was composed of some of the most accomplished climbers in North America, including George Lowe, Steve Swenson, David Cheesmond, Catherine Freer, and Greg Cronn. As the time drew near, I found myself feeling more angry, jealous, and hurt that I would not be part of the expedition, but when I confronted Alex, he said bluntly, "I think this is a trip I need to do alone. It isn't that I don't want you with me, but I've never been to altitude and don't know how I'll do. I will be with some very good climbers. But I'll be in a position of managing these other people, and it might cause problems if you were one of them." He tried to be diplomatic, but I had no trouble deciphering his fears. Alex would be on his first high-altitude climb on one of the world's most difficult mountains with a formidable group of teammates, and he wasn't sure how he would measure up. At the age of twenty-seven, he was the youngest member.

In 1937, the British explorer Eric Shipton and his team ventured to the Shaksgam Valley and its glaciers and climbed a nearby peak to survey the northern flank of K2. The technical difficulty of K2 is far greater than that of Everest, and the northern flank, which Alex would be attempting, had only two previous ascents, the first in 1982 by a Japanese team and the second in 1983 by the Italians. Alex knew it was a serious undertaking and he didn't want distractions. He was not a great manager of people, so the job of directing the load carriers loomed as a significant challenge. In retrospect, I think he didn't want me worrying in base camp, and he might not have wanted to be tempted by the opportunity to head down to my tent. He just wanted his shot at climbing K2.

It was a bitter pill for me to swallow, but I knew he made sense. We simply didn't have the money for me to join the trek. I also would have had to miss school, setting back my projected date of graduation. So I cried my fair share, feeling sorry that I wouldn't get to ride a camel across the remote desert to the Shaksgam glaciers in the footsteps of Shipton and look up at the incredible Karakoram Range of the Himalaya.

When I married Alex, I knew he was an alpinist. He seemed part of the wild world that I admired, a bird that couldn't be caged, a spirit with the same sense of confident drive and inquisitive need for adventure that sent forth explorers of old. I believed in his extraordinary talent. His sense of freedom allowed me to push myself, not accepting limits imposed by others. I never wanted to take that same freedom from him. So I made peace with the K2 expedition and went about focusing on what I would do while Alex was away.

At school, I found out about a summer program in art history at Warwick University in Coventry, England, and decided to go. I managed to scrape together enough money for travel and tuition, so while Alex was laboring to climb K2, I would be finishing up the spring quarter at MSU, showing some of my artwork in a Bozeman gallery, then touring about England viewing art and architecture of past eras. Alex left Bozeman with Choc Quinn late in April 1986, bound for China and K2. His first letters arrived ten days later.

I'm in Urumchi which is a city of 1 million people in North Central Xinjiang Province.... All day long, workmen chant as they dig and build. Everything involves hand labor here. We see men breaking rocks with hammer and chisel, working on highway construction and laying foundations of stone for big concrete buildings. With 1.5 billion people there is no shortage of hands in China. Wish you were here sweet one. I miss you already and know I'll miss you more and more. The group seems to be quite good, lots of spirit and no major problem types, but we've got some real characters on the trip. It will be wonderful to finally start walking into base camp. How's the fishing and school?

Fly-fishing was becoming one of my favored pastimes, and Bozeman had no shortage of streams to try. I loved losing myself in time, picking my way along the bank of a stream or wading into the cold swell of a current. It provided a calming diversion from the pressure of school and work. Alex wasn't cut out for fishing—he found it too difficult to stand still—but was delighted that I enjoyed it without demanding his participation. "Catch a lunker!" he'd say, grinning, as I ducked out the door.

His next letter told me all about his surroundings, and began with the Chinese rendition of my name:

This is the beginning of a long letter to the person I love more than any other. Today, we awoke at 8:00 and began our walk in. We have an incredible entourage; 50 camels, 15 sheep, 20 Americans, 2 Chinese, and 12 Kirghiz camel drivers.... Oh yes 3 mangy wild dogs and a half a dozen burros. Quite a group! Let me describe the camels. They are both stately and gangly. You would love them I know. They have absolutely serene faces with huge soft brown eyes. They have furry heads which they turn slowly from side

to side taking in their surroundings with composed disconcert. Their necks curve gracefully down to their bodies, which is where grace ends and awkwardness begins. Their legs are far too long for their seemingly scrawny bodies. Right now their winter wool is shedding off in great clumps like mountain goats in spring. To load them, the drivers jerk them down to their knobby padded knees. They look like a big dog when they kneel down with their long legs folded under them, and even more so when they lay their heads down between their "paws." Their sound is a wild shriek which seems strangely in place here in these wild remote mountains. They plod along with huge loads (200 lbs.) passively all day at about a person's easy pace. Their feet are wonderful, huge furry pads with two bird-like toes.

We walked all day through a deep gorge whose walls tower four to seven thousand ft above us. This is one of the most hostile environments I've encountered. The only vegetation is scraggly bushes eking out an existence in the dry rocky soil. I'm sitting by a fire drinking tea with Du, our interpreter. I must introduce him to you. . . . Du is fast becoming a good friend. He works for the C.M.A. [Chinese Mountaineering Association] and resides in Urumchi with his wife and son of three months. His wife is a medical instructor at a university. He's a lovely person who laughs all the time and has a great sense of humor. He teaches us Chinese and we reciprocate by improving his English. I walked all day with Du and we chatted of many things. I've told him all about you and he has told me all about his family. The camels have come near to be fed. The Kirghiz drivers grunt at them in their guttural Uighur tongue and they respond with loud shrieks, almost like apes but also something like the noise the lion makes on the Metro-Goldwyn-Mayer films. The whole effect seems like something out of the past. I feel so far away from you tonight. Goodnight my love.

Alex and I loved wild places and the feelings they invoke of traveling back in time. One of my favorite escapes was into my own past a few hours away near the town of Dillon, and I made the trip that spring, driving a seldom-used highway over the craggy sage-covered hills of Badger Pass. I glanced lovingly at the silver curls and smiling face of my grandmother as we buzzed along the empty roadway, enjoying the lush green of early spring. We were en route to the cabin that was her summer home, and as we dropped into a wide grassy valley, a cluster of grazing antelope scattered from the roadside, running in nimble unison. "Oh my!" Grandmother exclaimed. "How they can run! Aren't they beautiful?"

We rounded a long curve, slowing to turn on a dirt road that snaked its way between greening bottomland of wild hay and sage-brush hills. I slowed as we passed a weathered log house, gazing at the homestead of my great-grandparents, the place where Grandmother was born and grew up. "I remember riding in my father's wagon to our little schoolhouse, just there on Scudder Creek," she told me. Her voice was soothing as she recalled the past, telling the now familiar stories of her youth and invoking a timeless quality that I loved. We continued up the valley, over corrugated cattle guards and into a grove of quaking aspen. Nestled among the aspen, on a patch of green dotted with yellow dandelions, was a red log house. Behind it, the proud peaks of the Pioneer Range rose crisply white above the new growth of spring in the high clear air. "Oh, I love the little sage hens!" exclaimed Grandmother as we caught sight of a few watchful grouse.

Originally built as a ranch home by Grandmother's much adored older brother Ted, the log house at Polaris had been a quiet refuge and gathering place for our extended family for many decades. We entered the cool cavern of the kitchen where bottles and glassware, blue with age, lined the counters and shelves. The wood-burning stove stood cold and silent, but a stack of split wood and kindling held promise. "Let's take the chill off the house," Grandmother said as she laid a fire. I drifted through the rooms, gazing at familiar contents.

"Jensey, would you bring in a load of sticks?"

"I'd love to." I headed for the springhouse that straddles the trickling stream of Billings Creek. Its roof extends out over an open porch crowned by a small wood bell tower, a rusted iron bell hanging within. When I was a kid, running wild in the willows and hay meadows with my sisters and cousins, the ringing bell meant dinner, but we were admonished not to ring it just for fun. Grabbing the cable now, I pulled it slowly to hear the resonating *dong*. A rusty pipe protruded from the wall at the end of the porch, where water used to gush forth, splattering into a round hole in the floorboards to the stream below. The white enamel dipper still hung against the wall, and I pictured little hands grabbing it from its nail to catch a swirling cup of icy water. "The good old days before we had to worry about giardia," I mused.

Across the bridge in the aspens, I passed the old blacksmith shop sandwiched between ghostly relics of hay rakes, mowers, and tall white trunks of trees that bear the black scars of time and carved initials. I looked for mine and Alex's, where he had carved them inside a heart during our first visit. They were already as black as my father's initials, which he had carved in 1937 on a tree close by. Dad was seventeen then, working the hay fields at the heels of his uncles' horses. A wisp of drifting smoke reminded me of my original task: to bring in an armload of wood.

My little grandmother had an enormous heart and energy to match. She taught me an appreciation for nature and for the simple life that we found in this peaceful hideaway. "We're country mice," she said. I was content with her in this place that spoke to us of our own lifetimes and of those who came before us. As evening approached, we sat together in front of a warm fire and I read aloud to her, sharing Alex's letters and adventures from afar. "Now let's hear from that man of yours," Grandmother teased, settling into her chair with blue eyes dancing. "Where will he take us tonight?"

May 11: Tonight we camped at 14,300' just below Aghil Pass. It snowed off and on today with patches of sun revealing pinnacled granite peaks all around us. Hanging glaciers come down quite

near the pass, which is a broad, rocky, gentle break in an otherwise extremely rugged range. Should the clouds lift tomorrow we
may glimpse K2.

. . . I walked up onto a ridge above camp earlier and had a fine
view of Aghil Pass and the surrounding peaks. . . . I found a little
stone hut used by the nomadic herders which had two rooms
with fireplaces included. Quite a little refuge on this cold bleak
pass! Yesterday I slit the throat of one of our sheep. A couple of
camel drivers gave me a hand and it was great to see how these
hill people do their daily tasks. Following its certain death, one
cut a slit in the lower rear leg and put his mouth right over the
hole. He began blowing and blowing until it was blown up like a
balloon. This pulls the skin away from the meat and makes skin-
ning a breeze. Ray and I cubed up the quarters and tenderloins
while others sliced up loads of potatoes, carrots, onions, turnips
and garlic, and we all enjoyed a lovely mutton stew. . . . Dad did
us boys well by taking us out hunting.

Grandmother smiled, and I read on.

May 12: I'm sitting on a gravel bar on the Shaksgam River
tonight, the sun is warm and I'm wonderfully relaxed. The walk
up Aghil Pass was gentle but long. I felt fine at almost 16,000 ft.
From the top we got our first view of some of the world's highest
and most remote peaks. The Gasherbrums marched off to the
east surrounded by dozens of peaks over 25,000', all unnamed
and unclimbed. Absolutely breathtaking! . . . We're camped in a
thicket of bushes by a lovely stream. A little hawk was sitting on
a rock when we arrived. He was almost unafraid of us and I got
within 6' of him before he flew. He had the most fierce, yellow
eyes and watched me in wonder. I'm in good spirits but I really
miss you. It's going to be a long summer in here. . . . I trust all is
well with you, and your art show must have been a great success.
Your talent won't remain unannounced for long!

"I once had a beau who wrote letters like that," Grandmother said. "Marvelous!"

I arose early the next morning, ducked under the jack fence, and made my way across my cousin's hay field toward thick willows flanking Grasshopper Creek. The sky was clear and the grass frosty as I clunked along in green rubber waders, my fly rod in hand. Two mule deer dove from their beds and bounded off to a safe distance, then turned to survey me. High in the meadow I heard the gravelly call of sandhill cranes and watched them soaring overhead, voices echoing and long legs trailing. I crossed the bridge and a skunk waddled off, its black-and-white tail held high; then I followed the stream to my favorite hole, standing back to watch the water and tie on a fly.

Fishing this stream brought back memories of my first time out at Dad's heels, scurrying to keep up and spending the entire time trying to untangle my line or pull it from a willow or a seedy head of tall grass. I cast and watched the fly land above the swirl at the top of the hole. Within an hour I had caught and released a few brookies and kept two rainbows, which I gutted, cleaned, and slipped onto a green willow branch. "Oh my, rainbows, aren't they lovely?" beamed Grandmother when I laid them in her sink. "Our favorite breakfast!" I answered, and she had them frying on the wood fire in no time.

A few weeks later, I packed my bags for England. The summer program at Warwick University was a roving art history course, with lectures and field trips that took me all over the United Kingdom viewing museums, cathedrals, private art collections, and historic sites. My classmates were a mix of ages. I befriended Leone, a warm, inquisitive woman who was excited to learn that my husband was climbing K2. Such an endeavor was completely foreign to most of the people in the group. In fact, few had heard of K2, and even fewer knew it was the second-highest mountain on earth.

I toured castles and shops of artisans and wandered through the Cotswolds' lush hills of sheep farms and age-old houses. We studied John Ruskin, William Turner, and James McNeill

Whistler, romantic artists who had celebrated landscapes and mountains as art forms of nature. A visit to Stonehenge captured my imagination like nothing else. The megalithic blocks from the third millennium BC form a ring enclosing an area of some twenty-five acres. Though fans of literature like to think of it as the work of Merlin the magician, it is now thought to be an incredibly accurate calendar. To see this miracle, massive and elegant in its simplicity, was to marvel at the intellectual and physical tenacity of ancient man.

Though I was miles from home, Alex's letters still found me.

May 22: We still have two tons of gear at C.1 to bring 20 kilometers and 2500 ft. up to Advanced Base Camp. It's a staggering job. We have a wide range of strengths, personalities and abilities here. I'm definitely the strongest of the bunch for hauling loads but not the best people manager. I like most to be on the trail working hard rather than mediating at Base Camp. I'm learning a lot though and I'm making an effort to be fair and accommodating. It's good for me I'm sure. It's my job to get everyone pulling equally to accomplish a huge task. We've been waiting for a break in the weather now for almost one week. This morning, Choc and I decided to set off despite zero visibility. We stumbled through 18 inches of snow over loose moraine for 8 hours and are now camped in the middle of God knows where and the snow still falls. . . . Ah yes, this is climbing expedition style. Huge packs, long carries and endless days of snow and grey.

On the eve of our anniversary, he wrote:

May 27: Today, I thought of you constantly. A friend and I had a conversation about marriage, and he claims that partners change too much over time for marriage to work. I told him that I disagreed—that true commitment to each other requires each person to accept and love the new person who is continually evolving. That's what I want our future to hold. I love you deeply.

*We're so far apart but I feel very close to you tonight. Walking
up today with a heavy pack, I found myself drifting off in my
imagination. I pictured us walking up to the old cabin at Polaris
in the fall under the golden aspens. I hope you get over there this
summer with your grandmother to mow her dandelion lawn
and catch trout out of Grasshopper Creek.*

When my course at Warwick ended, I visited our friend Ian Parsons and his parents at their simple, charming cottage in the seaside village of Somerset. There, near the soothing sound of the sea, Ian's parents treated me with great kindness and warmth. One evening Ian led me down the narrow cobbled walk with a flashlight to show me a tiny visitor to the garden. "Look here!" he laughed. It was a hedgehog, magical, like a storybook character come to life. It had an innocent and fragile demeanor, rolled up like a ball to hide from the world.

Ian had heard through the grapevine that it was a season of bad weather and tragedy on K2. He didn't tell me until he knew who had died, but all were climbers from groups on the south side of the mountain. There was no news from the north. Ian quietly told me of the eight deaths, at the same time assuring me that Alex was fine. "No news is good news," he said. When I arrived home in August, the magnitude of the K2 tragedies made me eager for news, but the only word from Alex was the last letter he had sent out with the trekkers. I read it and cried:

*June 5: This is to be my last letter to you. I'm sending along a
postcard of the route in this letter. It will be two long months before
I see you again. The climbing is finally going to begin! I think
maybe I'm crazy to stay here and not come out with the trekkers.
Right now the wind is blowing down the valley at its normal 50
mph creating a classic desert dust storm. It blows every day and
coats everything with dust. Dust in the food, grit in your teeth,
sleeping bag, tent, everywhere! . . . I'm going to miss you badly
without being able to write and I'll think of you every day. Don't
worry about me, please—I'll return to you. Much, much love, Alex*

I rationalized that if there was bad news, I would have heard. I hoped they had made their ascent before the storms that had claimed so many lives around August 5. But I worried. I resumed work as a waitress and watched the days tick past. One day, walking home deep in thought, I was stopped by an acquaintance who said, "I'm sorry about Alex, I heard he died on K2." Shocked, I caught my breath in surprise, staring at her. I wondered if she knew something I didn't, but instantly decided not. "Not that I know of," I replied. "I think you got the wrong news!"

A few days later I made a weekend trip to Jackson Hole, staying with Jack and Joanne at Lupine Meadows. Perhaps I was seeking the company of other climbers in case I did get bad news, or perhaps it was a way for me to feel closer to Alex in spirit. In any case, I determined to climb the Grand Teton via the Enclosure Couloir, which includes several pitches of ice climbing, and I fished around for a partner at the Climber's Ranch. We packed our gear, rope, and food, hiked to the lower saddle of the Grand to camp, and then arose early to find our route to the Enclosure. I led the ice pitches, but near the top of the couloir, a storm moved in and we were enveloped in a thick cloud pelting us with snow. Lightning illuminated the cloud and a roar of thunder followed, giving no option but to get down fast. With ice tools humming and fear coursing through us, we made a rapid rappel and returned to the lower saddle for the long descent. I recall the beautiful site of Lupine Meadows and the relief of being down and safe, but I longed for the relief of knowing that Alex was also down and safe.

Early in August, Alex, Steve Swenson, and George Lowe reached their high camp on K2 and were poised to make a summit bid. The month of June had entailed leading and fixing rope to the high camp, with Steve, George, and Alex all climbing strong above Camp II. Storms came, one after another, with barely enough time between them for snow to settle. Twenty-six days of bad weather in July made climbing impossible, but it looked as though a window of opportunity finally had arrived. They were psyched and eager, but as evening came on, George didn't feel well. Coughing and tired, he announced to the others that he had pulmonary edema and needed to descend immediately. Both Alex and Steve wanted to accompany him to the lower camp, but George would not have it. He thought they had a good chance of summiting and would not let them give up. They radioed down to Catherine at the lower camp, and with reluctance Alex and Steve agreed that George would descend the fixed line alone. If he didn't reach Catherine within two hours, she was to call and they would descend after him. They waited anxiously as George descended and Catherine radioed the news.

Steve and Alex then prepared to make a summit bid, but with George gone, it seemed to Steve that Alex had lost his enthusiasm. The weather looked perfect, but Alex wasn't sure and Steve didn't want to pressure him. They did not know each other well, and Steve had climbed more on his own up to that point, while George and Alex had functioned as partners. The two discussed their options from their separate tents. "What do you want to do?" Steve asked. "Let's go up," Alex decided.

They set out but made slow progress through deep unstable snow. Alex was nervous about avalanche conditions, and about weather as it began to change; ultimately they decided to turn back at an elevation of 8,100 meters, only 500 meters from the summit. It was Alex who chose not to summit that day, and Steve was unwilling to go on alone. Perhaps Alex was worried about George or lost his nerve when his favored partner became ill. He had trusted in the judgment and experience of his older partner and was uncertain of his own and Steve's. "Alex was very cautious about snow conditions," Steve told me. "He was really the most cautious partner I've had in the mountains."

"And perhaps he just made the right call. That's what I believe," George told me recently. That night, it began to storm. The same storm trapped and killed five people on the other side of the mountain, bringing the season's death toll to thirteen. Had they pushed on to the summit, Steve and Alex may very well have stood atop K2 with the climbers who subsequently died. Alex did not make another summit attempt, and before long they were on their way down the glacier and out to the torrid banks of the Shaksgam River. They had brought along rafts, thinking they could cross the river and make a quick retreat through Pakistan, but one look at the river told them the folly of that. The long trek out began, and at the end of August, Alex came home from K2.

Responsible Family Man

SUCCESS
To laugh often and much;
To win the respect of intelligent
people and the affection of children;
To earn the appreciation of honest critics
and endure the betrayal of false friends;
To appreciate beauty, to find the best in others;
To leave the world a bit better,
whether by a healthy child,
a garden patch or a redeemed social condition;
To know even one life has breathed
easier because you have lived.
This is to have succeeded.
—RALPH WALDO EMERSON

ALEX CAME HOME FROM K2 with no evident disappointment over not having made the summit. He told me he had been reluctant to make an attempt without perfect conditions and minimal risk. "It just didn't feel right," he said. "I kept thinking about all the other things I want to do in my life, and it wasn't worth the risk." From K2, he had written, "I'm getting sick of hauling 80-100 lb packs and will definitely never do an expedition like this again." Once home, Alex referred to the K2 experience as a dinosaur of an expedition, telling me he had discovered that expedition-style climbing was not his thing. "I'd prefer to go light and move fast," he said.

I believe that was a turning point for Alex in that he did not regret his decision to retreat and did not dwell on the bad luck of weather. He was saddened by the loss of the other climbers and felt lucky that he had trusted his instincts and escaped a similar fate. I already knew that his endurance and ability were extraordinary, but this decision gave me confidence in his judgment, his mountain sense. In the five years we had spent together, it seemed to me that Alex had matured and settled. I could envision a long future for us with a home and some sort of real jobs—and a family.

The issue of whether to have children has strained or split apart many couples I have known. It played a major part in my decision to escape my first marriage, so when Alex and I chose to marry, children were part of the equation. It was a decision that we thought about carefully and that he was very much a part of. Although I knew Alex would always be a climber, I didn't worry that he would die and abandon me with children. I had a youthful sense of immunity, but I'd also learned long before that I could not sway the destiny of life's path, no matter how painful it might be.

When my father left our family in my thirteenth year, I did not want that new reality. I wanted to hang on to the security of my parents together and whole. I made a plan to run away to my grandmother's cabin at Polaris, where I would hide out and somehow ransom my parents into reconciliation. The safe haven of that log house beckoned with a notion that I could live alone rather than accept a painful change. To run away would certainly make them aware of the importance of my feelings. I arose from my bed one night to creep down a dark hall to the kitchen, slipped an apple into my coat pocket, and stared at the back door. Then I stole down the basement stairs to where my older sister slept and went to her side. "Jan," I whispered, touching her shoulder.

"Jenni, what's the matter?" she asked.

"I'm running away. I'm going to ride Mo to Polaris," I said, referring to my horse.

"But that's two hundred miles away!" she countered with grown-up concern. "It could take a few days. Where will you sleep?"

"I'll be fine. I have matches and food at the barn, and I'll sleep under the saddle blankets."

"That's so brave," she said. "Be careful!"

I hugged her tightly, then took the stairs three at a time and burst into the night. My heart raced as I ran into the dark field, looking back at my simple home in a neat row of houses. Images of rolling snowmen, running on freshly mown lawns, and birthday celebrations with my three sisters and two parents flooded my thoughts. A dog barked, and I turned to stride through the dried yellow grass of the field I had once thought of as endless. I had come to know it bit by bit, the call of its killdeers and hawks, its dirt piles and ditches and far boundaries. I ran most of the three miles to the barn where my horse stood in a black stall of fresh sawdust and hay. He nickered softly as I went to his side, grabbed his mane, and swung onto his familiar back. I lay there, burying my face in his sweet smell and feeling the warmth of his shifting weight beneath me, and began to cry. I sobbed for some time, trying to muster my courage but knowing I couldn't run away. Then I gathered myself to walk home as dawn approached, resigned to the fact that I could not change the way things were.

⸙

Isaac and I peered from our kitchen window recently to watch a downy woodpecker feed at the suet hanging from a dormant lilac while a red-breasted nuthatch made its way down a neighboring branch, headfirst as is its habit.

"Mom, do people come back to life as something else after they die?" Isaac asked.

"Well, some people believe that they do," I answered, "but I really don't know. It's a comforting thought, isn't it?"

"Yeah," he answered, nibbling the middle out of his grilled cheese sandwich.

"What would you come back as," I asked, "if you could choose?"

"I'd be a bird. Maybe a hawk . . . or an owl."

"Me too," I said. "I think I'd be an owl."

A few weeks before, Isaac and Sam discovered owl pellets in our backyard below the spruce that towers fifty feet above it. "We have an owl, Mom, we have an owl!" Isaac yelled, bursting into the kitchen with fuzzy grey lumps of fur and bone in his palm. Owls regurgitate these indigestible tidbits after gulping down their prey and we examined them with excitement, guessing they were left by a great horned owl.

In the spring of 1987, while I did my student teaching in Dillon, Montana, I had the fortunate opportunity to watch a family of great horned owls on the outskirts of town. After teaching art each day, I would bike to a grove of stately cottonwoods outside of town, and there I discovered an owl nest one afternoon. I caught sight of the adults first as one of them swooped into the upper branches of the towering tree, and then I noticed the tangle of nest nearby. It became my treat at the end of the school day to ride out to the old grove and watch the owls for a bit before pedaling back to my grandmother's place, where I was staying.

Grandmother shared her house with three of her sisters, my great-aunts, who were all in their eighties and nineties at the time. They loved hearing about the owl family each time I came sprinting back from my ride. There were three chicks like tiny creamy snow-men in their juvenile down, visible above the mass of sticks that was their nest, with parents perched close by, turning their heads slowly about. I took Grandmother and her sister Margie to see them one day as we traveled to our favorite picnic spot along the Beaverhead River. "Aren't they darling?" Grandmother enthused. And I had to agree.

I sometimes think of the young owlets as a precursor to my own three children, for it was then that I began to long for a family. Alex wasn't as eager as I was, even though we had agreed to it before marriage. As my clock began to tick and babies looked cuter and cuter, as school was behind me and I had a good job, I leaned on him. "I'm ready," I said.

"I'm not," he answered.

"But Alex, I'm thirty-one. I can't wait forever, and we have good health insurance while you're still a student, so the baby won't cost much."

"But I love our life the way it is, Jen. I love the freedom we have to travel, and my climbing is so important to me. I'm not sure I want to share you with another person yet. I'm scared that things will change, and I'm not sure I'll make such a great father just yet."

Alex's own father had been exacting and full of high expectations for his sons, with the added challenge of a short fuse. When angry, Jim was formidable. He was from the South, where good manners and obedience are expected, and though he was a bit of a rabble-rouser himself as a young man, he expected his boys to toe the line. Alex felt he had never met his father's expectations, somehow always falling short in his behavior, grades, athletic ability, or prowess as a hunter. "I was always grounded," he told me. "I thought I was a bad person and so was always being punished for that." His climbing had begun as a rebellion against those perceived expectations. For a few years, Alex refused to do anything he thought his parents wanted him to do. He dropped out of college and took off to the oil fields to make money for climbing.

Alex punished himself with criticism long after he had left home and the confines of his parents' upbringing. "I'm really not a great climber . . . if only I was stronger," he would say. "I'm the jack of all trades and master of none," he professed to audiences for his climbing slide show. The modest and humble nature of his character came from politeness, but it was combined with the belief that nothing he did was truly extraordinary. "It's just the result of a lot of hard work," he'd say. Friends and acquaintances always thought Alex had a positive outlook; like most of us, he saved his low moods and bleak outlooks for those who loved him unconditionally. "I suck at math," he would say to me while studying. "I just wish I was smarter and could understand this better."

"Must be hell," I'd try to joke. "I can hardly manage algebra, Alex."

"You know, Jen," he once said, "I have this fear that sometime people will find out how really mediocre I am."

Although he was humble and exacting of himself, Alex found criticism from others difficult to take, even unbearable. When he was criticized by *Climbing* magazine for putting an ascent of Hunter's North Buttress on his résumé even though he hadn't reached the true summit, he took it as a personal affront and was quite unforgiving of the writer and editor, still complaining years later about the scurrilous attack. "Self-righteous journalists trumping up controversy!" he'd grouse to me.

In our first years together, Alex carried some resentment toward his father for demanding perfection while falling short of it himself, as everyone does. But it was that little bit of anger and the ingrained self-doubt in Alex that fed his constant drive and desire to push himself beyond what most people do. It drove him to study madly and it drove him to work out like a fiend, doing hundreds of pull-ups, push-ups, and marathon runs in the backcountry. The adrenaline addiction that many risk takers speak of certainly played its part in his drive to climb. This powerful force, together with the intense love he felt for the mountains and the desire to be among them while testing his mental and physical prowess, all came together to make up his passionate character.

But the core of Alex's drive, I believe, came from the inner angst he had felt because of his father's tough love. He had a hard time with his dad's quirks, but of all the Lowe boys, Alex was the most like his father in many respects. Like his dad, Alex was a magnetic person whom people were drawn to and instantly liked. They both had a way with people, extending themselves genuinely to put others at ease and make them feel important, but around their own families, they could be intolerant, quietly critical, and impatient. And both had an incredible work ethic. If something needed doing, by God, they got after it. They also had the same affinity for laughter, silly jokes, and pranks. I believe that Jim was largely responsible for the man Alex became.

Jim had come from a broken home in the South where poverty

made life a challenge. His father, James Harry Lowe Sr., was a handsome red-haired fellow who, like Jim and Alex, was charismatic, intelligent, and good in music and math. But his weakness for alcohol led him to disappear repeatedly. Eventually he abandoned his family when Jim was twelve years old. The only boy in the family, Jim was raised by his mother and two older sisters.

"I owe everything to my mother, Anna Lacks Lowe," Jim told me. "She was a totally devoted mother who gave her life to her children. And I was a handful," he admitted. He loved nothing more than escaping to his beloved Smoky Mountains, where he learned the ways of the wild. He was bright and tough and he worked his way through the University of Tennessee, then Yale graduate school and a PhD. His sense of adventure and desire to protect his precious woods led him to become a smoke jumper, a job that required both physical and mental stamina.

Jim's strictness with his boys was likely overcompensation for the lack of fathering that he himself had experienced. He had no role model and had done the best he could. As parents, we always want our children to have a better life than the one we have lived. It's ironic that in our struggles to provide that, we may sabotage the parent-child relationship with our admonishments meant to impart knowledge. "I know I was too hard on the boys," Jim has said to me with true feeling, and I know that, like Alex, he is hard on himself. "I only hope that Alex knew how much I loved him," he told me quietly, tears welling, after Alex died. "He did," I assured him.

Two summers ago in Tennessee, hiking through the Appalachian old-growth forest with Jim and Dottie, it was a joy to see Jim share his knowledge of plants, trees, and the creatures of the Joyce Kilmer Preserve where we walked with his grandsons. "Grandpa, what's this bug?" asked Sam. "Ooh, that's a good one," he answered, excitedly explaining that its long stingerlike tail was actually for laying eggs deep in the wood of a tree.

In our first years together, I encouraged Alex to forgive his father for the perceived blunders of parenting and be thankful for all of the wonderful things Jim had imparted. Alex had written me from K2:

> I had the weirdest premonition that Dad is not well today
> which made me sort of sad and melancholy. I hope it doesn't
> mean anything. I'll send a long letter to Mom and Dad with the
> trekkers. Dad sure gave us boys a strong background of skill in
> the outdoors. It seems so easy and natural to get along in a cold,
> snowy environment. . . . I believe I can carry 75-80 lb packs easily
> as a result of having packed elk out of the mountains with Dad
> and Andy from a young age. Anyway, he taught us a lot of good
> things, which I value very much now.

"I know you'll be a great father, Alex. Everything you do, you do it well," I lobbied.

Finally he said, "OK, Bird, you've been so patient and supportive of my climbing. I want to do this with you. I'm ready."

We learned of my pregnancy early in 1988. Surprising both of us, it had taken a year to achieve. "All those years of birth control for nothing!" I fumed impatiently as each barren month went by, but six weeks after ringing in the year, we knew. I think Max was conceived on New Year's Eve.

That spring I made a trip to Ventura, California, where I taught art to employees at Patagonia. The Chouinards offered a variety of classes to their employees, from fly tying to cooking to art and languages. The paintings they had purchased from me and hung in the offices stirred enough interest to elicit the invitation.

While there, I learned of their plan to move Patagonia's mail-order operations to Bozeman later that spring. I eagerly applied and was hired for a job as a Patagonia telephone operator, taking orders from all over the country and world for the coveted outdoor clothing. It paid the bills while I painted on the side, selling a few pieces of art here and there. The work environment was creative and fun, with some of the best coworkers I've ever had. Alex began working on a graduate degree in engineering mechanics while finishing his undergraduate degree in applied math.

In early spring we drove west to visit Jan and Perry in Squamish, British Columbia, north of Vancouver. The maritime community of Squamish was an entirely new environment for us: ferries, rocky beaches, seaside cliffs for climbing, lush rain forests, and abundant wildlife. It was a refreshing change from the arid western landscape of Montana. Alex and Perry climbed each day on the cliffs above Squamish, then strummed their guitars into the evening while Jan and I hiked, climbed, or just hung out, feeling lucky to share so much as sisters and best friends. My sisters are each wonderful and unique. I have become closer to Paula and Camilla in recent years, but with Jan I had always had the feeling that she loved me fiercely and admired everything I did. If she didn't, she was discreet enough not to let on. We were both definitive about what we liked or didn't, so my tendency to be frank never offended her. She was thrilled over my pregnancy, and I shared my secret fears of birth and parenthood with her while she showered me with praise and confidence to meet the challenge.

On an earlier visit, Jan and I had decided to climb a route together on the Chief, a commanding granite wall along the sound. The route was graded 5.9, which is fairly moderate, but it had a pretty run-out section with no protection that ended with a sling around a horn of rock. Watching Jan lead it remains one of my fondest memories of her. When I arrived at the belay and exclaimed, "Way to go! That was sketchy and you were solid!" her smile was enormous. "I know—can you believe it? It's so amazing to be up here—just the two of us!"

Summer arrived and I stayed in Bozeman, working at Patagonia, while Alex spent his first season as part of Exum Mountain Guides in Grand Teton National Park, four hours to the south. I drove through the winding Gallatin Canyon and Yellowstone National Park to visit Alex in the splendor of the Tetons as often as possible. I'd stop for lunch in green meadows along the Firehole River and watch fuzzy merganser chicks bobbing on sunlit ripples behind watchful parents, while young bison and elk calves frolicked among their herds. Wildflowers splashed colors along the banks with changing displays as weeks passed. I walked the weathered boardwalks of spewing geyser basins and spitting mud-pots while breathing in sulfury steam, feeling particularly akin to the earth, pregnant and teeming with life.

Alex was an apprentice guide relegated to taking the leftover or overflow work, but he showed up at the office every day at the crack of dawn to sweep the floor and greet people as they arrived. If there was no work, he would run into the mountains and climb, but he made himself available at the drop of a hat for any guiding job that came his way, and in no time they came. He was a natural at guiding, with a gift for sharing his love of the mountains and his acuity for climbing. His clients were drawn to his charisma and modesty. He wrote to me of his guiding experiences between my visits that summer:

> Hi from the lower saddle (11,700'). I'm sitting in the hut with my single client plus Jack Turner and his crew. We've had dinner, lots of tea and contemplated the route for tomorrow. —I've now moved to my bivy spot. (Too much snoring in the hut.) The wind is blowing steadily, but it's quite warm otherwise. We'll be up at 3:30 and away by 4:30 in order to begin climbing at first light. My client is a great guy, Rodney Wright. He's from North Carolina where he works as a ranger at a small state park. It's his first trip out west and he's euphoric here in the mountains. We stopped for an hour and bouldered in the meadows this afternoon. We stopped again and walked out into the middle of the Middle Teton glacier. He was enthralled and overwhelmed by the whole experience. It's so enjoyable to watch the childlike enthusiasm and anxiety of these folks. They are trying to absorb so many new experiences so quickly.

> . . . We had fun at dinner with Jack Turner. He's an eloquent and loquacious storyteller. He related numerous adventures from his peregrinations in Nepal including tales of tigers, cobras

*and elephant rides at Tiger Tops. We must go there. It would be
a great experience for us to meet him in Nepal as he has spent
lots of time there and is intimately familiar with the country
and its inhabitants.*

When I showed up to visit Alex in Jackson, he was somewhat
unnerved by my advancing pregnancy and morphing body. "Be
careful, Jen!" he fretted as I climbed the ladder to his loft. It's not
uncommon for an expectant father to feel a bit "out of the loop" at
this stage. While a mother is acutely aware of every change in each
passing trimester, a father cannot help but be an outsider. But Alex
was very tender and loving, even though he did not yet feel a bond
to our unborn child. He paddled our canoe on String Lake while I
lounged like Cleopatra. We hiked the many trails, scaring up moose,
watching pikas build their haystacks among talus, and picnicking
along the rocky banks of icy streams with the Tetons rising over us.
When I wasn't with him, he wrote:

> *Hi again, dearest wife, I was assigned cube point 2 days ago with
> sixteen 13-, 14- and 15-year-olds from "Man and His Land," a
> wilderness venture group for city kids. ("Man and His Gland" is
> our moniker for them.) They were great fun if a bit rowdy and
> hard to manipulate. We told them to bring lots of water, which
> of course they didn't, and by 10:00 AM most had finished all they
> had. I anticipated this so the night before, I bought a 25 lb water-
> melon and loaded it in the bottom of my pack, unbeknownst to
> them. At the last creek, just below the start of the climb, I dropped
> back and deposited the secret melon in the icy creek. By 3 PM
> when we returned, they were parched. You should have seen their
> faces when I produced the melon. I was an instant hero! They
> fixed steak dinners for us that night at their campsite. All the
> guides that had worked with them were in attendance and Pratt
> handed out certificates of ascent around the campfire. What fun! I
> miss you and look forward to seeing you next weekend. Yours is a
> devoted and admiring husband.*

By mid-August, Alex was swamped with guiding opportunities for the rest of the summer, taking on the private clients of good friend and fellow guide Jack Tackle, who had back surgery. I was consumed with nesting. I had found a small brick house to rent near campus that some friends were giving up and was readying for the move, wanting to settle in before the baby arrived. Alex had his fill of guiding by the end of summer and wrote, "I'm missing you badly. I'm so happy about the house coming through for us and desire to be with you again soon . . . in it!"

Reunited, we painted walls and settled in. Alex resumed classes in math and engineering, while I continued work at Patagonia. My labor came two weeks early in mid-October, long awaited yet with some dread. We had attended Lamaze classes, puffing in rhythm to practice breathing, but I was still nervous. Alex's humor had lightened those tense moments. "Just think of it as climbing a 5.11," Alex said during a class while I draped my bulging form against him, trying to imagine the fierce pain of labor. He was referring to one of the harder grades of rock climbs.

"I can't climb 5.11!" I answered.

"Well, you can climb 5.10 and grade IV ice and alpine faces, so this will be a cakewalk."

"Right," I answered.

When the class watched a film of a birth, he leaned over and whispered, "That does look pretty grim. Are you sure you want to go through with it?" Then he cracked up while I rolled my eyes in amusement.

When Max came slipping into the world, Alex held him with enormous hands, fingers a good inch longer than my own gently wrapped around the wide-eyed baby as his cord was cut. Whatever fears had existed about fatherhood evaporated in that moment, and Alex was instantly smitten with his new son. As we lay together in the maternity ward just hours after Max arrived, Alex drew back the curtain to show his new son the stars. As if on cue, the northern lights danced across the sky above Bozeman. "You have the whole world in front of you, my son—a clean slate," he said. To me he whispered, "Thanks, Bird."

Our parents and siblings welcomed Max with the usual fanfare. In my family he was a firstborn grandchild, and I was shocked and touched to see my Dad stroll into the hospital room before Max was even twelve hours old. He had driven more than four hours to congratulate Alex and me and greet his grandson for a brief visit.

My mother arrived a day later, burdened with gifts to help me with my new role, even though I had encouraged her to wait a couple of days. I could understand her excitement, though, and appreciated her smothering of love. Mom hadn't had a mother when her own babies came. She had been far from her own family, and she wanted to be the best she could for me now. During my pregnancy, I'd felt a growing closeness to my mother that came from the shared experience. I was suddenly aware of the sacrifices she had made for me and my sisters, and I had a new understanding of her fierce love for me as I looked upon my own child. I took great comfort in knowing she was near.

It was difficult for Alex when Mom came, as she wanted and needed to care for all of us, cooking, cleaning, and dispensing advice that came from her own parenting experience and her heart. But her presence made Alex feel a bit displaced and less needed by me and the baby. He always felt insecure around Mom, thinking that he didn't measure up as a husband and provider in her eyes. Mother reprimanded him for being late for dinner one evening, and he stomped away to his graduate school office in anger. My heart went out to both of them during that time, when a new life had brought us together with emotions high.

Jim and Dottie arrived later with Max's great-grandmother Argo for a precious four-generation photo. Dottie is a devoted Christian, and although Alex respected her faith, he didn't want to be married in the church or have our children baptized. "We aren't Christians!" he said when I asked him to consider appeasing our parents. My own mother, an Episcopalian, would have loved to see our babies baptized too. "It's just a harmless ritual," I told Alex, remembering the baptism of my little sister, Camilla.

Both Alex and I had been taken to church regularly as children, sometimes against our will. My dad used to quietly bow out and disappear to the horses, his favorite weekend pastime, but Mother was adamant about our attending with her, even if we would have preferred to go to the horses too. I went with resignation and learned to recite the prayers and psalms, and to stand and sit and kneel when I was supposed to, but my thoughts were always somewhere else. I studied the intricate pictures in the stained-glass windows and the sweeping ceiling beams, imagining them to be an overturned ship, perhaps even Noah's ark. Then I thought of the whole church filled with animals, two of every species, and knew it would be packed. I wondered which would be left outside, doomed to extinction. I think of church as a dreamy meditative time in my childhood. I figured God knew that I wasn't paying attention and that I didn't buy into all those stories, since he supposedly knew everything, but I had the idea that he liked me anyway just because I was a child.

Sometime in high school, I decided I was more interested in hiking or skiing than church on Sunday and declared myself an agnostic. Alex said he'd had enough of church too and preferred to find his spirituality in moving through the great outdoors. In this we agreed. "To me there's definitely a spiritual catharsis to be found in movement," Alex wrote from Trango. "I think one of my favorite quotes is from Pascal, a French mathematician-philosopher, who said that man's true nature lies in motion, without which we die. And I can adhere to that."

He certainly did. Anyone who knew Alex can attest to his inability to be still. He reflected on this in a letter:

> Funny how sometimes life hurtles toward us at such a rate that
> we would give anything for an idle moment to reflect. And
> then those idle moments come in too large a parcel and we can't
> dispense with all the surplus moments. I like to think that I'm
> capable of using these days to grow spiritually, to develop personal
> philosophies more deeply and bond with my mates, but I'm weak!
> I'm restless. I find that I have my greatest moments of revelation
> and insight when I'm active.

Like many mountaineers, Alex found spiritual satisfaction in the sheer grandeur of the mountains and nature herself when he did manage to sit still:

You know, for me the climbing is insignificant compared with the moments spent reclined on a ledge watching clouds transmogrify from one ethereal shape to another even more evanescent shape. And while I'm lost in cloud reverie, an old tattered gorak drifts carelessly and silently upward, cocking his hoary head at me curiously as though asking why I struggle so hard for such measured upward gain. I'd love to borrow his wings for a magical waltz through these magnificent towers.

I settled into the long-awaited role of mothering with quiet contentment, joyfully caring for our new baby. The tree-lined streets near our home had donned their fall colors, and I bundled Max into a carrier and strolled beneath a canopy of yellow each day to lunch with Alex at the campus. Time slowed down. Three months passed and I found a caregiver, returning to work at Patagonia part-time. Alex helped where he could with changing and bathing, and he often cooked dinner. He toiled away in graduate school while continuing to work part-time.

Alex loved Max but I was obsessed, and conveniently so, since I was nursing. I lost interest in activities such as ice climbing and skiing for the first time ever. Instead I was immersed in the miracle of new motherhood, content to stay at home caring for my baby while listening to the offerings of National Public Radio. Folk, bluegrass, classical music, and the soothing voice of Garrison Keillor accompanied Max and me in the rocker. I often sat for hours, rocking and reading, observing the sleeping child in my arms until he awoke and stared up at me with large blue eyes.

That spring, Alex was invited to join an expedition to the Himalaya with well-known alpinists John Roskelley and Jim Wickwire. Alex's partner would be Steve Swenson, with whom he had climbed on K2. Before K2, Alex had heard that Steve was a strong climber but "intense," and wondered what that meant. That he had no sense of humor, perhaps, or that he was driven beyond reason in his goals? It turned out that Steve and Alex were well suited for each other as partners. Both were driven to climb, had an education in engineering and math, and were straitlaced, well-read fitness nuts with families.

I encouraged Alex to take off the spring semester and go. I knew he would be finishing grad school within a year or so and then would likely take a full-time job. He was haggard from the relentless schedule, and we were both sleep deprived because of our new baby. I figured the trip would give him time away from the grind of school and work, time to take an objective look at his life.

Funds and sponsors were gathered and preparations made for an expedition to climb Menlungtse in Tibet. But China turned down the permit at the last minute, and the climbers were left hanging. Roskelley and Wickwire dropped out, but Steve and Alex quickly came up with Plan B: to attempt a route on Kwangde, in the Khumbu region of Nepal. They headed off in April, and Alex wrote to us from Nepal:

> Dear Family, How are you two getting along? I expect you are good company for each other. I think of you every day and long to see you very soon. We are camped in a lovely green pasture in a village called Thame, one day's walk from Namche and directly under Kwangde. We arrived yesterday and lay around, sorted climbing gear and took a marvelous walk to a Buddhist monastery perched in cliffs above the town. The monastery is four hundred years old and we went inside where a young monk was beating the huge suspended drums. He blew on one of those huge long horns which produced a deep booming sound heard up and down the valley. Such a peaceful place.

Home was also a peaceful place without Alex and his frenetic energy, but I loved getting his long letters. I missed him, but not as much as I had on past trips, as the baby kept me occupied. I packed up Max for weekend jaunts to visit grandparents in Missoula, where

Jim and Dottie welcomed us and Mom delighted in every little milestone and spoiled both of us with new clothes, baby toys, and favorite dinners for me. I drove to Dillon to visit Grandmother and introduced Max to his great-great-aunties. When not at work, I hiked with Max in the backpack and walked with him in the stroller. We sat in the rocker listening to *Prairie Home Companion* on the radio while snow disappeared from hillsides and yellow hay fields began to green. Tulips and daffodils sprang forth in my garden, and robins arrived in force with the driving spring rains. When I came down with a bad case of stomach flu, I wished Alex were there, but not once did I wish I were anywhere else. And Alex wrote:

Dearest Family, I came down from high on a new route on Kwangde. Both literally and figuratively. I came down with bronchitis and we came down to base camp. We plan to spend 4-5 days getting well then go back up and finish the route. The route has been interesting. It's a big rock buttress—mixed climbing but mostly rock. We've done 25 pitches and have 7-8 more to go up a vertical rock headwall. Our plan is to reclimb to our highest bivy where we have a tiny ice ledge. We will fix our two ropes and then leave predawn, sans packs, for the summit in one day. But enough climbing talk.

I'm reading a wonderful book which I'd love you to buy and read. It's called The Solace of Open Spaces *by Gretel Ehrlich. You would love it and so would your grandmother. It is the most beautiful description of ranch life I've ever read. Ed Hillary is walking up here to Thame today to inspect his school. The kids are all excited about his arrival. They have songs ready to sing for him. . . . How are you? I hope very much that you are happy, healthy and enjoying spring in Montana. I've had a relaxing recuperative day but have been thinking about my role as father and husband with pensiveness and feelings of irresponsibility. It's a classic case of greener grass. When I'm home with you, I fantasize about being here and it seems perfectly normal to take off in pursuit of*

adventure. However, being here alone, I can't help feeling that
I'm living a self indulgent experience without two thirds of who
I am . . . You and Max. I love you two dearly and look forward to
seeing you at Gallatin Field soon. . . . Much, much love, Alex

I was touched by Alex's introspection and his ability to communicate his feelings to me. I realize now that his letters were his greatest gift to me aside from the children. He was wise enough to know that love needed such nourishment to survive his absences, and appreciative enough to thank me for the freedom I bestowed on him. But I really think that Alex's letters served another purpose. They gave him the satisfaction of sharing his thoughts and feelings, of giving his love. They created a lifeline to his more grounded, meaningful purpose as father and husband.

Alex loved his family fiercely and without question. As our family grew, he embraced each of the boys with equal devotion. His life was a balancing act; I know he was tormented many times by the desire to be in two places at once, and by guilt and loneliness when he was away in his beloved mountains. I felt sorry for him, knowing this inner turmoil was ever present. There were certainly times when he and I were at odds, when he may have wished he were single and able to devote himself to climbing without guilt. There were times when I thought him unbearably selfish for his insatiable drive to climb, which resulted in so much time away. But I loved his spirit and his passion for life. When Alex was home, he took on the workload eagerly and efficiently. He was a whirlwind in the kitchen and a neatnik like me. He always insisted on doing the cleanup after a meal, knowing that I did more than my share when he was away.

Alex never forgot a special day, whether he was home or far away. He helped the boys write wonderful cards and rallied them to serve me breakfast in bed for Mother's Day. On one of my birthdays, he presented me with a picnic basket but wouldn't let me open it until we arrived at our favorite spot in Hyalite Canyon. There, I opened it to find a picnic dinner that he had prepared, complete with a checkered tablecloth, bottle of wine, and homemade chocolate cake.

With so much time away from our own family, Alex found it difficult to make time for his parents and brothers. But even though he may not have returned home as much as they would have liked, Alex wrote to his parents religiously, informing them of his travels, reflections, and love for them. His mother, also an avid writer, kept their correspondence going.

Dear Mom, Your love has been like a steady beacon to me for so many years and I truly appreciate it. . . . When we'll see you again, I can't say but I do look forward to it. We'll all be thinking of you and Dad at Thanksgiving—Andy and Ted and their respective families. As always, I wish you nothing but happiness. Love, Alex

Alex expected good manners and follow-through from our boys even when they were small. But like all kids, they tested us and did not always do as they were told. When Alex was tired or stressed, he sometimes lost his temper over some small infraction such as leaving toys everywhere or splashing water about the bathroom. "You can be firm without anger," I said. I knew he did not want to be the strict disciplinarian that his father had been. He endeavored to have patience and convey his love in the limited time he spent at home, making time to play Legos, trucks, or trains, and every evening he would gather the boys into his lap and read them a story.

From the Atlantic Ocean Wall on El Cap: Pitch 18, 6:30pm Good evening all, You are probably having dinner right now and so am I except my legs are dangling over the edge of my porta-ledge with 2,500 feet of space below! I am having tortellini out of a can and I was thinking that Max really likes tortellini also. You might be a little scared eating way up here with me, Max, but someday I'd like you to come travel up this granite wilderness with me. I'll show you slides of this climb when I get home. We'll have an evening show as a family. Jenni, I've been reading this little book of Buddhist teaching—absolutely a delight. It is filled with truth and wisdom. My greatest challenge is to remember the simple ways of being mindful of happiness at each moment. I just read a great chapter which says that love and understanding are the same thing. If we work to understand ourselves and those we come in contact with, we are then loving them. We can't be angry at someone if we work at understanding how they feel. I was struck by how shallow the phrase "I love you" sounds. But "I understand you" takes real effort, commitment and focus on the other person's concerns and needs. I must remember all this when I get home. The coyotes are starting to sing down below while I lie on my back and watch the moon. I love and understand you three very well.

A couple of years later, during a Bozeman winter, Alex bought a blank book, which he took into a local gear shop, and wrote on the first page: "This book is dedicated to Brent Bishop, Barrel Mountaineering, climbers past, present and future, and the spirit shared by all those who love the hills. To share your love for ice-climbing is a gift. Write down your events." Alex was in the thick of pioneering ice routes in Hyalite, and in the book he recorded over a dozen of his own first ascents, including one with fellow dad John Wasson: "We had to climb up and do a scary traverse into the base which is seventy-five feet above the ground. One steep pitch . . . John and I, ever responsible fathers, left home at 3 AM, did the route and got home by 11 AM to do laundry and take care of the kids! Thus the name . . . 'Responsible Family Men.'"

They chose that name for the route in jest, but not completely. Alex took pride in his role as a family man and truly invested himself in our family as much as he was able. When home, he cooked, cleaned, did laundry, and helped with all of the household tasks. With determination, he fit his workouts into our life, rising at four or five in the morning to run or ski up local summits. Baldy Mountain in the Bridgers became a favorite for his dawn patrol, where he would swill coffee from his thermos at sunrise. Cutting turns through powder or running through meadows of alpine flowers would bring him back to the valley and back to the family before our day began. "Good morning, family!" he would announce at the back door. "You missed the best part of the day."

Everest Years

> What is the use of climbing Mount Everest?
> If you cannot understand that there is something in man
> which responds to the challenge of this mountain and goes out to meet it,
> that the struggle is the struggle of life itself upward and forever upward,
> then you won't see why we go.
> —GEORGE LEIGH MALLORY

MOUNT EVEREST WAS NOT A SUMMIT that Alex placed high on his list. The tallest point on the planet had a certain appeal, but it was not the kind of challenge he preferred. The difficulties that Everest presents are of an objective nature. The challenges posed by severe weather, avalanches, glacier travel, and sheer altitude were not as appealing to Alex as those presented by steep and technical rock and ice climbing, which demanded a wide range of specific techniques and knowledge that could be obtained only through years of study and practice. He felt that anyone who was fit enough and willing to chance the unpredictable aspects of high-altitude climbing could get up Everest. But climbing a 3,000-foot wall of rock and ice took skill that not everyone had. "I'll climb it when I'm an old guy," he'd say, "as long as I can put one foot in front of the other."

By January 1990, Alex had tired of graduate school. He had

had it with tests and long hours of study, and he dreaded writing a thesis. He paid a casual visit to a job fair on the MSU campus and interviewed with a couple of companies out of curiosity. When an oil service company, Schlumberger, offered him a salaried position with good pay, benefits, and moving expenses, he couldn't resist. The thought of a fat paycheck each month was enticing, and the job was available immediately. I lobbied for him to stick it out in school, knowing he needed only a few more months to finish his degree. But Alex quit his master's program anyway, assuring me that he would come back to it sometime, and we prepared to move to Casper, Wyoming, after a six-week training period near Calgary, Alberta.

While I was happy for Alex's opportunity, I worried over leaving Montana and the close proximity to my grandmother, whose health was failing. I had driven to see her often in Dillon over the previous months. The biweekly letters she had sent me for years had helped to shape my view of the world as nature's pageant, always unfolding for the lucky observers. I knew I would miss her terribly. "The years are rolling by too fast," she had written me recently, perhaps presciently. "This will be a memorable year for you and us all. You will be caring and loving parents."

In early winter Grandmother was hospitalized with pain in her abdomen and diagnosed with cancer. She passed away soon after the New Year, plunging me into grief. Though she was ninety, I felt devastated by the depth of my loss. The letters I had always looked for in my mailbox would no longer come. Soon after her service, Alex and I sadly said goodbye to Montana and traveled to Alberta, where Alex began his training to become an oil-well engineer.

We lived in a stark motel with a kitchenette for the six-week stay in windblown Airdrie, just north of Calgary. Alex went to classes during the week and I cared for Max while painting on the Formica table of our kitchenette, dragging out art materials each day after breakfast. I began a body of work for a show at the Danforth Gallery in Livingston, Montana, during the coming summer. I had promised the gallery ten pieces by late June. For inspiration and fun, I visited the zoo many times with Max, who was particularly enthralled yet terrified by the roar of the Siberian tiger. He wanted to go nearer and nearer to the plaintive cry, but at a certain point he would burst into tears. I wasn't sure if it was empathy or fear that triggered his response—or both.

On weekends the Canadian Rockies drew us into their craggy realm for hiking, climbing, skiing, and soaking beneath the winter steam of mineral hot springs. Alex hooked up with his old buddy Choc Quinn from the K2 expedition to climb the abundant frozen waterfalls around Banff. We drove to Jasper and I looked upon the face of Athabasca, which I had summited with Alex a few years before. I remembered soloing the Skyladder on Andromeda, crossing the glacier alone and front-pointing my way to the summit, then down-climbing the same route to avoid more unknown glacier travel. It was impulsive—I had just gone to look but kept going, feeling confident, lured by the sun, the serenity, and the exhilaration. It was a risk I had enjoyed, but—no more. With motherhood, my self-preservation instinct had kicked in.

In May 1987 two of the climbers from Alex's K2 team, David Cheesmond and Catherine Freer, had died in a Canadian climbing accident, falling through a cornice on the Hummingbird Ridge of Mount Logan. Alex and I were shocked to hear the news. They had both been so vibrant and skilled. Catherine and I had become friends when we lived in Boulder in 1983. She'd come to buy bagels from me nearly every morning at the shop where I worked. "I want to lead the Rigid Designator," I had told her. "Go for it!" she had encouraged. And I did, becoming the first woman to lead the steep frozen waterfall near Vail. I could picture Catherine's funny smile with arms crossed, and then I pictured her and David falling through the cornice in a blur of snow to their deaths. It was so sad, and it made me worry. But Alex had reassured me. "I have no interest in that kind of route, Jen—too much objective danger."

Choc was David's best friend and had come to the aid of David's wife, Gillian, and their daughter as they grieved in the months after his death. Eventually Choc and Gillian were married. Alex and I shared evenings and weekends with them during our stay in Canada, but fear gnawed at my stomach whenever they recounted the shocking experience of losing David. Yet they had found love and comfort in each other, and their lives were going forward. I held great admiration for them both, and to me Choc seemed a hero. I knew that he had been close to David too, and I found it compelling that he had chosen to step into David's shoes. I felt sadness for Gillian as I tried to imagine myself in the same position, knowing full well that it was always a possibility. "Would I be as strong as she?" I wondered.

Once settled in Casper, Alex began a schedule of work comprising ten days on and four off. His work often took him into the field for the entire ten days. I was left to find us a home, as we had hastily rented a dismal apartment in a crowded complex mostly housing transient oil-field workers. I scoped out the city of Casper and found an appealing neighborhood in the old part of town. Charming houses with gardens beckoned from tree-lined streets near a large grassy park. The Norman Rockwell–like serenity drew me there each day to look for possible rentals.

I searched like a lost bird looking for my flock and a safe place to nest. Max slept in his car seat as I slowly steered our Subaru one morning, eyes peeled for rental signs. I saw a young mom herding two little kids along the sidewalk. She was decked out in Patagonia fleece, and her wide smile met my gaze. Sensing a kindred spirit, I stopped the car to leap out and introduce myself. "Hi, I'm Jenni, and I've just moved here. . . . I'm feeling a bit lost and . . . you look like someone who'd make a great friend." Her name was Mary Sue Marsh, and she welcomed me into her community like family.

When Alex quit school for the position with Schlumberger, he had said, "Jen, I want to work this job for about five years. We'll save enough money in that time to buy a sailboat. Then we can take off and sail around the world."

"Wow! How are we going to get sailing experience in Wyoming?" I asked, ever practical.

"We don't need experience—we'll get it as we go. We just need the dream!"

"OK, sounds good to me," I answered.

And so, thinking we'd be in Casper for a while, I enlisted Mary Sue to help me find a wonderful old two-story house that we could afford to buy. Alex liked the idea of not throwing away money on rent but was nervous about the commitment of a mortgage. I pressed him, wanting out of the gloomy apartment complex, and so we bought our first home.

Soon after, I began to worry that we had made a big mistake. The house was lovely, but Alex was not happy with his new job. He was, after all, still in the oil fields, the very environment that we had gone to school to escape. In the field he worked out during his downtime, running on the open prairies, doing push-ups on pavement or rocks, and seeking out beams around the rigs for pull-ups. He suffered stares and coarse remarks from the ever-present rednecks roaring by in their dust-covered pickups. "Hey fagboy, nice legs!" was typical.

Although he enjoyed his fellow engineers and they respected him, most could not relate to his level of athleticism either. Alex sought out the few climbers in Casper, but he did not find a close friend among them. Through Mary Sue I'd found a bevy of new friends, but young mothers were easier to find than climbers. I was happily nesting, ecstatic to have a studio space at last, and focused on my work for the art show in Livingston. But within a few months, I realized that Alex had sunk into depression. He came home after stints of working all night, powered through six-packs of beer, and collapsed into bed for twelve hours at a time. I was deeply concerned.

"Alex, you're drinking too much," I ventured.

"I know," he answered, "but it helps me feel better about the bleakness of my future. I think I made the wrong decision. I don't know if I can do this job, Jen. My spirit is being sucked dry. The light at the end of the tunnel is so far away, but I've got you and Max to think of. I can't quit." That was the last thing I wanted to hear.

"Let's figure it out, Alex. If you hate the job, you can always do something different," I said bluntly, hoping to pry him from his self-pity. "You can look for another engineering job . . . or pound nails and guide. We can go back to Montana or Jackson. I'll do what I can to help." Relief washed over him once he knew I would support whatever decision he made.

The Danforth exhibit opened in July, and we traveled to Livingston for the unveiling of my new work. Mountains and plains had inspired images of antelope frolicking with sheep, ravens holding world peace talks against blood red skies, and bison dancing beneath a round white moon. They were simple and playful yet serious and filled with color. To my surprise, I sold nearly every piece in the show on opening night.

About the same time, Alex was invited to join an expedition on the south face of Mount Everest as a guide. In 1985, David Breashears had guided Dick Bass to the summit of Everest, setting a new precedent. Up until that time, only expert and professional climbers had ever attempted it. In the five years since, other guides had quickly recognized the opportunity for commercial trips, and business was beginning to thrive. I was confident that Alex could climb Everest if the conditions were good, but the guiding aspect worried me. It seemed to me that Everest was difficult enough without having to be responsible for less experienced climbers. We discussed the offer, and I reminded him that he had claimed to be finished with expedition climbing and 8,000-meter peaks. "This is different," he said. "I'll be paid."

"It better be a lot!" I said.

"It is—a third of my current yearly salary." Time off from Schlumberger was not an option, and it seemed to be just the out he was searching for. We talked it through and figured that the pay for Everest would tide us over until he found another job. And so, after seven long months at Schlumberger, he quit.

By mid-August Alex was on his way to Nepal, with the agreement that Max and I would meet him in Bangkok after the climb. I felt a mixture of sadness, worry, and vicarious excitement. I had once entertained thoughts of climbing Everest myself, but the objective dangers were more of a gamble than I wanted. Now that I was a mother, my interest in climbing had waned. But I was greatly relieved to see Alex so happy again. He was not cut out for a nine-to-five job, but that was part of why I loved him.

His letters helped us track his journey:

August 27: We're in Khumjung—about an hour above Namche Bazaar. The mountains are magnificent! Every kind of flower is here—both domestic and wild flowers including forget-me-nots and edelweiss. I've never seen so much edelweiss!

September 6: I'm sitting here in base camp taking a rest day. We've been here now four days. The first two, we acclimatized by lounging at 17,500'. We've been to 19,500' and established Camp I. The notorious Khumbu Icefall is very benign this year and only takes two hours to negotiate anyway.

October 1: I'm at Camp II and all talk is about going home! The end has come fast as motivation dwindles. I've been on 2 summit bids (unsuccessful) and Dan and I will go back once more. . . . This has been one interesting trip. I wouldn't do it twice but it was amazing once. I'm ready to walk out of here and my only regret is that I now must wait so long to see you two.

On October 4, 1990 Alex became the fortieth American to summit Everest and the first person to summit postmonsoon that year. When it looked as though the season was finished and most groups were giving up, Alex broke trail through deep snow, leading the summit bid to the top of the world. In Wyoming, I received a phone call from a national news station. I had a panicked moment until they told me that Alex had reached the summit of Mount Everest and they needed to verify his background information. I was ecstatic and called everyone I could think of. One week later Max turned two, and we celebrated his birthday by building his first snowman. A jet flew over with a dull roar, and Max looked to the sky. "Daddy?" he asked. "No," I answered with a phrase that would become routine, "Daddy's on the mountain."

En route from Casper to Bangkok, Max and I went trick-or-treating in Bozeman with friends, visited grandparents in Missoula, and stayed with our old friends Eric and Alice in Seattle.

My sister Jan drove down from Canada to visit, and I was shocked and saddened to see her. She was thin and depressed; her marriage was ending, she told me with sorrow. Perry had been working in the film industry, which resulted in too much time away and a lifestyle she couldn't tolerate. She still cared for him but thought it necessary to move on. In doing so, she hoped to find her way to a happier life.

When Max and I deplaned in Bangkok, exhausted from the long flight, I barely recognized the thin man with the dark beard who approached us waving an enormous bouquet of flowers. I'd never seen Alex with a beard, and Max was skeptical too. It took some convincing before he would believe that this guy was someone he knew well enough to leave my arms for. Alex had lost some twenty pounds in the three months since we'd seen him in Casper.

Thailand was hot, humid, and delightfully foreign, a perfect place to reacquaint. We walked the streets of Bangkok with Max perched atop Alex's shoulders, visiting temples with gilded Buddhas and gardens with leaping monkeys. By longboat, we toured the floating market of Damnoen Saduak. Women in flat wood boats filled with baskets of ripe papaya, bananas, coconuts, and pineapple jockeyed to sell their produce. Floating stalls sold steaming bowls of noodles, woven hats, and bolts of bright cloth. We traveled by train and then boat to the islands of Koh Phi Phi and Krabi to relax in breezy grass huts near sandy beach coves. Like other tourists, we snorkeled, lay around, and feasted on Thai food. Alex was thrilled to be with us, basking in the slower pace and the company of his family. He gave Max his full attention, wandering through tide pools and collecting shells, building huge sand castles, and then smashing them together. It was great fun—until Max became ill. He began to vomit one night, and by morning he was burning with fever and had diarrhea. It took a boat trip and an entire day to find a local clinic. By then I was filled with fear and guilt over the state of our listless toddler, and I stroked his damp blond hair with worry. In only two days, he had lost almost one-fifth of his body weight. We were given medicine and he recovered quickly, but the experience gave me such a scare that I refused to bring the children to Asia again until Isaac was four and I had my own arsenal of drugs and fattening snacks.

Just after Christmas, Alex took a job with Black Diamond Equipment in Ventura, California, as a product-testing engineer. The newly formed Black Diamond had sprung away from Lost Arrow, the parent company of Patagonia. We were relieved when the offer arrived just as our funds were getting scarce. It seemed the perfect fit. Alex could have the intellectual challenge of an engineering job and work for like-minded individuals who would understand his need to climb. The company was owned by its employees, and most of them were climbers who had learned the business under the tutelage of Yvon Chouinard.

That summer we lived out of duffel bags wherever we could find space in various friends' apartments and houses, sleeping on their floors and enjoying meals of bagel sandwiches and fish tacos on the beach. Weekends took us up the coast to Monterey Bay or down to LA for some cultural offerings such as the Getty, the Natural History Museum, or the La Brea Tar Pits. We camped on beaches and the high plateaus of the Channel Islands, where we kayaked with another climbing friend, Rob Raker. Max sat tucked in with Alex while I nervously tried to keep up on an island circumnavigation that took us near giant sea-lion bulls and into magical tidal caves to look at purple sea stars, shiny mussels, and crabs clinging to black rock.

The Black Diamond employees became our surrogate family, with many climbers and adventurers among them. Andrew McLean was one. Alex honed in on his fun-loving spirit and athletic ability and identified a perfect partner—the kind who never says no. Andrew would join Alex in any harebrained scheme he dreamed up. From Ventura, they did marathon drives to Yosemite for weekends of climbing. Andrew did his first wall climb with Alex on El Cap—not a beginner's route like the Nose, but a difficult overhanging route called Sunkist. A few days before they were set to go, Alex cut his finger badly while washing a wine glass. Relief washed over Andrew, as he figured the climb would be off. "Oh, no," said Alex. "It'll be fine—nothing a little tape won't manage."

As they approached the base of the climb, its serious nature became fully evident to Andrew. "Alex, I'm terrified," he admitted. "I don't know if I can do this."

Alex leaned toward him and grinned. "Be brave, Andrew. It'll be a blast."

"It is," says Andrew today, laughing, "one of my finer memories."

By late summer we were on the move again, as Black Diamond was relocating. "Mom, I wanna go home," little Max pleaded as we drove toward Salt Lake City. "Do we have a home?" We had all grown tired of being transient by the time we settled into our own place there. The Wasatch provided a paradise of rock climbing, skiing, and ice climbing, the three basic food groups for Alex's soul and that of his new company. I discovered the Flat Rabbit Gallery, a whimsical new place in Park City that agreed to represent my work, and planned for shows in Santa Monica, Livingston, and Missoula. I was happy to see my career begin to accelerate.

I recall a sense of relief in all of us that autumn when Max turned three and we joyfully learned that we were expecting another child. "I can't imagine not having had my brothers as I grew up," Alex had told me. "I want Max to have a sibling." But I lost the baby to miscarriage at ten weeks. Perhaps it was a blessing, as everyone said—"nature's way of eliminating defects," they assured me in tones I knew were meant to be soothing. Still, I thought of the little thumping heart that I had heard during doctor visits and grieved for what might have been. By New Year's, though, we were anticipating Sam's arrival on the next Labor Day. A good omen, we thought.

Spring arrived early. It had been a year and a half since Alex's last expedition, and he was chomping at the bit to get away to the big mountains. He managed to talk his boss, Peter Metcalf, into giving him time off and an endorsement of cash for an expedition to Pakistan. The trip had been in the planning phase for five months, and Alex had sent out more than a hundred letters to a vast array of sources, soliciting money and gear and organizing food, menus, and logistics for the trip. Endorsements were not easy to come by, but he searched far and wide:

Greetings, I am involved in a trip to Gasherbrum IV, a 26,000 ft
peak in the Baltoro region of the Karakoram range in Pakistan.
I've included a photo of the route so you can get an idea of the
striking nature of this mountain. Our intended route, the south
ridge, is the right-hand skyline in the photo. The route has never
been climbed and the peak has only had two ascents by any route
as of the time of this writing. . . . Our expedition brings together
a veteran group of talented and experienced Himalayan climbers.
The members include George Lowe, Steve Swenson, Andy Tuthill,
Naoe Sakashita and myself. I'm convinced that the important
objectives in climbing today are exactly this kind of route:
light-weight, low-impact, highly committed small groups on big
unclimbed lines.

The money trickled in for the expedition and our everyday
routine took shape in Salt Lake City, with Alex bicycling to work
each day. Max and I often joined him for lunch at Black Diamond,
where we were eagerly welcomed by Alex, Andrew, and their fellow
employees. We packed picnics and drove up the canyons for rock
climbing—and rock throwing, as Max never tired of chucking rocks
into any available water, be it stream or puddle. Alex would join in
by hefting massive boulders to create the biggest splash imaginable,
while Max would squeal in delight. Dinners by campfire brought
out the pyro that must be latent in all males; by the age of three and a
half, Max was well versed in building a fire. In winter we taught him
to ski at Snowbird's Chickadee, alternating between spending time
on the beginner slope and on solo runs in the moguls or powder of
the steep slopes above.

On evenings and weekends Alex took Max on "boy adventures,"
giving me time to myself. The adventures included riding the public
bus around Salt Lake City with no particular destination, visiting
the museum to wander among dinosaur skeletons, and becoming
regulars at the zoo and the aviary. And, of course, visiting the train
yards to watch the trains switch tracks was high on the list. Alex
even managed to meet an engineer who let them climb up into an

engine. where Max was allowed to blow the horn. "Dad, let's go to the bus," Max would say.

By the time Alex departed for Pakistan in May, the members of his expedition had changed. All but Steve Swenson had dropped out for various reasons. Charlie Fowler and Tom Dickey replaced them, joining in the last month before departure. Alex wrote to us as usual, charting their progress:

> May 8: We had a great bus trip from Islamabad to Skardu. It is about 200 miles and took 16 hours. Now, this was not like the buses in Salt Lake City, Max. It is a big colorful noisy bus covered with chrome, wild painted pictures, flags, pinwheels, lights and Arabic writing. It smokes awfully, has a loud horn which the driver blows constantly, and it goes where Salt Lake buses never would. It drives on dusty, bumpy roads over high mountain passes, then switchbacks down, down, down to the Indus River and over rickety old suspension bridges. All the while, loud Pakistani music plays on a scratchy old tape deck. It drives up roads blasted into sheer cliffs high above the river and finally it arrives at Skardu where we are now. You would love this bus ride, Mr. Max, and someday I will bring you here.

> May 13: Today is a rest day—our third day of walking from the end of the road. We washed hair, bodies and clothes in the Braldu River today on sunny warm sandbars amidst the splendid backdrop of Paiju Peak, Cathedral Peaks and the Trango Towers. This evening we will walk up the flanks of Paiju peak, about 2,000', for our first glimpse of Gasherbrum IV. We're all very excited to be moving into the big mountains now. The porters . . . are baking lots of bread today since from here, there will be no more wood for cooking since we will be on the Baltoro Glacier now for 60 miles to base camp. . . . They make chapatis on flat hot rocks. This bread is like round pizza crust—thin and chewy. They make roti, which is a thicker, hard loaf—they bury a chunk of dough in the hot ashes to bake it. . . . The cook we hired is an old friend of Steve's from past trips named Rasool. He is the most gregarious, happy person and

*a superb cook. He has a wife and two daughters in a small village
called Hushe . . . he loved my picture of you two.*

*Under a nearly full moon on the bank of the Braldu we danced
wildly with 50 of the local people, called Baltis after the region of
Baltistan. The night air filled with loud and boisterous folk songs,
drums, and rhythmic banging on pots and pans. We all danced
madly around a fire in the most infectious manner—truly
mystical with the looming granite walls bathed in soft moon-
light. I'll remember this night forever. I truly wish you were with
me—both of you. Max, you are such a good dancer—you would
have loved to dance with us. It's late now. We have slipped away
to bed but the Baltis dance on into the night.*

At home, Max beat on our pots and pans and we danced together
in the living room. I took Max to ride the bus, and we went to "mom-
tot" swim classes, library hour, and the park. We hiked among spring
wildflowers that sprouted in the greening hills of the Wasatch. We
baked cookies, read stories, and were together always. I loved it and
looked forward to the arrival of his sibling as I prepared for another
show, painting diligently with Max playing at my feet.

But juggling all of my roles could be exhausting. One day while
I was cooking lunch, I left Max playing on the floor of the studio
and returned to find that he had climbed into my tall chair to add his
own touches to my newly finished piece. Of course it was red that
he had chosen to scrawl across the work in wide whirling circles. I
went ballistic, screaming at my toddler as I whisked him away from
the ruined work. He cried as I had never seen him cry. My anger
frightened him, and his fearful reaction frightened me as I realized
I had broken his trust for the first time.

Apologizing, I hugged him to me and began to cry too, feeling
how tired I was from the daily tasks of mothering, the needs of the
growing baby within, and the pressure of having to finish my work
for the coming show. I wished Alex were there. "Mom," I told her
on the telephone that night, "I think I'll come up to Missoula for a

visit." I called my mother nearly every day when Alex was away to relate the various events of our daily life, and although she was full of advice that was sometimes critical, she was a great support, always sending care packages and eager to hear of any small achievement or funny tale about her grandchild. "Wonderful!" she said.

Mom welcomed our visits with fanfare, preparing special meals and leaving gifts for me waiting on my bed: earrings, bath soaps, or a new outfit or nightie. She would put her guest crib out, made up with blankets and bumper pads that she had sewn. "What do you need?" she would say. "I want to take you shopping." And she was filled with ideas for outings. We would visit the greenhouses together in spring, pick raspberries or corn in summer and apples in fall, and take Max to various parks or the pool or carousel. My mother was never idle. We made raspberry jam and apple pies or casseroles to put in the freezer, and they would be carefully packaged up in newspaper and boxes for my trip back home.

Jim and Dottie always welcomed our visits too, and the drive to Montana was well worth it for me in R & R. Between Mother and Dottie, Max was well cared for and I got some time to paint, go for a hike, or relax.

On May 26 Alex wrote me in celebration of our tenth wedding anniversary:

> I am a lucky, lucky man to have wed you. I really feel that you
> have enriched my life in ways I never would have even been
> aware of had we not met up. In reading The Road Less Traveled,
> the author states that two individuals need to maintain their
> separateness and individuality to have a healthy and mutually
> beneficial relationship. We have certainly done just that, if not
> too much so. I admire and respect your ability to be yourself—an
> artist and mother among many more talents—in the face of my
> inconsistent support for those things. You inspire me to define who
> I am and to have confidence in being that person. For this, I thank
> you very much. I love you dearly now after ten years of marriage
> and I always will.

Steve and Alex climbed as a team and got on well as always, but were thwarted time and again by bad weather and route-finding challenges through icefalls and slopes that were loaded with snow. Steve told me that Alex was never very settled on that trip; once on the mountain, he was nervous about snow conditions and more conservative than Steve. As the lead party, they began a traverse up a slope one day, but Alex fretted. They retreated to go through the icefall instead, and that night they descended to a lower camp. The next morning they watched two Italian climbers descending the very slope they had avoided. It fractured above them and slid, carrying the climbers down to a depression and burying one of them. Steve and Alex ran to the scene, arriving within five minutes, and dug out the man but could not revive him.

Eventually Steve and Alex reached a high point of 7,000 meters, but the weather remained unsettled and they had lost enthusiasm for the climb after the sad event, according to Steve. Once home, Alex wrote to a friend, "Cheers, We're back from our gallant attempt on Gasherbrum IV. Bad weather, deep snow and a reluctance to die in avalanches cost us the summit but I guess that's always one of the possible outcomes of these adventures. Since coming home our second son was born—Sam, healthy, happy, and a real joy."

Sam arrived two weeks early, after an unbearably hot summer in Salt Lake City. I'd made frequent trips to the grocery store with Max just to stroll the air-conditioned aisles and pine for the cooler weather of Montana. A successful summer with respect to my art sales prompted me to find us a different rental house in a quieter neighborhood. It had a lovely garden space in back where climbing roses had grown into a wild bramble, two bedrooms, and a little closed-in porch that could do for a studio. We painted walls, and Alex sanded wood floors and refinished them in the nick of time.

One evening when Alex and I went for a Lamaze refresher course at the hospital, my water broke and I ended up checking in. The day after Sam was born I had a few visitors at Saint Mark's Hospital, including one who surprised me. A climbing buddy of Alex's came shyly knocking, with flowers in hand, to get a peek at the new baby and pay his respects. I'd met the tall handsome blond only once before, at Black Diamond, and couldn't recall his name. "I'm Conrad," he said quietly. "Alex wanted me to see him. Is it OK?"

"Of course . . . well, this is Sam," I said, and held out the day-old baby for him to meet.

"He's beautiful!" he said, holding him awkwardly for a few moments, before carefully placing him back in my arms and then departing. It was a casual meeting but is now dearly tucked away in both of our memories.

* * *

Max was less than thrilled to have a younger brother join the household after nearly four years of being the star, and after a few weeks with the baby he emphatically announced, "I wish Hurricane Andrew would blow him away!" The hurricane had hit just two weeks after Sam was born, devastating southern Florida, wiping out coral reefs and mangroves, and destroying cities. I felt as though I was in the eye of my own hurricane—complete calm with our newborn son, while Max's energy increased and Alex's was never-ending.

Alex began to work part-time for the Wasatch Avalanche Forecast Center, helping to further knowledge of avalanches and snow conditions, which meant that he started going into the backcountry as often as possible. I recall rising to nurse Sam in the early hours of a winter morning and finding Alex already up . . . and baking biscuits. "Jesus, Alex, what time is it?" I stammered. "Four," he answered simply. Soon a knock came at the back door, and in trooped Andrew and a few other brave souls. The coffee machine hissed as my kitchen was transformed into an early morning diner. It was a meeting of the "dawn patrol," Alex's idea of a breakfast club. He wrote of it to a backcountry skiing chum, Richard Siberell:

> Cheers! We skied another "dawn patrol" this morning. A lovely
> little 800' chute into the North cirque of Wolverine peak above
> Alta. You would love this place! One hour from the car. Back to
> work @ 8:05 with shit-eating grins and a great work attitude

*induced by mid-calf powder. So next time you come out this way,
let's do a "dawn patrol."*

Alex went ice climbing whenever conditions allowed and he
could solicit partners. He pioneered some desperate new routes
that winter, including one called Prophet on a Stick. Named for
the gilded Mormon angel that stood atop the Tabernacle high over
the city, the climb set a new precedent for difficulty and helped
make mixed climbing more popular. By ascending a steep rock
wall behind a massively overhanging icicle, Alex was able to lean
out and snag onto the ice dagger. Then, with feet dangling in space,
he pulled up gingerly, hung by one arm, and planted his other ax
higher until his feet had purchase.

But of course he was not sated by occasional weekend climbs and
early morning adventures. The failed expedition of Gasherbrum IV
ate at him. He longed to do another expedition, but we were barely
making ends meet. We had lost money on our house in Casper and
had just managed to pay off that debt after almost two years.

Alex grew frustrated with his job that winter, feeling over-
worked and underpaid. "I'll never be able to do another expedition,"
he lamented. "It's impossible to make a living and be a real climber,
Jen. Nobody in the States appreciates mountaineering—it's what I
love, but I'm just a freak, some fringe nutcase instead of a real athlete." He complained about "trust funders" who had the money to
do what they wanted, and he envied his single friends like Conrad,
who could live on a shoestring and were always free to go.

Alex worked out obsessively at a local gym and told me one evening that a woman from work had started showing up at the gym
when he was there. "I think she has a crush on me," he admitted.
"What shall I do?"

"Oh, that's nice. Maybe she'd like to babysit your kids so I can
go skiing. Or babysit you," I snapped. I had less time to stay active
now that I had two kids, and I mourned the loss of my athletic self.
Although Alex had dubbed me "Saint Jennifer," alluding to my patience and understanding, I didn't feel too saintly then.

Meanwhile, I was feeling increasingly unhappy in Salt Lake City. I felt closed in by winter smog and isolated by the predominance of the Mormon religion in Utah. I had a few good friends but felt no sense of community, and I longed for the open space that I had grown up in. I wanted to be closer to our parents as our children grew up.

"We'll make a change," Alex said when I finally told him how I felt. "I want you to be happy. I want us to be happy." We decided to move once again, to go home to Montana in the coming summer. Alex would work as a guide and try to make his living from climbing. Out of the blue, he was offered a sponsorship from The North Face through his friend Conrad, and another lucrative guiding job appeared on Everest. With my encouragement, he took it. I knew that the money would enable us to make the move, and the expedition would give Alex a much-needed change.

He departed March 16, but not before leaving me a beautiful letter:

> Dearest Jennifer, I want to leave a few things in writing as I prepare to be absent from your life for three long months. First, you must know that I love only you. . . . I am devoted to us as a family. I absolutely adore my beautiful sons and it is my ambition to provide for them in all ways. Although I will always want to climb, I will continue to weigh my decisions according to the desire to grow old with you three and give you myself. I will base my mountaineering judgment on the promise and commitment to return to you. My greatest goal as I try to organize my life is to acquire or discover peace within so that I may bring peace to you, Sam and Max. This is something that is very difficult for me but which I must do. I admire you as a human, as a mother, as an artist and as my lover. Take care of your self as you selflessly continue caring for Max and Sam. Until I return, holding you in my heart, Alex

Spring came to Salt Lake with the promise of change, and I prepared for another show in Montana and one in Jackson Hole. The previous year, I had decided to combine my works with the whimsical willow twig frames of my friend Peter Bartlo, who lived in Bozeman. Peter created twig frames for mirrors and also built small folk art structures. I proposed that he frame some of my work, and we were pleased with the collaboration. I worked with the seven-month-old Sam at my breast and Max at my feet and painted into the night while they slept.

I lost myself in images of cowgirls performing daring tricks on paint horses that raced beneath the stars. My sister Jan and I had ridden our horses across wild hay fields in adolescence and rode stirrup to stirrup on a western drill team, performing in rodeos, horse shows, and parades. I painted to capture that feeling of youth, of endless meadows and a sweat-soaked horse beneath me. I thought of my grandmother and painted the magpies and skunks and red-winged blackbirds that she loved. I painted the Montana that I longed for with bison and bucks and billowing clouds above blue mountains.

I was reassured of Alex's devotion to us and had sent him off to the Himalaya with the knowledge that he would be happier and thus make my own life happier. Knowing that he loved and needed me was integral to my staying with him, and both of us appreciated each other more after periods of being apart. It was a pattern we seemed to have followed since the beginning of our relationship. We both needed our space and needed to feel independent, yet relied on the other as a constant. For Alex, his family was a port in the storm and I provided his calm. For me, he inspired a storm of endless possibilities in setting my own goals. I also enjoyed his adventures in a vicarious way, knowing that I no longer wanted to take the risk personally but sharing in the thrill of his accomplishments. We both looked forward to a day when we could take our children to faraway places and share adventures with our whole family. Until then, the boys and I would read Alex's letters together:

> April 2: Base camp is a small city but a unique one. Literally hundreds of prayer flags radiate outward on strings anchored to altars, central to each campsite. Gaily colored tents and people

*dressed in bright apparel create a delightful collage of color in
this stark land of ice and rubble. Yaks are arriving in droves and
their tinkling bells mix with chatter, gorak croaks and the songs
of tiny birds inhabiting base camp. All this of course, beneath the
mightiest peaks on earth. It's breathtaking!*

*April 7: There is a New Zealand commercial team here. The
leaders are great folks, Rob Hall and Gary Ball. Gary has invited
me (us) to spend a season guiding for him in New Zealand. . . .
The Brits are here with a huge 40 year anniversary climb. . . . The
Koreans are here for another attempt on the SW face. There is an
Indian-Nepalese women's expedition, a Korean women's team, a
Russian West Ridge team, blah, blah, blah. . . . It's a circus.*

*I got a taste of what this is going to be like over the past two
days. Andy Politz and I started up to Camp I @ about 5 AM, just
as the sun begins to ignite the summit of Pumori behind base
camp. We were fairly far back in the commuter traffic which
consists mostly of Sherpas hauling loads plus the occasional
expedition member, huffing and gasping upward. We got to a
steep section where you ascend a fixed line up an 80' ice wall.
Well, there were more than 50 people backed up, waiting to
ascend! We stood for at least 1 hour waiting in the cold dawn
wind, shivering as we witnessed all sorts of cumbersome
gyrations as Nepalese, Koreans, Spanish, Indians, Russians,
Kiwis, Americans, Czechs, Brits and Australians thrashed and
struggled upward. It was scary to see how inept 90% of them
were. We finally gave up and returned to base camp, resolved to
set out at 3:30 AM from now on.*

When I read letters like these, I worried. I had known it was
crowded, but Alex's descriptions sounded like lunacy. The technical
difficulty was fairly benign, but it seemed to have lulled people into a
false sense of security on a mountain that had taken many lives. Alex
reassured me over and again that he would be safe, but those reassur-

Here in Eldorado Canyon, Alex beckons me toward the first climb we shared in 1980—and down a road that changed my life. I carried this photo in my wallet for years. (Lowe collection)

With a piece of gear between his teeth, Alex spiders his way up the classic Clean Crack during one of our many visits to Squamish, BC. (Photo by Jan Daly)

Alex snapped this around 1983 as I followed a thin crack called Bird of Fire *in* Joshua Tree National Monument. (Lowe collection)

The Bitterroot Mountains outside of Missoula offered the first wilderness experiences for both Alex and me. Here, we posed for the timer at a winter camp near Trapper Peak where we spent several days backcountry skiing in 1985. (Lowe collection)

The arrival of Max did not curtail our wilderness excursions. We packed him along on this trip into the Wind River Range in 1989. Alex is wearing the elephant hat that I knit for him when we first fell in love. (Lowe collection)

Though Alex loved climbing of any sort, I believe that ice and mixed climbing was truly his favorite. He forged many routes in Bozeman's Hyalite Canyon which is now a known destination for ice climbers. Here, he makes his way up Come and Get It.
(Photo by Gordon Wiltsie)

In 1997, Alex and I realized a dream of traveling abroad with our children. Here, Alex pauses on a trail in the Italian Dolomites with Sam and Isaac, in the pack. (Lowe collection)

Aid climbing takes focus, skill, and organization to move efficiently. Alex searches for the right piece of gear as he leads a difficult pitch on Great Sail Peak. (Photo by Gordon Wiltsie)

Canoeing was a favorite pastime for the boys and me during summer stays in the Tetons where Alex worked for Exum Mountain Guides. (Lowe collection)

At the base of Great Sail Peak, Alex cranks pullups on his ice ax while Mark Synnott and Greg Child look on. His boundless energy enamored Alex to their Inuit guides but drove his climbing partners to distraction. (Photo by Gordon Wiltsie)

Conrad looks on as Alex scrubs up at the base camp of Rakekniven in Queen Maud Land, Antarctica. (Photo by Gordon Wiltsie)

Conrad and Alex stand atop Rakekniven in Queen Maud Land in 1996. Alex proclaimed the expedition, his favorite ever, a place of spectacular beauty that is seldom seen by men! (Photo by Gordon Wiltsie)

After returning from Trango Tower in the summer of 1999, Alex was home for one month before departing for Shishapangma. We made a trip to Wyoming where Alex and Max summitted The Grand Teton and we took this family photo to commemorate the occasion. (Photo by Al Read)

The summit of Half Dome in June of 2000 was the first mountain we climbed after Alex's death ten months before. The boys piled on top of Conrad in tired bliss after ascending the cable route. (Lowe-Anker collection)

South Georgia Island is home to an abundance of extraordinary wildlife. Isaac and the king penguins found each other equally intriguing in 2003 when we followed the footsteps of Shackelton—and Alex—across the southern ocean. (Lowe-Anker collection)

The lofty village of Namche Bazaar, en route to Everest, was a place that Alex wrote about in letters home and dreamed of bringing his family to see. In 2004 Max, Isaac, Sam, and I arrive in Namche Bazaar and stand with friends Sherrup, Lhakpa, and Chhongba Sherpa. (Photo by Steve Gipe)

On our anniversary in April 2007, Conrad, Sam, Isaac, myself, and Max celebrate six years as a family. Above the fireplace behind us is the original painting of "Into the Dawn." (Lowe-Anker collection)

ances only served to make me more nervous, as I worried that he was trying to convince himself of the sanity in his own undertaking.

> It's a pretty amazing task ahead with a vastly diverse group. By and large they are people who don't climb and are looking to us to be told exactly what to do to stand on top of Mt. Everest. We'll break them into 2 groups of 9 and move them along in waves. There is no "slow" or "fast" group—they're all slow!! It will be a personal challenge to remain open and accepting. This is completely foreign from any of my prior climbing experience. The Sherpas haul everything, fix the route, and do all camp setup and cooking. My task is: walk the clients to the summit. This is very different from the last time, where we were also guides but climbers as well. This time our major task is to walk clients up fixed ground, ultimately to the top.

> It is very important that I feel I have a purpose here to justify not being with you, and I feel I am finding that purpose in helping others to meet the internal challenge of climbing Everest. Of course, I'm also charged with bringing them down safe and sound! I want you to relax and know that my safe return is a #1 priority. We have a great Sherpa team who, by the way, all agree that I am the strongest westerner they have ever seen. I have a Sherpa's attitude that this is a job and not worth dying for.

Alex was not one to brag and would never say something like this publicly. I knew he was telling me this to reassure me that he wouldn't risk his own life for someone else's ambitions. I also knew that he was trying to make sense of what he was doing there as a guide. He was in his beloved mountains and earning an income for his family, but felt he might be compromising his own values of what the mountains meant to him. "I just want to move gracefully through the mountains as long as I am able," he once said, and the purity of that quest struck a chord in my heart. I knew that the scene on Everest did not fit that picture, and I sensed he was struggling with that.

I tried not to think of Alex's daunting job too much but focused on my work and the kids. Sam was becoming an active little guy, crawling about to try to keep up with Max, and I had my hands full watching them both. Max was still not totally keen on having a sibling to share toys and attention with, so I didn't trust him alone with Sam. One day when Sam was napping and I suddenly missed Max, I went to the crib and found him with a pair of scissors, quietly snipping away the sleeping baby's blond hair. "He needs a haircut!" he wailed as I snatched him up and removed the scissors, then hauled him from the room for a time-out. The next thing I knew, he had his little backpack on and was heading for the door.

"Where are you going?" I asked.

"I'm going to Kathmandu to find Dad," he said matter-of-factly.

"Well, how will you get to the airport?"

"I'm going on the bus. Goodbye!"

"Goodbye," I said.

I watched him walk along the sidewalk until he was about halfway down the block and then stop. He turned around and came back slowly, deep in thought. When he opened the door, I asked him if he had changed his mind.

"No," he said. "I was just wondering if you would give me a ride to the airport?"

Alex sent notes for Max written on paper in the shape of a whale. He asked me to place them on the table for him at breakfast.

> Good morning Max—We have a huge tent here that we will live in. This tent is as big as our living room and kitchen combined. We all gather for our meals in this tent and the Sherpa people cook for us. The Sherpas are the people who live here in the mountains called the Himalayas. They are very strong folks who can carry heavy packs up the snowy peaks much faster than you or I can. . . . I'm thinking about you waking up at home and having pancakes or waffles with Mom and Sam.

Alex surprised us with a call from base camp on May 5 just to make sure we were OK before he set off to the summit. He told me he planned to summit by May 10 if the weather held and would be home by the end of May, but at twenty dollars per minute, he didn't talk long. He left the next day and made the summit on May 10 along with nearly thirty other climbers and Sherpas. Soon after, he began the long trek home.

We moved our things to Montana in June and put them into storage until fall. Our summer home would be a little one-room cabin at the Climber's Ranch in Grand Teton National Park, where Alex would work as an Exum guide. There we cooked and ate at shared picnic tables beneath a kiosk, and Sam learned to walk by holding on to benches, making laps around the eating area. We bathed and washed dishes in a communal shower house and had one shelf of a refrigerator for food. It was all we needed, a divinely simple existence in the shadow of the most beautiful range of mountains in the Lower 48. I felt that I could breathe deeply again, and our friends there held the same values dear that Alex and I did, a deep appreciation for the wild being foremost.

Alex went off to guide each day and returned by dinner most evenings. We ate among the rotating guests and retired to our cabin in fading light. The boys and I found our place among the alpine meadows and lakes. We swam and canoed and searched for frogs in the muddy reeds of String Lake. We hiked and fished and filed onto tour boats with names like Curley Bear Two to ride across Jenny Lake and picnic on the willowed shore. We lay in wildflower meadows reading books and wandered trails to pick huckleberries until our tongues were purple.

One day while picking berries for the next morning's pancakes, we startled a young black bear. My heart leaped as he rose to his hind legs and woofed in surprised aggression. I slowly backed away with Max behind me and Sam peering over my shoulder from the backpack. "Doggie," said Sam. "No, Sam, that's a bear!" Max admonished. The bear dropped to the ground suddenly and turned to run into the safety of thick underbrush.

When the nights grew frosty and elk began to bugle, we left the park reluctantly and returned to the quiet streets of Bozeman, where we rented a century-old house on the south side of town. It was the end of our search for the right place. Many of our old friends were still there, and it felt as though we had never left. The following spring, we would buy the house with a down payment from one last guiding trip on Mount Everest. It has been our residence ever since, and in a way, it was Chomolungma, Mother Goddess of the Earth, who brought us home.

A Hero

A hero ventures forth
from the world of common day
into a region of supernatural wonder;
Fabulous forces are there encountered
and a decisive victory is won;
The hero comes back
from this mysterious adventure
with the power to bestow boons
on his fellow man.
—JOSEPH CAMPBELL

"THE BEST CLIMBER IN THE WORLD is the one who's having the most fun," Alex always quipped in response to the oft-asked question, and his playful yet heartfelt answer has been quoted many times. Still, people love to quantify and compare. That is the nature of most sports, after all. There must be a winner or a best. Alex said he wasn't comfortable with the label of best climber, claiming that climbing is a lifestyle, not a competition.

Before the advent of climbing competitions, no climber I ever met admitted to being competitive, yet most were at least quietly so. Alex was no different. Climbing brought him the personal rewards of joy and satisfaction, but the accolades of peers and eventually a climbing public were certainly boosts to his ego and an incentive to keep pushing. Over time, his climbing achievements attracted more and more attention. He was flattered but worried that he didn't deserve the attention. "Jen, I'm just an average climber, no different than many and not as good as some," he'd say.

The November 1992 issue of *Rock and Ice* magazine ran a feature article on Alex, along with George and Jeff, who all shared the Lowe name. The latter are cousins, and both are well-known and respected climbers but no relation to Alex. "Alex is superior genetic material," George joked in his interview, saying he was "phenomenal, the best guy I've climbed with." Similarly, Jeff called Alex "the best climber I know." His alpine ascents were listed, along with his most impressive rock and big-wall ascents and numerous ice climbing routes that pushed modern limits. The article, written by Nancy Prichard, placed Alex at the forefront of the American climbing scene, referring to him as "the quintessential renaissance man of climbing." Over the years, other articles followed in *Climbing* and *Outside* magazines, all alluding to Alex's accomplishments but highlighting his modesty and character.

Although this was not his intention, Everest had given Alex an arena in which to perform, and his reputation grew as he moved up and down the mountain with speed and grace. Fellow guide Dave Hahn said, "There's Alex Lowe up here . . . and then there's the rest of us down here. The guy's just that much better than everybody else." Dr. Kenneth Kamler, who was on Alex's 1993 Everest trip, told me how Alex quietly amazed his clients with strength and speed in mountain terrain and endeared himself to them with his modesty. "It was hard to pry his accomplishments from him," Ken told me. "He always managed to make his feats seem like no big deal." His style was to show what he could do and then play it down.

Hooman Aprin, an expedition leader on Everest in 1990, had similar tales. When it became apparent that the South Pillar was too dangerous and difficult for their group, Hooman requested permission to climb the regular route. He radioed Alex at Camp III on top of the pillar, expecting him to rappel down and then climb up to Camp III on the South Col. He was shocked to see Alex jog along the forty-five-degree slope that separated the two routes. "I watched him run along this face. No one would have believed it. That route had never been traversed before! He was the first to do it."

At the South Col, Hooman and Alex discussed whether to attempt a summit push without oxygen but decided that because they were responsible for the welfare of others, taking such a risk would not be ethical. Alex would have liked to climb Everest without oxygen, as that bar had been set by renowned mountaineer Reinhold Messner and his climbing partner, Peter Habeler, years before. But he reasoned, "We're guiding. We're not here just for ourselves."

One night on the South Col, that fact became hauntingly evident as Alex watched climbers from various expeditions drift into camp. Long after everyone had retired to their tents, Alex noticed a headlamp still far below the camp. He descended to find a French woman collapsed and exhausted. With effort he brought her to camp and the safety of her tent. "I think I saved her life," he told me. Years later, after his death, I received a letter from Chamonix. "I shall never forget the flashlight which appeared in the night. I'll never forget the strong arms who helped me to walk to the tents. He will be in my memory forever."

Sandy Hill Pittman was another Everest client who was impressed with Alex. Sandy had failed to summit in the spring of 1993 but was determined to return in her quest to be the first woman to reach the Seven Summits. She felt she would have a good chance at it with Alex as her guide, so that summer Alex began planning for Everest once again, in 1994. David Breashears was the expedition leader, and Sandy would be Alex's sole client. David would film "Dispatches from Everest," a chronicle of Sandy's quest, to be aired on the *Today* show.

Alex recruited his close friend Steve Swenson with a letter that read in part, "Whenever I'm thinking of strong climbers to join a group you are the first person I contact. I love climbing with you." Barry Blanchard, considered one of Canada's best alpinists, completed the team. It was a strong team, but their proposed route was not standard. They would attempt the remote Kangshung Face, which rises from the Tibetan side of Everest in a difficult technical wall of rock and snow. "Don't you think it's dangerous to guide an amateur on that route?" I asked him with concern. I wasn't an Everest climber, but I was certainly experienced enough to know what he was getting into. "Jen, I have confidence she can do it, or I wouldn't take the job," he argued.

Though Breashears was the expedition leader, it was Sandy who propelled the expedition forward, finding sponsorship through Vaseline for a team dubbed the Vaseline Research Expedition. The name brought endless ribbing from Alex's peers as they conjectured about what the research would entail. Sandy was beautiful, confident, and wealthy. Her husband was Bob Pittman of MTV and Time Warner, and her friends were the social elite of New York City and Washington, D.C. I felt more than a bit threatened by the thought of this glamorous woman traveling to the other side of the planet with my husband as her personal guide.

Alex spoke of her fun-loving nature, spunk, and drive. I grew paranoid. "You'll be with her constantly in extreme conditions, and there's no way around the intimacy. How do you know what you might feel?" I fretted. Alex rolled his eyes, saying, "Jen, come on! She's married to an amazing man! I'm not interested in other women. I love you." I knew that—but still I worried.

Sandy came to Jackson in late summer, and Alex arranged for me to go fly-fishing with her to set my mind at ease. He knew I'd be in my element, and his plan worked well. After breakfasting with Alex and the boys at the Shades Café, she and I drove to a ribbon of stream where we donned waders and went casting for cutthroats among the moose-eaten willows of Teton Basin. In the quiet of streams dammed by beaver, we fished as any two fishermen must, going our separate ways, giving each other berth for throwing and stripping our lines, then coming together to share lunch and conversation. We talked of our families, fishing, and climbing. In doing so, the fears I had harbored were stripped away. I sensed that Sandy respected Alex not only for his climbing skills but for his character and dedication to his family.

That evening we met Alex and the kids in downtown Jackson, where Sandy was staying in a hotel. Over dinner, she and Alex discussed the proposed climb. She was a fireball, as Alex put it, with energy and determination to rival his own, and she looked fit. Sandy had just picked up a new puppy, a yellow Lab named Bell that she was taking home to New York. Since dogs weren't allowed in her hotel, she enlisted Alex, the kids, and me to smuggle the puppy into her room by handing it to her through the window. My view of her softened even more after that. But I also realized that she was from a different world than the one that Alex and I had chosen. "How can you stand to live in New York?" I had asked naively during the peaceful day. She bristled and answered, "I love living in New York. It's the most exciting city on earth!"

Alex gave me the final say on the trip, saying, "Jen, you need to be comfortable with this." I told him I trusted that all would be fine. And so they departed in mid-March. Two weeks later, he wrote:

We are at the end of the road where we start the six day trek to our base camp. We left Kathmandu with three tons of food and equipment loaded onto 2 big trucks. This is the most encumbered expedition I've ever seen. I look forward to getting to the mountain and doing what I am here to do—guiding Sandy, climbing safely to the top of the world, earning my wage and getting back home to you. It is dark outside now and thousands of stars shine through the silver clouds floating above ghost peaks illuminated by the pale full moon. It is lovely, yet I am lonely for you all. I have been gone only two weeks now and the two months ahead seem unendurable.

Lots and lots of little boys and girls watch us pack all day long. They wear wool boots, usually bright red, that are very warm, coming up to their knees and made of hand-felted yak wool. They have turquoise earrings that are beautifully contrasted against their chocolate brown skin and wild stringy black hair with red

ribbons in it. The kids are very curious about our equipment and
we made a line with little rocks around our camp. We forbade
them to cross this line and they are very cute as they crowd
behind the perimeter trying to see all our things. They laugh and
play just as you do, Max. When they venture over the line, I run
toward them, roaring and waving my arms. They dash back
behind the stones laughing and chattering excitedly in Tibetan.

While Alex was away that spring, his dad drove from Missoula to spend a weekend building a cedar fence around our backyard, providing a safe place for the boys to play and a secure place for a dog. I had fallen for Sandy's puppy and found a litter of yellow Labs available in April. Max and I built a doghouse and prepared for a puppy. Alex had more than his share of dog chores as a kid and he wasn't wild about dogs, so I purposely planned to get the puppy before he came home. I knew he wouldn't have the heart to say no once we had her. It was devious on my part, but I saw it as an advantage of my sole authority in his absence.

Whenever Alex was away, I tackled major projects like painting the house, creating a garden, adopting a new pet, or even buying a car. Perhaps it gave me an illusion of control over my life that felt reassuring. Over the years we had a menagerie of pets including a magpie, a raven, rats, chickens, rabbits, cats, fish, frogs, and a lovebird. I guess it's the latent ranch girl in me plus an inability to say no to the boys where critters are concerned. Alex and I had an understanding that when I was running the show I had full authority, and I must say that I liked it, being an independent sort. I executed decisions with glee and took pride in getting things done.

The women I look up to are strong and capable like the pioneer women of the West, my own ancestors. "Jenni functions perfectly well without me around," Alex often said, and he was right. If I had a tough day, I'd lean on Mom or Jan or my girlfriends, who were ever present. Alex once wrote: "Wow, you never cease to amaze me dear one, herding boys, toting artwork and scoring major successes in your sales. You are definitely my hero!"

Alex gave me his power of attorney as a matter of convenience since I usually did our taxes, managed our money, handled legal matters, and paid the bills. That spring I closed on our house, using Alex's Everest salary as the bulk of the down payment and signing all of the papers twice. It was a lonely feeling, scratching my name and Alex's at the bottom of the endless forms as I thought of the responsibility attached to the signatures and had a fleeting moment of fear.

Though we missed Alex, I was accustomed to his absences and found a routine that was simple and efficient. While I sat to paint, the kids lounged on the floor of my studio to create their own bright drawings or piece together wooden train tracks snaking down the hallway from beneath my chair. I built a sandbox in the yard where Max and Sam played for hours, making mountains, rivers, and roads. From my studio window I watched them beneath the tall spruce while magpies swooped about with finches and chickadees in pursuit. I ordered pizza or whipped up macaroni or grilled cheese sandwiches, and the boys learned to forage for fruit and snacks that were always on hand. After bedtime stories, I returned to my studio and worked into the night.

One day I answered the doorbell to find two strangers on my porch, young men who looked a bit awkward when Max and Sam peeked from behind my knees. "Is this where Alex Lowe lives?" one of them asked.

"Yes," I answered a little hesitantly, "but he isn't here right now."

"Cool! We're climbers. . . . Do you mind if we take our picture in front of your house? We're just traveling through and . . . he's our hero, so . . . "

"No problem," I said with surprised amusement.

I would work obsessively and then take a few days off to clean the house or bolt to Chico Hot Springs in Paradise Valley. It was a favorite outing for soaks in the hot mineral pool, where Max and Sam never tired of leaping from the edge into my arms. We camped impromptu near Mammoth Terraces in Yellowstone, where elk and bison grazed nearby and carefree coyotes jogged through our campsite, giving inspiration for my work. We walked through clouds of steam over weathered boardwalks to look into the veins of the earth and watch them boil and spill over the snow-white mineral terraces.

Easter at Mom and Papa's had become a tradition since Alex was usually away on expeditions in spring. Mother and I shared the ritual of hiding eggs and setting out baskets for the boys late at night. Mom hauled out malted eggs, chocolate eggs, and plastic eggs jingling with nickels and dimes and packed with jellybeans to hide about the house. Church was required on Easter, and though the boys looked like little gentlemen, they were revved up on sugar by the time the service rolled around, making it challenging for them to sit on the hard wooden pews. But it was my gift to Mother, and she prayed extra hard on our behalf.

"Jennifer, how are you?" Mother inquired. "You work so hard, and I worry about you."

"I'm doing fine, Mom," I replied. "Life is good."

"How much longer do you think Alex will do this climbing?" she asked, her brows knitted.

"As long as he can, Mom . . . until he's an old man. He's a climber, Mom. Try not to worry."

Alex wrote us about his Easter in the Himalaya:

March 27: It's Easter Sunday and Sandy scattered chocolate and malt eggs all about our dining tent early this morning which set off choruses of "Here comes Peter Cottontail. . . . " It was quite fun actually and typical of Sandy to remember to celebrate such occasions. I of course got horribly lonely, thinking of you three enjoying Easter egg hunts together.

We divvied up loads to 140 porters today. . . . The usual yelling and haggling over weight ensued but the first day is always the most chaotic. . . . When we got to camp last night, I pulled out my dozens of family photos for the porters. They expressed delight at Max, Sam and your pictures and I've definitely been accepted as OK for having a fine family.

There was no TV in our house, but we watched the *Today* show at a friend's and saw glimpses of Alex wandering through markets, then traveling and trekking to the mountain. When Sam first saw him he burst into tears, thinking his dad was trapped in the strange box. "Get him out!" he pleaded, while I tried to explain how it all worked.

Once they arrived at base camp, enormous avalanches were dramatically depicted cascading from the face as the route was pointed out nearby. That was disconcerting for both me and Steve's wife, Anne, whom I spoke with often. They were a mile and a half from the face, but their camp still felt the windblast from the avalanches and received a dusting of snow from them.

> *April 4: This is our first day at base camp. It is absolutely the most dramatic place I've been. To the north and east, the Kama valley, which we walked up to get here, drops away to the Tibetan Plateau. The mountains in that direction are gentle and only the highest of them are covered by glaciers. The hills are vegetated with grass and heather while the valley itself sports tall juniper bushes and eventually pine forests far below. But . . . turn 180 degrees and I am confronted with giant peaks surrounding us for almost 270 degrees. In some ways, it's oppressive and ominous. I feel a little pit in my stomach looking up so far above me, like I'm in the bottom of a deep cauldron. When I awoke this morning, Everest, Lhotse and Chomolonzo were shedding new snow in avalanches that fell in surreal silence, 10,000 vertical feet into the basin above our camp. I could feel the wind generated by their descent. I feel small and vulnerable here but simultaneously overwhelmed by the beauty and power of nature. It's snowing today so we've spent a day relaxing in base camp. I'm listening to Mozart piano sonatas, which are calming yet simultaneously invigorating in technical perfection. The clouds envelop camp here at 17,900', and even over the lyrical strains of Mozart I hear the omnipresent thunder of avalanches roaring off the faces surrounding us.*

The snow kept falling and one of the avalanches came close enough to blast tents from their stakes and send them flying with occupants inside, strewing gear and supplies about the glacier. They moved their base camp down valley, but as Alex waited out storms and toiled on the mountain, fate dealt a harsh blow to his family. His grandmother Argo, Dottie's mother and the last of his grandparents, passed away. Within the same month, Alex's brother Ted and his wife, Kathy, got the heartwrenching news that their infant daughter had leukemia. She died before Alex returned.

> *April 19: Yesterday, we spent our first day climbing on the route with Steve and me in the lead fixing 2,200' of rope two-thirds of the way up the buttress toward Camp I. We climbed in ten hours what took the Chileans three days in '92! Steve is a formidable and synergistic partner. I'd forgotten how fluid we are together. Steve, Barry and I finished the steep buttress and put in Camp I at 21,000'. It's a spectacular campsite atop the 3,000' buttress. The climbing was great—very exposed vertical mixed, overhanging ice and all reasonably safe on good rock. It's all fixed and we've been carrying loads the past 2 days. I'm enthralled with the climb and the setting.*

But he wasn't enthralled with the avalanche conditions, which grew more dangerous as they pushed to Camp II. With the fragility of life on his mind, Alex would not risk going higher. He was one of the most conservative of his peers in that sense. "I thought if anything ever happened to him," Steve Swenson told me, "it would be from some technical stunt that went bad." At Alex's urging, the expedition called it quits and headed for home—aside from Steve, who managed to join another team on the North Ridge and went on to summit without oxygen.

Sandy eventually reached the summit of Everest in 1996, thus finishing her Seven Summits quest, but was caught in a tragic and infamous storm that took the lives of nine people, including her guide, Scott Fischer, and left her entangled in controversy. Alex was devastated by the tragedy, which also took the life of his good friend Rob Hall. Asked by the *Bozeman Chronicle* about guiding on Everest again, he was definitive: "I saw myself in the situation that Rob got himself in, perfectly capable of walking off the mountain, but obliged to fulfill his professional obligation to his clients. The difference between climbing and guiding is enormous. If a guide wants to take on Everest, that's fine. I'm not going to do it again."

Alex climbed at a pace that stunned his peers. In the summer of 1993, he had traveled to the Tien Shan range in Kyrgyzstan to compete in an alpine speed-climbing contest on a 23,000-foot peak called Khan Tengri. He and Conrad were the first Americans to participate in the international event. Alex won the contest, running to the summit and back in ten hours and breaking the previous fastest-ascent record by more than four hours. "Alex is due in camp in a few days," Conrad wrote in a letter home. "The folks here think I'm fit (the Brits call me the fit bastard) and the Russians tell me 'Yes, you strong.' I tell them, wait until the Fiend pulls into town." Conrad came in second, but he and Alex forged a partnership amid the goodwill and camaraderie of the Russian climbers who hosted the event.

"Conrad is the most selfless person I've ever climbed with," Alex confided once home. He described Conrad as contemplative and quiet but ready to help wherever needed. Conrad brought watercolors to base camp, Alex told me, and painted lovely sketches of the mountains, then gave them all away. He told me that Conrad had caught a fellow racer who slipped and fell high on the route after becoming fatigued. Had Conrad not made a timely appearance, the man might have suffered a tragic end. Conrad then stopped mid-race to make sure the fellow was OK before resuming the climb. "That's the kind of partner I want," Alex said, and that's the kind of partner Alex wanted to be.

In June 1995, Alex was in Alaska with Steve Swenson to try a route on the east face of Huntington but never got a window of weather. When Steve went home, Alex and Conrad had planned to meet at Kahiltna base to climb the Cassin Ridge on Denali, known to most as Mount McKinley. Alex flew into the Kahiltna Glacier at the base of Denali a few days before Conrad and hiked to the rescue camp at 14,000 feet to acclimatize. Feeling strong, he decided to go to the summit with friends Mark Twight, Scott Backes, and Colin Grissom, who were heading up that night. En route, they passed a team of Spanish climbers who were bivouacked on the West Rib.

The next day, after Alex and his friends had summited and were back down to 14,000 feet, the Spaniards radioed for help. A storm had hit and their tent was shredded. Alex, Scott, and Mark were enlisted for a rescue, and a Chinook helicopter was called in to make a dicey landing above the stranded climbers at an elevation of 19,500 feet, the highest ever in a Chinook. Alex was no stranger to helicopters, but he told me it was the scariest flight of his life. The pilot managed to set down on a relatively flat section of the mountain and instructed his rescue team to be back in two hours.

Mark, Scott, and Alex climbed down the technical route to the Spaniards on June 9 and found that one had already fallen to his death. Two others were in bad shape with extreme frostbite and hypothermia. Mark and Scott took the first climber, who could still walk, and left Alex attending to the second man, who was in worse shape, thinking they would be back to help. But Alex decided there was no time to wait. He tied the collapsed climber to his harness and began dragging him up the route. When that became impossible, he hefted the man onto his back and carried him toward the waiting chopper. "We couldn't believe it," Mark told me. Alex was hiking steadily up the steep slope with a man on his back at an elevation where most people struggle to keep moving.

When Conrad arrived, he and Alex were enlisted for yet another rescue of three Taiwanese climbers who had become separated from their team in a storm. Conrad and Alex arrived at near 19,000 feet to find one climber dead and two others close to death, with severe hypothermia and frostbite. They had lost their judgment and were lying out in the snow with no gloves or shelter. With great effort, Alex and Conrad brought down the two survivors, dragging them by their harnesses nearly 3,000 feet to a waiting helicopter.

Their time was now short, so Conrad and Alex decided to go for a fast ascent on a 4,000-foot route of difficult rock and ice called the Moonflower Buttress on Mount Hunter. They left Kahiltna base about 2:00 AM to approach the mountain, skiing across the glacier. By 6:00 AM they were on the buttress, which consists of three technical rock bands and three steep ice bands. They climbed with no tent or sleeping bags, only a stove to melt snow and a small stash of food. Their intent was to do the climb in one push, though it had never been ascended in less than three days. They each led three pitches, aiming to move as fast as possible. Some twenty hours into the climb, Conrad says they watched a helicopter effect yet another rescue on Denali across the valley. "It was surreal to be climbing this difficult technical route, feeling so out there in one sense, and watch another drama unfolding across the glacier." But as they neared the top of the buttress, storm clouds began to build. They watched them engulf Mount Foraker to the southwest and decided to rap off as snow began to fall. In six hours, they were back on the glacier where they had started twenty-eight hours before.

Before they flew home, Alex and Conrad stopped at the hospital in Anchorage to visit one of the Spanish climbers they had rescued, Xavier Delgado Vives of Barcelona, as well as the Taiwanese climbers. The Spanish climber wept with gratitude and later wrote to Alex, "You will not have to choose a mountain to climb or route to climb, you are in all of them. Our encounter was brief, just a few hours but you are forever a light, in the future and in life for me. My gratitude is eternal."

The Taiwanese climbers, on the other hand, were not demonstrative but rather seemed embarrassed by their rescue. "They would surely have died had we not brought them down," Alex told me, "yet it seemed as though that reality wasn't obvious to them." Their leader, who was also being treated for frostbite, was named Makalu Gau. We were shocked to see that he was one of the men with extreme frostbite rescued on Everest the following spring, a victim of the storm that spared Sandy Hall Pittman but claimed the lives of Scott Fischer and Rob Hall. Kenneth Kamler, the doctor attending Gau, said it was the worst case of frostbite he'd ever seen—until he saw Beck Weathers, from the same expedition.

Alex continued to guide for Exum, whose concession has a small enclave of cabins in Grand Teton National Park for their guides. We bought a one-room cabin on the piece of ground near Lupine Meadows called Guides' Hill, where we would spend our summers. The tiny cabin was in such close proximity to the handful of others that it felt like summer camp with one big bedraggled family. Climbers drifted in and out for coffee, a beer, or simply to chat. Max fell in with the casual rhythm, to such an extent that it was hard to keep tabs on him. I would miss him and go searching frantically, worried about the rushing stream nearby, only to find him having a visit with one or another of the guides, his favorites being Chuck Pratt and Jack Turner, two of the senior guides. One day I found him in Jack's spiritual retreat, where books lined the walls. He and Jack were quietly engrossed in painting with watercolors while sunlight and the songs of mountain chickadees streamed in through the open doorway.

Guiding had taken Alex to places far and wide, from South America to Everest to New Guinea and Europe. He wrote to me from an ascent of El Cap in Yosemite:

> It's lovely here as always and I have wonderful memories of our time together here. I see other male-female climbing partners and I feel kind of sad. It's not that I long to climb with you so much as I long to simply be with you more. I'm only going to do this much guiding until our house is mostly paid off. After that, I want to slow up and be with you three.

Alex loved walking out the door of the Teton cabin in the morning to guide, and coming home to the kids and me at dusk. Dinner on a picnic table in front of our door, with the sun casting a pink glow on the mountains, was his idea of heaven, and each night he reclined on our one big bed with the boys leaning into him to read them a chapter from a book. Stories such as *My Side of the Mountain,* *Jenny of the Tetons,* and *Call It Courage* sent us all into our dreams.

On the rare occasion that I took a notion to climb and found a babysitter, Alex made a big deal of us going together, bringing along gourmet chocolate, smoked oysters, and a flask of wine for toasting on summits. Alex's father and his brother Ted joined us on a climb of the Exum Ridge on the Grand Teton one summer while Dottie watched the boys. I got to see Alex's guiding skills in action and was duly impressed. Jim was not feeling great on the second morning when we set out for the summit. The altitude and the long hike the previous day had him wondering if he could make it up. "Why don't you all go on and I'll go down. I'm just holding you up," he said. But Alex coaxed him along in a loving and respectful way, and Jim did just fine. It meant a great deal to Alex to have climbed the Grand Teton with his father and brother, and he looked forward to climbing it with his sons. Alex told me that he loved the Tetons more than any range of mountains.

Once in a while someone would poke their head in our cabin as he did pull-ups and make a comment: "Jesus, Alex, can't you get enough on the rocks?" But he couldn't. His workouts were a crucial part of his training as well as an outlet for his insatiable drive. The job of being a mountain guide required him to sometimes plod along at a snail's pace with clients, reining in his normal lope. His clients never saw any frustration, though, as he was a paragon of patience in their presence and wanted them to experience the same joy that he felt in the mountains. Instead he would crank pull-ups or take a ten-mile run at the end of a mellow day of guiding.

One morning after checking in at the Exum office to find that he had the day free, he took off trail running and managed the Grand Traverse, which is ten peaks including the Grand Teton, in his tennis shoes. "He was back to the office by four," his fellow guide Doug Chabot told me, laughing.

"I could have done it faster," Alex told me privately, "if I hadn't slipped in a boulder field and sliced open my butt on a rock." He patched up the bleeding wound with some athletic tape and continued on his way, only realizing that he needed stitches after he arrived back at the office, hours later. There he inspected the gaping wound and his blood-soaked leg in a mirror while the office staff looked on in combined horror and admiration. Henceforth, the wide white scar marked his bare butt as a badge of honor for the Grand Traverse.

Under the leadership of Bill Simon, then president of The North Face, 1995 saw Alex and Conrad's sponsorship from the company grow into salaried positions for the two climbers as the company endorsed a group of athletes dubbed the Dream Team. For Alex, it was a dream come true. No longer would he be forced to find time and money for his climbing while trying to make a living somewhere else; now he could do it all in one fell swoop.

Kyrgyzstan beckoned once more. Alex joined the Dream Team for a sponsored expedition to the Ak-Su, where the climbers spent three weeks and put up new routes on the countless granite towers. In a letter he enthused about the "terrific" climbing, but still remembered to wish me a happy birthday. At home, I opened the gift he had left me, in a large box marked FRAGILE. It was a beautiful antique wall clock with a note that said, "To measure many more years together."

And it wasn't the only gift he had left me.

Alex called from Kyrgyzstan as soon as he was out of the mountains to let me know he was safe. "Hi Bird, how are you? I can't wait to get home. How're the boys?"

"Alex, I'm pregnant."

"What?"

"I'm pregnant. We're going to have another baby."

"Are you sure?"

"Yes, I'm sure."

Silence and then, "OK, wow!"

Once home, he held my hands and spoke quietly. "I know the boys are a lot for you, and I'm away so much. . . . Is this what you want?"

"I'll manage. It's what I want," I assured him.

"OK, then it's what I want too," he said, wrapping his arms around me.

In January 1996 Alex took a trip that opened his eyes to one of the least explored and most pristine places on earth. He was invited to join a unique expedition being filmed for ESPN called Sailing to Climb, bound for the Antarctic Peninsula. Gary Jobson, a renowned sailor and winner of the America's Cup who had never climbed, would be featured along with Alex, the mountaineer who had never sailed. Whitbread race veteran and mountaineer Skip Novak would pilot his sailing vessel *Pelagic* through the most notorious passage of rough water on the planet, teaching Alex the rudiments of sailing along the way.

It was Alex's first experience on a sailboat of any kind. The *Pelagic* was designed by Novak to have a retractable keel for navigating through bergs and brash ice. But on seas where the waves reach heights that break over the bridges of large ships, she was not your average beginner's boat. I was in my last trimester of pregnancy, and though I was excited for Alex to try sailing and to see Antarctica, I was definitely nervous. Alex wrote to us via satellite link:

> Dear Jennifer, Max and Sam, and soon to be Isaac, Are we going
> to spell Isaac with a "c" or a "k" as in Isaak? Important matters.
> . . . We're tied up in a secure bay waiting for weather to clear
> enough to do our climb on Wiencke Island. We had an incredible
> run of good weather, sailing well down the peninsula under
> sunny skies watching humpback whales, dozens of orcas that
> curiously followed the stern within five feet, and hundreds of seals
> including leopard seals lolling about on ice. Skip and I managed
> to climb a new route on Mount Scott along the way . . . a lovely
> ice couloir, slightly mixed about 2,500' long that led directly to the
> summit with fabulous views.
>
> Yesterday I got to do a fantasy ice climb on a huge iceberg in the
> middle of the ocean. It was close to 120 feet high and slightly
> overhung most of the way. Skip nosed the bow of the Pelagic up
> against the berg and I slammed my tools into the overhanging

side and stepped boldly off the boat. The seas were high so Skip
immediately pulled away, leaving me wondering if I liked what
I'd started. The sea is 28 degrees and looks mighty black and deep.
The view looking down between my legs was really wild.

"Whoa!" exclaimed Max and Sam over the sighting of whales, but as I read Alex's letter over my large belly, I pictured him soloing above the icy southern ocean and cursed. I had to believe that Alex would assess the situation to be safely within his ability, though. I imagined he was so pent up on the boat that he would do anything to escape the inactivity, including climbing icebergs with no rope. I was greatly relieved when I heard that they had made it back to land and he would be home the first week in February. And even as I fretted, I looked forward to his stories, slides, and the film and hoped to see the beauty of Antarctica for myself one day.

When Isaac arrived, Alex held the dark-haired babe aloft and announced over his screams, "Hi little man, you were meant to be." Isaac was only five weeks old when we packed the family into our van and drove south toward California. Our destination was Yosemite via the town of Big Oak Flat, California, where we would be guests at Priest Ranch, the home of Conrad's parents. Alex had stayed there before and enjoyed the warm hospitality of Conrad's German mother, Helga, with whom he had practiced his rusty German. Conrad's father, Wally, had grown up on the land, his grandparents and parents having owned and operated Priest Station, a gateway into Yosemite Park. The ranch sits high above the Central Valley, where oak forests turn to pine, and offers a stunning view toward the ocean.

Perhaps the most enchanting resident was Albert, a great horned owl who strayed from wildness to visit the clothesline each evening, burbling to be fed by Conrad while we looked on in awe. The stately bird would turn his head, blink his yellow eyes, and spread his lovely wings to fly to the porch and grasp a chicken leg from Conrad's gloved hand. Wally and Helga were accustomed to having Conrad's climbing friends drop in, as Priest is an hour's drive from Yosemite Valley and the perfect place to stage for a wall climb.

In the driveway Conrad, Alex, and Andrew McLean spread out their climbing equipment and food to organize and pack into haul bags for climbing El Cap. Max and Sam caught the drift of excitement and dove into the thick of it, playing with cams, slings, and carabiners. Andrew and Conrad snatched up the boys to swing them about, and Max crawled in and out of haul bags, pleading, "Dad, I can ride in here—can I come too?"

Though I spent more time with Conrad's parents than with Conrad himself, I could see the synergy he shared with Alex, and I sensed his quiet pride in sharing his parents' home with us. He was enthusiastic about having the kids around, and Wally and Helga were overjoyed to have us all. "Jenni," they said, "you give us hope that Conrad might have a family someday. You don't have a sister, do you?"

We accompanied Alex through towering pine and cedar forests thick with dogwoods to the valley floor, where he and his partners headed up El Capitan. Max and I pitched our tent to enjoy a few days of exploring our favorite places with his little brothers. The spray of the Mist Trail christened tiny Isaac in his baby pack as we ascended the rocky pathway to the Nevada Falls Overlook, and three-year-old Sam made most of the hike without being carried. I held Isaac next to me in my sleeping bag at night and nursed him to sleep while reading stories to Max and Sam by headlamp.

On Mother's Day morning, we unzipped our tent to find an enormous pile of bear scat less than five feet from the door. Though I wasn't normally afraid of black bears, knowing their shy character, I shivered to think what a morsel Isaac would have made. Alex surprised us by appearing in time for a Mother's Day brunch at the Ahwahnee Hotel. He and his friends had bailed from the climb to regroup after Alex took a long leader fall and banged himself up. As we strolled across the Ahwahnee parking lot, we were approached by a couple of young climbers. "Are you Alex Lowe?" they asked. "Sure am," he answered jovially, extending his hand and asking their names. "So what are you here to climb?" they asked. "Oh, I'm just trying not to fall off things," he said. "I think Max and I will attempt After Six today," he said, referring to a beginner climb.

The North Face job sent Alex on dream expeditions of his own design but also required him to appear at trade shows, annual meetings, dealer events, slide show presentations, and climbing demonstrations. His reputation spread with the appearances, which were promoted heavily by the company, and films of him ice climbing were seen widely on television. Alex felt lucky to have found a way to make a living from his passion and to have financial security and a life in Bozeman, but he was on the road or away from home far more than either of us had ever imagined. Meanwhile, my own work was getting more demanding as I expanded my market and my clientele grew.

In the summer of 1996 Alex decided to sell our cabin at Guides' Hill, since his work with The North Face did not allow him time to be an Exum guide. It was bittersweet and difficult for both of us. The cabin had been crowded and chaotic at times that summer with five of us, and the Exum "family" seemed larger than ever. As summer drew to a close, I packed up the children and left Alex alone to soak in the last few days of that place we all loved, knowing that it had special meaning to him. Guiding for Exum had set him free by providing a job, an outlet, and a refuge at times in his life when he had needed that most. And for all of us, the Tetons had been a place where family and climbing could mesh.

At the end of September, we drove to the quiet park for a last weekend at the cabin. It was sad for both of us as we emptied our little space of belongings and bid farewell to the Tetons. On our final morning there, we took a walk with the children beneath the craggy mountains that Alex had come to know intimately. Max ran ahead with Sam on his heels and Isaac swung between us, gripping each of our hands, as elk bugled and frost covered the yellow grasses of Lupine Meadows. "Someday, we'll come back here," I told him. "You can always come back to Exum."

"Bird, you're my hero," he said.

Polar Dance

There's a land where the mountains are nameless,
And the rivers all run God knows where;
There are lives that are erring and aimless,
And deaths that just hang by a hair;
There are hardships that nobody reckons;
There are valleys unpeopled and still;
There's a land—oh it beckons and beckons,
And I want to go back and I will.
—ROBERT SERVICE

"ANTARCTICA HAS A SPECIAL sort of tug on my heartstrings," Alex said. "It's the last true wilderness left on the planet, in my opinion." He had barely tasted the vast frozen continent from the *Pelagic* and was more than eager to get back to its unclimbed summits and spires. Alex had contacted photojournalist Gordon Wiltsie for information and advice when he traveled to the peninsula on the *Pelagic* and Gordon was happy to oblige, having already taken part in eight expeditions to Antarctica. Thus the acquaintance was made and Alex and I became friends with Gordon, his wife Meredith, and their two young sons, who were close in age to our own. We joined them for a family dinner one evening, and the air was charged with excitement as Gordon pulled out photos from a recent trip he had taken to Antarctica. He and Alex began to scheme.

Queen Maud Land, one hundred miles inland on the continent, beckoned as an extraordinary photo opportunity for Gordon, whose curiosity had been piqued when he had flown over its otherworldly spires. His animated stories about his adventures instantly endeared him to Alex, who convinced him that it would be no problem to climb one of the imposing spires. To Alex, the granite spears sprouting from the ice looked like a climber's dream. Gordon put forth a proposal to The North Face and *National Geographic*, which ponied up funds for an expedition that Alex ultimately would cherish as the best of his life.

Conrad was keen to come on board, having climbed in Antarctica in 1992 and 1994. He had successfully guided the Vinson Massif and pioneered a new route on the unclimbed Mount Craddock. Jon Krakauer, who had not climbed since the tragic expedition on Everest seven months before, signed on as a journalist, tentatively hoping to write about a far different mountaineering experience than the one he had recently survived. Filmmakers Rick Ridgeway and Michael Graber joined at the last possible moment after struggling to secure funding. Their goal was to climb and film the proposed ascent of the breathtaking unclimbed spire called Rakekniven, Norwegian for "The Razor." It is a fin of granite rising over 2,000 feet from the ice, with an overhanging face to rival any big wall.

The place and the climb were spectacular, but it was the group dynamic that made for the greatest reward, according to Alex. His partnership with Conrad was solid, and he knew that the two of them would forge the route with easy confidence born from their countless big-wall ascents in Yosemite. An inherent trust and a sincere enjoyment of each other's company had developed from their past expeditions. Rick Ridgeway was Alex's hero when he became the first American to summit K2 and was the author of several books that Alex had devoured as a young climber. He was delighted to discover Rick's naturalist streak, and they came away from the trip as fast friends. Michael Graber had an impressive résumé of climbs around the globe but also possessed enough talent and wit to rival the best stand-up comics in a tent-bound storm—"the funniest guy I've ever known," Alex said. Jon was the only one in the group who had not visited Antarctica, but Alex was enamored of his talent as a climber, his obvious love of the woolly places on the planet, and his ability to write about them with such passion.

Christmas provided the best weather window for the expedition, so unfortunately Alex would have to be away from our family on that holiday—Isaac's first Christmas. "Couldn't you go earlier—or later?" I had asked, disappointed. But the answer was no. We packed him off with a bundle of special gifts to open at the other end of the earth. The boys drew pictures, and Max took a great deal of time to make an assortment of Christmas bugs in green and red cut from construction paper "so Dad can decorate his tent."

Alex blinked back tears as he handed me a collection of gifts and notes to tuck under our tree on Christmas Eve. "Thanks for understanding, Jen," he said. And I did understand. The expedition was a rare opportunity in my mind, with little objective danger and lots of appeal. I was proud and excited, knowing he would be exploring an extraordinary, rarely seen place and that his adventure would be documented by National Geographic, whose hallowed pages I had grown up turning. Though I would have loved it if he could do both, I could not let him pass up the chance to go to Antarctica in order to have Christmas in Bozeman.

Antarctic expeditions are usually staged from Argentina or South Africa. In this case it was South Africa, where the climbers explored Cape Town's rock climbing, surfing, and sightseeing while waiting for the right window of weather to make the long flight and, more importantly, the landing on blue ice. Fine limestone crags enticed them out with Ed February, a well-known black South African climber. "I have a better understanding of this place and the political injustice it has seen through Ed," Alex wrote. "We are so fortunate to have spent time with him."

Gordon had told Alex that they would have the opportunity to rock climb in South Africa but made the mistake of saying that he wasn't too keen on it because of his fear of snakes. When Alex packed his duffel, he had purposely thrown in one of the boys' rubber snakes with the intent of having some fun at Gordon's expense. So on a Cape Town climb, as poor Gordon belayed from below, Alex pulled the rubber snake from his pack and placed it carefully on a ledge. When Gordon climbed up and came nose to nose with the rubber snake, he let loose with a bloodcurdling cry that sent Alex into hysterical laughter. It took Gordon a moment to realize that the snake was a fake before he started laughing too.

While a storm in Antarctica kept the expedition delayed in Cape Town, snow fell on Bozeman. Christmas approached, with the usual rituals of cutting a tree and decorating it. Max took part in his school program, marching to the stage of his school to stand and sing Christmas songs, while I sat alongside other adoring parents and Sam and Isaac wiggled in their seats next to me. We feasted with friends at holiday parties, and Isaac sat on Santa's lap for a brief moment before assessing the situation and bursting into tears.

Finally, the C-130 Hercules had a window of weather to fly and deliver them safely to Queen Maud Land's bare ice landing, where they switched their cargo to a smaller ski-equipped plane for a forty-five-mile flight to their base camp. Three weeks after he had departed Bozeman and four days before Christmas, Alex and his partners stood on the frozen continent beneath their imposing goal. The sheer face of Rakekniven provided a combination of difficult technical challenge and incredibly remote environment that promised a profoundly unique climbing experience.

My sister Jan and her new partner, Murray Journeay, traveled from Bowen Island in British Columbia to share Christmas, bringing the sounds of bluegrass. Murray played fiddle with the boys while Jan strummed rhythm guitar. On Christmas Eve, also Alex's birthday, I bundled the boys into snow pants. We rolled the fresh wet snow in our front yard into balls and created a life-size snow bear, standing upright with paws across his chest. In early evening, the boys and I placed a candle in one paw and lit it in honor of their dad. In front of the illuminated snow bear, we sang happy birthday to Alex while he slept in a yellow tent on a desert of ice at the bottom of the world.

With six people on the route carrying heavy film equipment, a fast alpine-style ascent was impossible. They began a traditional wall-climbing style of fixing pitches as far up the face as they could, climbing higher each day and then rappelling to their base camp each night. Actually, night didn't occur, just a sort of twilight during which the temperature dropped dramatically; that was chosen as the time to rest. In the morning, the climbers ascended the ropes. Mechanical ascenders allow a climber to slide the handheld device up the rope as far as they can reach; there it catches and holds their weight as they stand in a stirruplike sling. One ascender is used in each hand and efficiency takes practice, fitness, and nerve, especially when one is hanging far out from the rock on a spinning rope. In this manner, the fixed ropes allowed for a quick descent in the event of a serious storm.

When storms did occur, the temperatures could drop drastically in gale-force winds, whipping up snow into a blinding whiteout. Exposure on the rock face in such weather was out of the question, so only the calmest days were chosen to climb the difficult rock pitches that required climbers to use their bare hands to make their way up delicate holds. The rock was a mix of solid and crumbly granite; thus rockfall was a constant danger to the lower climbers. Rick took one hit directly on the nose, which resulted in a dramatically bloody mess but no serious damage. Once they had climbed high enough to make the return to base camp inefficient, they camped in free-hanging tents called portaledges, suspended from the rock, with two members in each ledge.

Alex shared his ledge with Gordon, who was a novice to vertical camping. Gordon had climbed all his life, but wall climbing was new to him and he was not especially relaxed in the precarious tent. In ledges the climbers are always tied into an anchor, but Alex delighted in teasing Gordon by leaping from his end of the ledge as if slipping from a teeter-totter, causing it to drop suddenly and spin over the ground far below. Alex also pulled the rubber snake out every now and again to elicit a laugh. All of the gear, food, and ice to melt for water had to be hauled in enormous durable bags that were literally dragged up the face using pulleys and brute force. "An arsenal of swearwords helps," Alex explained to Gordon.

Alex and Conrad did the majority of leading up the steep granite spire, climbing and reclimbing the strenuous pitches for photos and film. Their hands became bloodied and swollen by crystalline rock and dry cold. Their team ascended the wall over a period of thirteen days, but nearly half were weather or rest days. Alex knew that the fifteen-pitch climb could have taken a fraction of the time were it just Conrad and him. But the joyous moment of attaining the summit belonged to their entire team and was a pleasure he didn't regret. Success was all the sweeter for Jon's restored sense of confidence and joy in being a climber among kindred spirits. They christened their route the Snow Petrel Wall for the tracks of the birds they found on the summit snows.

A few birds had been the only sign of life during the weeks on that barren landscape, making the team's status as privileged guests obvious. Alex stood on Rakekniven's snowcapped summit with a group of men who were like himself in at least one respect. In his words, they "had a lust to experience as much adventure as possible in the one precious pass we get at life." Pinned down by storms for most of the next two weeks, Conrad, Alex, and Jon managed one more ascent, summiting a nearby spire called the Troll Castle, which they climbed in a day. When the Twin Otter appeared, Alex and his mates climbed into the plane and rose up over the vast white horizon, leaving nothing behind but their tracks, along with those of the snow petrel.

The snows of Bozeman began to melt, and bright paintings lined the walls in my upstairs studio. *Trixie and Fly Race the Magpie* was the title of the invitation piece for an art show I had scheduled for Sun Valley, Idaho, the following July. I dreamed up a life of daring deeds for Trixie on the backs of palominos and paint horses as they galloped across mountain meadows beneath yellow moons. Magpies swooped across my paper with bold black-and-white wings, and bison danced to the tune of "Buffalo Gals." As spring progressed, I tore myself away from the studio to tend my awakening gardens, eagerly noting each bulb that pushed out of the dirt and watching the lilac buds grow fat and break into fragrant lavender clumps.

In August, when my summer shows were over and a number of my paintings had found new homes, Alex and I made plans for our long-awaited trip to Italy with our young family. Alex traveled ahead to guide in the Italian Dolomites and Switzerland. A couple of weeks later, the children and I made our way across the Atlantic to meet him in Zurich. Keeping track of one-year-old Isaac and four-year-old Sam during layovers was a difficult task. "Max, help me watch your brothers!" I implored my eight-year-old. "Sammy, you have to stay by Mommy!" I chastised after he pulled away from me to run through the Atlanta airport. We arrived exhausted and bedraggled from the long flight to find Alex with a fistful of flowers. He gathered us up and took us to a tiny cramped hotel room, where we all promptly fell asleep even though it was morning.

A couple of hours later, Alex awakened me to help carry the sleeping children out to a rental car packed with our duffels, handed me bakery goodies and a stiff cappuccino, and drove us out of Zurich toward the mountains on a scenic winding highway. We spent a few days in the magic of Swiss mountain villages, where cows with tinkling bells wandered near our campsites among alpine wildflowers. Alex pulled to the roadside for more than one sick child as he navigated the endless switchbacks en route to the Dolomites. George Lowe, his wife Liz, and their two young daughters met us in the village of Cortina d'Ampezzo for a week together, during which George and Alex managed to slip away and climb the well-known Marmolada.

When George and Liz's niece, Alta, offered to babysit, Alex and I jumped at the opportunity to escape the duties of parenting and headed for a nearby rock climb with one difficult overhang. He led the climb quickly and easily, going beyond the standard place to belay, and was so far above me that communication was difficult.

I began to climb, feeling rusty as the rope pulled tight, but when I reached the overhang, some twenty feet above a ledge, I fell. To my complete surprise, I fell all the way to the ledge, landing hard on my thigh. For several minutes I thought the leg was broken as I gasped to get my breath. "Alex," I yelled in tears, wondering why he hadn't caught my fall. "Can you come down?" Moments later, he appeared, looking ghostly. "I'm sorry, Jen! The rope must have hung up." He convinced me to climb the rest of the route, which I did, powered by adrenaline, then limped back down the trail with his assistance and utmost remorse. "I'm sorry, Jen," he kept saying.

When I told the story to Conrad a few years ago, he said, "Alex told me about that . . ." Alex had been nearly to the top of the climb on an easy section, and to save time he had chosen not to belay but continued to climb as I did, in an alpine style, placing protection as he went. When I fell, I pulled him off to his last piece of protection, which had held us both. But the ledge caught me first. Though I was surprised by the real story, I was not surprised at Alex's boldness. "That little rat!" I said to Conrad. "No wonder he looked so scared and guilty when he rapped down." He always overestimated my abilities, forgetting that I rarely climbed, and likely thought we could fit in an extra climb if we were fast.

Venice was enchanting to the boys, who delighted in the fitful dance of thousands of pigeons in St. Mark's Square. Again and again Max, Sam, and Isaac enticed the motley beggars to their feet with fistfuls of feed, then jumped and swirled to watch wings explode into the air. In Florence we climbed hundreds of steps spiraling into the top of the Duomo, then wandered from Caravaggio to Michelangelo to gelato. Alex piloted our car through hair-raising traffic for a last jaunt to the coastal villages of the Cinque Terre. There we strolled along narrow cobbled streets, sat on sandy beaches, leaped into ocean coves, and dined on Caprese salad and squid.

In retrospect, I assume that Alex's relative calm on the remainder of our trip was due in part to our close call in the Dolomites. He likely realized that he had put us both in a compromised situation, and appreciated that we had both been very lucky.

Back home in November, I received a call from my sister Jan with heart-wrenching news: she had been diagnosed with breast cancer. "Oh Jan . . . shit," I stammered.

"Yeah, that's what I thought too," she replied. "It's really scary. I'm afraid my life will be shorter than I'd hoped."

"Don't say that," I begged, trying to keep my voice normal. "You'll be OK," I told her, willing it to be so. When I told Alex that evening in tears, he put his arms around me. "I'll be there for you through this. We'll both be there for Jan." He visited her a short time later while on a business trip to Vancouver, and they shared a heart-to-heart talk about facing the disease. "It was great to see Alex," she told me afterward. "He really gave me a boost."

Jan loved Alex for his intense yet sensitive nature. She knew why I had made the choice to live with his risky pursuits. "I can sort of understand now how it must feel for you, Jenni," she told me. "Just living with fear and trying to put it aside. Not really having any control, but hoping for the best."

"Well, it's not quite the same," I told her. "I make the choice to live with Alex, but you don't have that choice with cancer."

By the following May, Alex had departed for another polar adventure cosponsored by *National Geographic* and The North Face, but this time it was in the northern regions of the planet. Greg Child, Mark Synnott, and Jared Ogden were Alex's climbing companions this time, Gordon Wiltsie was the photographer, and David Hamlin and John Catto were the filmmakers. Their goal was a tremendous monolith called Great Sail Peak, which stood in a mighty cirque of granite around the Stewart Valley on Baffin Island. "How appropriate," I had told Alex when I learned of their destination, for Stewart Alexander Lowe was his given name. The remote valley is nearly three hundred miles north of the Arctic Circle, and Alex was to attempt a northern counterpart to his successful Queen Maud expedition.

The expeditions had their similarities, but for Alex this one would be a far different experience. He did not know his partners well, though they were all North Face athletes. Greg Child is an alpinist of stature whose beautiful writing has brought him as much notice as has his extensive climbing résumé. Alex and Greg had shared one expedition to the Ak-Su, but they had not been partners on any extended climb. Mark and Jared were new talent to the North Face team and more than a decade Alex's junior. The idea of the expedition was to pair the old sages with the young guns and see what they could do as a team. Greg was expedition leader but Mark had the most experience on polar big walls, having pioneered several routes in Baffin's Sam Ford Fjord, including the 4,400-foot Polar Sun Spire, which Alex considered the most impressive polar wall ever climbed. Jared was Mark's favored partner, and Alex was equally impressed with his vast array of climbing skills and notable ascents. "We'll see if the old dogs can teach them any new tricks," Alex said.

Gordon was the only one on the trip with whom Alex had spent considerable time. Though Gordon didn't claim to be a climber of the same caliber as the rest of the team, his résumé of polar adventures and his solid mountaineering background gave him the skills needed to get up the wall with the team's help. Alex wrote of Gordon, "I'm engaged in another wonderfully insane adventure with one of my favorite, wonderfully insane companions."

When the Queen Maud Land article was published in *National Geographic*, Alex's disappointment revealed his vanity: the majority of the photographs, including the cover, were of Conrad—probably because he had been more available to rig and assist Gordon in the sometimes arduous task of getting a shot. In retrospect, Alex was a little bitter about the work he had done to get the team to the summit without compensation, and the lack of photos felt like salt in his wound. "The writer got paid, the photographer got paid, the film-makers got paid, and the two climbers who made it happen didn't get a dime!" he groused.

"But Alex, you do get paid by The North Face," I reminded him.

"I'm aware of that," he said, "and they're getting their money's worth! I'm gone from home half the year, I'm risking my life, and I earn a fraction of what other top athletes make! I should have been a golfer."

He was being facetious, of course; Alex knew in his heart that making a living from climbing at all was a gift. But the experience influenced his planning for Baffin; he prepared to do whatever Gordon needed to get the best shots possible for *National Geographic*, with whom he and Greg had negotiated for a small stipend for the climbers in return for rigging. "I've learned my lesson!" he said, "Climbing with a photographer and film crew is a whole different ballgame than just climbing."

Alex wrote me in May from the land of the Inuit, whose enduring, calm spirit he appreciated; he called them "solid, tough people who accept their harsh environment unquestioningly."

We reached the coast at 4 AM where 2 little huts—summer fishing camp—gave us shelter for 12 hours of sleep. That's where we are now and will remain until the weather improves for we now head out across 30 miles of ocean with no landmarks or shelter. The wind howls outside but we're cozy with a little kerosene stove purring, card games raging between us and endless hot cups of coffee. I'm incredibly happy but for missing you and the boys, curled up on a bed with my feet toasting in my down bag. . . . The cabin bears the scars of polar bear entries and years of families summering here during the char runs. A little pair of child's tennis shoes, an old swing set outside, nearly drifted under. I'm aware that I see just the skin of a land with a deep history, tradition and story. It would take many years to really begin to know what life is like in this harsh land. And it is changing so fast for the inhabitants. . . .

May 23: Well, we've been holed up over 36 hours now—reminds me of most climbing trips, 90% killing time and 10% climbing! I took a walk in the snow and saw a flock of lovely white ptarmigan. . . . I walked back to the beach on the return and found a thirty pound vertebrae from a Bowhead whale, probably killed

years earlier. I carried it back to the cabin for the others to see.
It sparked a conversation with the Inuit telling us of Narwhal
hunts yielding 7 foot tusks and old days when the Bowheads and
Belugas were thick. Few remain today.

May 26: Yesterday finally cleared up enough to travel again.
... We stopped for tea next to a magnificent blue crystal iceberg
jutting majestically from the sea ice flatness. The Inuit fired up
Coleman stoves and we all ate their bannock bread, sliced raw
caribou meat from a big chunk of rump they unwrapped from
its canvas cloth covering, and even sampled the contents of the
caribou stomach! Greg and I were the only ones brave enough
to try stomach content—awful! It simply tastes just like horse
manure smells—grassy and bitter. The Inuit love it and I'm sure
it's nutritious—lichen, grass, and shrub leaves partially digested.
But I'll pass on it until I'm starving! The raw caribou is wonder-
ful. Cut in thin sheets, it tastes like rare beef—excellent.

... Just before arriving here last evening, about 10 minutes out on
the ice, we crossed a pair of polar bear tracks. The Inuit conjecture
they are less than 12 hours old, and I watched with binoculars
for several hours from camp hoping to catch a glimpse of them.
Nothing. But it gives me a thrill to know that these majestic
creatures are in the area.

The boys and I were more fascinated by the thought of Alex seeing
a polar bear than by any other aspect of this trip. To be in the presence
of one of the fabled white bears in its own environment seemed like
a dream come true. Max and Sam pored over books about the Arctic
to get a feel for the place that their dad was exploring. Looking back
now, that time seems like a dream too. Like Alex, Isaac has developed
an empathy for wildlife, especially the creatures that inhabit the most
inhospitable places on the planet. He is concerned about the plight of
the polar bear, whose existence is threatened by global warming. He
once told me, "Mom, if an asteroid hits the earth, I hope that humans

don't re-evolve." I was a little shocked but recalled having similar feelings as a child when I realized the extent of humans' impact on the otherwise harmonious balance of nature.

> Awakening this morning after a full blizzard to the sunniest skies yet! The arctic showed us what it could do last night in no uncertain terms. We had to lash down tents and dig out drifting snow several different times. Yesterday, I went hunting with Ben and Romeo. . . . Romeo shot a ptarmigan and then I shot a huge Arctic hare and Ben shot another hare. Everyone else in my group were typically squeamish about the whole affair so I skinned them, gutted them and butchered them into a lovely rabbit and pasta dinner. I invited the Inuit to join us for dinner and they delighted us with stories of the old days in Clyde as we consumed our rabbit repast!

> Jushua's 63-year-old Uncle Ikakrialaq and I have struck up quite an amicable relationship. I've been riding on his sled and enjoy pushing furiously when the snowmobile gets stuck. This has apparently really impressed him because Jushua said he claimed I was like his Inuit son. I think the rabbit episode impressed all of them who otherwise consider us helpless babes in the wilderness.

> We went over a low pass and back down to the sea at a place called Refuge Harbor in Gibbs Fiord. We passed the grave sites of Jushua's grandparents who died there sixty years ago and never saw white people. Imagine—true hunter gatherers who lived in this desolate but majestic place, existing upon caribou, Narwhals and Belugas, and Bearded Seals that they hunted. Passing the long arctic winter night at −60°F, in a stone hut in this forlorn place with heat provided by skin blankets and blubber oil. Pretty incredible!

Alex bonded with the residents of Baffin in a way that was touching and sincere. Jushua's wife, Beverly, even wrote to me and proposed that their son, Benjamin, come to stay with us when he was older. In exchange, they would take Max for a season of Arctic education in the ways of the Inuit:

> *Alex made an impression on many people here. To some he gave jackets or other bits of equipment. To others he was the tall, self possessed and very kind climber walking about town. To our family he was an inspiration and a person to delight in, a man with a shine and a gentleness about him that was remarkable. Our son Benjamin, who has worn the boots Alex gave him all year with pride on snowmobile and dog trips, was especially impressed with his honesty and his commitment to good health. Jushua has been warmed a full year by the jacket Alex gave him and has often expressed his thanks for the gesture of kindness. For my part, I was impressed by Alex's steady love and joy in his family. Thank you for sharing him with us and for the light he spread in our lives.*

Finally the caravan reached the remote Stewart Valley, where their destination stood. As they crossed the valley, the granite wall grew to a magnificent size and Alex turned his attention to the dizzying task at hand. Great Sail Peak stood above the shores of a solidly frozen lake, but according to Jushua, the snows would start to melt quickly over the next couple of weeks. The Inuit would remain with them for a couple of days to fish and hunt, then would head back to Clyde River before breakup made travel impossible. David Hamlin would travel out with them, leaving John to the task of filming. "It will seem quiet here with merely six of us," Alex wrote. "I'll have lonely moments no doubt but activity will be the antidote." How, I wondered, could Alex have felt lonely with five companions?

Stormbound days had provided an abundance of downtime. Alex had hoped to make a good impression on the young climbers but didn't find opportunities to engage. "They were more interested in Greg's sharp wit and somewhat acerbic mood after his recent divorce," Alex told me once home. "Greg had this book with some really descriptive sexual stuff that he would read to us," recalled Mark. For his part, "I was depressed," Greg admitted to me. To him, the frat-style hilarity was a release and pretty normal for climbing trips. But Alex was straitlaced compared to his contemporaries; he soon tired of raunchy conversation, and looked to the Inuit and his old buddy Gordon for companionship instead. He also wrote me about some of his more thoughtful interactions with his mates:

> Mark Synnott is struggling with the news that his girlfriend Lauren is pregnant! They found out three days before he left. I've got a real interesting job now—counseling him on fatherhood. He's younger than I was of course, but probably even more travel restless. Lauren will have her hands full. The good part is that they seem to be honest and realistic about the challenges they are taking on and I hope it works for them. It's really interesting to hear all the differing advice he gets from the group . . . think of his own happiness and make his decision based solely on consideration of his own personal desires. They all miss the most important and most often forgotten truth about love: "Love is the only rational act"—a quote I picked up from this wonderful little book I read that I can't wait to come home and give you. Love is something you do, you work at, you learn to do—for your own happiness and for the happiness of other people—I'm pleased that we have this catalyst for meaningful conversation rather than the degenerative adult potty talk!

Alex knew that life as a professional climber was not an easy thing to combine with having a family, but he encouraged Mark to embark on a journey similar to his own, touting the joys of parenthood. Now, nine years later, I'm sure Alex would be happy to know that Mark and Lauren have three beautiful children and a lifestyle that works for them, and that Jared and Greg have also found joy in fatherhood.

Trixie Does Backbends for the Moon depicted a blond cowgirl, modeled after my sister Camilla, stretched out in a backbend over a black-and-white paint galloping across a wheaten meadow. "It's really me," I thought as I painted, "bending over backward to make our life work while racing blindly ahead." I scrawled words across cloudy skies and into painted grasses, professing "Cows are better than condos," "Open space," and "Save a piece of Paradise for me," as I worried that my wild Montana would be tamed.

I ferried the boys to soccer, where they ran among herds of teammates after a black-and-white ball. Isaac ran laps around the yard and around the dining room table, pulling a piece of string for the cat to chase. Max and Sam practiced their violins reluctantly, sawing old-time tunes between lessons that I raced to get to on time. "Come on, guys—we're late, we're late," I urged, buckling seatbelts.

"Mom, I don't want to go to fiddle," Max whined.

"Mom, Isaac broke my favorite truck!" Sam cried.

"Ai ai ai ai," Isaac shrieked gleefully.

Bedtime was my only respite.

Snow fell one morning in slow motion, floating in fat clumps to cling on daffodils. A chickadee's clear note accompanied the spring dance from the sky. Green leaves turned white and branches bent. Tulips bowed to the performance as I clomped about through the cold wet blanket, a broom in hand, smacking the lilacs to free them from their heavy load. From the window, the children, still in pajamas, watched branches snap skyward as wet snow plopped to the ground. I looked at the three noses pressed to the window and threw a snowball at the glass, watching them squeal with laughter.

Once school was out in early June, I packed the boys into our minivan and drove through Spokane, Seattle, and Vancouver, British Columbia, to the Horseshoe Bay ferry terminal. There we lined up for the ferry bound for Bowen Island. As I steered our van off the dock at Snug Cove, Jan waved us down with her usual enthusiasm. "I have hair again," she said, enthused about the close dark curls that had come back after chemo. My sister Paula and her son, Jake, also joined us for a reunion filled with laughter, a few arguments, tears, and a hopeful feeling that Jan's cancer was at bay. Jan played rhythm guitar while Murray played fiddle tunes with all of the boys. We visited the aquarium and museums in Vancouver, sat on the beach, wandered in tide pools, and subjected Jan and Murray to as much Lego construction and "boy" energy as they could handle.

On June 15 Alex wrote in his journal, "Cloud bank moves in from East. Alex leads Pitch 6 to bivi site. Greg belays but doesn't clean. Photo shoot with Gordon—major attitude problem brewing with Greg." I asked Greg about this, and he said he recalled belaying in a stream of icy water for hours that day, which left him frozen and furious at both Gordon and Alex after their long photo shoot. Greg remembered trying to coil the rope with wooden hands. Alex grabbed it from him, offering to do the job, but with an impatience that insulted Greg. They retreated back to a lower ledge to camp and prepared to haul their gear to the top of Pitch 6 for a hanging bivy. Alex's journal notes:

June 16: Snowy and windy—no climbing.

June 17: Still snowy & cold (below freezing) but periods of sun—windy. Mark & Alex haul first load to bivi—should be climbing—Alex finishes rigging bivi—Greg does not emerge from tent now for nearly 60 hours! Uh Oh!

"Yeah, I was pretty pissed off," Greg said.

On the side of the journal page Alex had written, "ACL tear!" He had torn his anterior cruciate ligament years before when we were living in Salt Lake City. He skied off a small cliff, landing in bad form, and snapped the ligament in his knee. Surgery, a common remedy for this injury, was something he could never face, not for the cost or fear of it but for the time required for rehabilitation afterward. The thought of being inactive for months while a surgery healed was worse than anything Alex could envision. So he had nursed the knee with ice and a brace and exercise. He had worked his leg muscles in gyms to build compensated strength, and he had run up and down the Grand Teton and climbed Aconcagua, Denali, Everest, and every other summit since 1992 with a torn ACL.

Alex thought he would find approval by doubling his work for the team. He mistakenly thought that setting an example would also light a fire under the others, but his attempts to guilt them into moving faster backfired. While preparing to haul, he shouldered more weight than he should have, straining his knee on the rubble-strewn ledge, causing it to balloon to an alarming size. At that point he became truly depressed, thinking that he might have to go down and simply wait for the others to finish the climb.

Greg realized that his team was not off to a good start. "Alex's energy and impatience were irritating to me," he said. "The guy drank like ten cups of coffee a day!" But he did not want to send Alex down alone. "I told him to give it a couple of days' rest." So Alex stayed below on the ledge for a few days, and recovered enough to do the remainder of the climb. After returning home, Alex favored the knee for months until he was forced to admit that surgery was his only option. Injured knee and injured feelings both continued up the wall. "The atmosphere was not cordial," Gordon told me. "There was plenty of backstabbing going on."

Alex sounded positive in the postcards we received:

Dearest Max, I got your email that you sent. I had already left Clyde River but an Inuit man named Eesah came into our base camp to bring more gas for the snowmobile return journey and delivered your message. You are so smart! You picked up on email really quickly. Mom said your recital went well. Sorry I was not there to enjoy it but I look forward to hearing your lovely voice and beautiful playing when I get home. You are really wonderful, Max—smart, kind, strong, handsome and talented. I love telling my partners all about you.

But I sensed his unhappiness. When he arrived home from Baffin, I was not surprised to learn of the discord. "It was a different dynamic than Queen Maud," Alex said sadly, admitting that he had felt like an outsider on his team. "Why?" I asked. Alex thought the elements of film and photography had brought forth a jockeying of egos that none of the climbers could openly address, but he also admitted, "I had too much energy for them." Between storms they had climbed fourteen pitches from the top of the slabs, many of which took eight to ten hours to lead, a tedious twenty feet per hour. Greg told me that one of his leads was the single most difficult of his career. But still, it is lead pitches that all expert climbers covet, and the most sought after of all may be the summit pitch on a new route.

Mark led what he thought was the final summit pitch, but after 120 feet, rope drag was slowing his progress and he called down to let the others know that he was close to summiting while bringing Jared up to his stance. Mark said that all the parties below asked that he wait there. Alex was next in line for leading, but Mark argued that he wanted to lead the last fifty feet to the summit, since his pitch had been short. Gordon and John wanted to get up to shoot the drama of topping out.

Alex demanded that the lead be his. He was proprietary when it came to leading, and having to split the entire climb between four leaders was probably at the edge of what he could handle. Had he been more patient and charitable, he might have given Mark the pitch, but by that time he had climbed for more than three weeks and had had only three leads. Reluctantly, Mark gave Alex the pitch, but it rankled. Mark ended up being the last to top out after thinking he would be first. The feeling at the summit was not one of joy, by all accounts.

Perhaps Alex disengaged from his partners in the early stage of the trip when he found the party atmosphere distasteful. They in return found his unbridled energy and impatience tiring and saw him as trying to hog the limelight, rigging relentlessly for Gordon. "We rubbed each other the wrong way," said Greg. "Greg was the leader on the trip," Mark said, "but Alex was the alpha; there was no other position for him."

An eloquent description of male polar bear behavior appeared in a 1984 article written for the journal *Natural History*. "A bear that wishes to play, slowly approaches another suitable male and the two begin a massive slow motion minuet," Fred Bruemmer wrote. "They circle and sniff, heads low, mouths closed, eyes averted, and they are silent, signaling by attitude and posture, peaceful intent and mutual respect." This dance between male bears has been documented for years. I wonder if it is so different from the dance that people engage in. Sadly, Alex and his partners did not find that place of peaceful posture and mutual respect on Baffin Island. So I was surprised when Alex told me that he was going to Great Trango Tower in Pakistan with Mark and Jared, but he was optimistic. "They're good climbers," he said, "and every trip is different."

Trango Tower Triumph

If you can dream—and not make dreams your master
If you can think—and not make thoughts your aim;
If you can meet with triumph and disaster
And treat those two imposters just the same . . .
—RUDYARD KIPLING

ALEX AND I STOOD ATOP the Empire State Building with Max, Sam, and Isaac in the late summer of 1998. We peered out at the famous skyline in every direction, referring to a map of well-known landmarks to identify them. The boys were fascinated most by the pigeons that fluttered from the eaves and strutted their rainbow feathers along perilous skywalks. Max and Sam begged for high-priced hot dogs and immediately began tearing bits of bread to throw for a flying fetch. "That's damned expensive pigeon food," Alex groused, but then grabbed a piece of bread to toss as well.

With measured purpose, Alex and I marched the boys through the echoing halls of the American Museum of Natural History and the Met, taking in everything from woolly mammoths to Egyptian tombs. We strolled Fifth Avenue to ogle skyscrapers and succumbed to our children's frantic consumerism in the most elaborate toy store we had ever seen. Peering at scraggly penguins in the Central

Park Zoo, Alex related the contrasting image of an entire colony in Antarctica. We took the boat to Ellis and Liberty islands, where we climbed as high up into the Statue of Liberty as possible after reading dozens of immigrants' stories. Part of the adventure was traveling by train to Keene Valley in upstate New York, where we bedded down at a country house in a quiet meadow. Nightfall delivered the sweet sound of frogs.

Lakes were abundant. On one outing, Alex and Max navigated our wooden canoe through inlets thick with lily pads and families of ducks. When Max became tired, Alex propelled us along, refusing my offers of help. "I need the exercise," he answered, digging his paddle in on one side and then the other, propelling us to a tiny, forested island. The kids tossed rocks and floated sticks at the shore while Alex and I fixed bagel sandwiches beneath the pines. It was an idyllic and peaceful day.

"Alex, I wish you could stay home more," I ventured. "The boys need you now. They're not babies, and I need you too. It's great when we're all together." We had both tired of his hectic schedule, which took him away from Bozeman for more than half the year. The climbing trips were something I had reckoned on, but the business travel doubled his time away. Although I had always loved my independence in his absences, I noticed lately that the boys seemed more settled when Alex was home, and they loved his impulsive adventures. He would whisk them off to the train museum or pile them into the van for a trip to some obscure pond full of tadpoles in the woods that he had discovered on a run. Alex was able to engage them in homework, chores, and music practice more easily than I, and I felt less strung out when he was home.

"I'm trying to figure that out, Jen. I want to be home more too," he answered, and I knew he spoke the truth. Two years before, Alex had written me from an expedition in Nepal, telling me of a job possibility with The North Face that would allow him more time at home. But the job didn't materialize, and Alex continued on the track of "professional athlete," with a packed schedule of what he referred to as "dog-and-pony shows" in between climbing expeditions. We talked of him returning to a job in math, engineering, or computers, and taking expeditions when he could. But I feared that wouldn't make him happy. We both thought perhaps he could make a living as a professional speaker, but he wasn't sure how to make the transition. In the meantime, we had grown accustomed to the benefits and comfortable wage that he earned at The North Face, which had enabled us to remodel our house bit by bit to accommodate our growing family.

In the winter of 1998, just before leaving for an expedition to Antarctica with Conrad, Alex was practicing soccer with Max when his bad knee gave out. He left on schedule, but as they waited for a connecting flight the team doctor told Alex that he needed to go home and have surgery immediately—or "you won't have a knee in ten years."

Alex finally listened. He flew home and scheduled surgery for a meniscal tear and an ACL replacement: two knee surgeries back to back. He brought home a little chunk of his meniscus after the first surgery, that smooth cartilage that coats the ends of bones. His physician had given him the souvenir, floating in fluid in a plastic baggie, and Alex placed the bag in our refrigerator, bringing it out now and then to show friends. "Alex, that's gross!" I said, not wanting to confront the "specimen" each time I searched for mustard, but it remains there today, a tiny piece of Alex that I could never bear to part with. I keep it tucked in next to the wasabi, a condiment he loved.

The first months that Alex spent rehabbing in midwinter were the most difficult. Although his doctors and therapists thought him an ideal patient who worked harder than any they had seen to regain his strength and movement, at home he was a depressed invalid, prone to making sweeping statements that he would never climb again. He also worried about his job as The North Face changed ownership and moved its headquarters to Colorado.

I decided to throw him a birthday party to cheer him up. More than fifty friends and family members from near and far gathered in our house one evening while Alex and his father went on an errand. Andrew McLean came all the way from Salt Lake City. At the appointed time Alex and his dad walked into the dark house, mumbling "Where is everybody?" Lights went on, cheers of "Surprise!" rang out, and Alex celebrated his fortieth birthday in fine style with a glorious cake that resembled a mountain, complete with tiny climbers arranged and rearranged by our children. At the end of the evening, he thanked me profusely for his first surprise party ever.

After Christmas, Alex and I wanted to do something adventurous with our family in the mountains, so we rented one of the nearby backcountry cabins from the Forest Service to celebrate the New Year. Max and I skied cross-country for several miles to reach the rustic cabin while Alex drove the snowmobile with Sam, Isaac, and all of our supplies in tow. We settled in with a blazing stove as the sun set and had just unpacked when Alex went limping out the door in his down booties to fetch more firewood.

His scream was piercing. "He's had an accident with the ax," I thought, and ran out frantically with the kids at my heels, but there was no blood; he had fallen in the slippery boots and was writhing on the ground in pain, clutching at his bad knee. The kids and I stood wide-eyed as he screamed unsavory words into the starry night. At last he calmed down enough for me to help him into the cabin, where we decided to stay until morning.

"If the ligament is ripped out, Jen, I don't know if I want to go through with it again," he fretted. I found a strong painkiller and packed snow into a plastic bag to ice his knee, then propped him on a bunk with down bags. Before long, he was reading books to the boys in a state of drugged bliss while I prepared our New Year's dinner. We opened wine for me to toast the New Year alone, and the patient drifted to sleep with his little boys. I read by headlamp until midnight, then walked out into the snow under the Montana sky for a quiet look at 1999, wondering what it would bring.

The March issue of *Outside* magazine put Alex on its cover. Writer Bruce Barcott began his story about Alex, "The Mutant and the Boy Scout," this way: "For the preternaturally talented Alex Lowe, world's best climber, the path to every summit passes directly through his living room. Which, as he is discovering, is a tricky route to take." I thought Bruce captured Alex's passions with insight. Alex was pleased too, feeling that the article focused more on what he considered the valuable things in his life—his family—rather than his "heroic" climbing feats. "The greatest accomplishment for me in life is to raise happy, self-confident, and kind children," he wrote to his mother.

By Isaac's third birthday, Alex was looking forward to his expedition, as his knee continued to heal nicely and he had gained more strength than ever from his obsessive gym routines. His demeanor was always much improved after a foray into the outdoors. I am now thankful for the injury because it allowed Alex more time with me and the boys that winter and spring. I had an overly booked year of art shows in Park City, Sun Valley, Jackson Hole, Missoula, and Livingston, and thus spent most of my time in the studio frantically trying to produce work. Alex practiced violin with Max and Sam, and took the boys on outings to the museum and on overnight campouts. He delivered them to skiing lessons even when he couldn't ski, and would sit in the lodge or stand at the base to watch them. His time at home was a great help to me with shopping, cooking, and schlepping the boys around.

The expedition to Trango Tower in Pakistan's Karakoram, which Alex had planned with Mark and Jared, was shaping up to be a massive media event. It was to be sponsored by Quokka Sports and The North Face, and would be filmed by a crew led by Michael Graber. For the first time in climbing history, an interactive website would be created and would host daily updates, both written and recorded, plus film clips and photos. The climbers were slated to answer email queries from fans, and Alex and I would be in email contact with each other for the first time ever during an expedition.

I was happy for him to go, knowing how difficult the long winter of inactivity had been for him, and knowing that we could communicate each day of the six-week trip made his absence easier. But when he told me that Quokka wanted to post some of our letters to each other on their site—and some from the boys—I was livid. "What are you thinking?" I asked him angrily. "To exploit your family while you do a dangerous climb? What if the worst happens and I'm . . . at my most vulnerable, for the entire world to see?"

"Jenni, it isn't that dangerous—and you and the kids are a big part of my life. They want to show Jared, Mark, and me as the whole people we are—not just as climbers," he countered. "I want to do the best job I can for Quokka, Jen. It's an opportunity that might be a goldmine for us. . . . I think it's a whole new world for media. And it's a way for me to share what I love."

In the days before Alex left, I agreed to allow a few of my correspondences onto the site, as long they weren't too personal. I thought perhaps Alex was right about its being an opportunity, and I wanted to be supportive of his vision. We made a plan for me to send a number of messages and photos from home that could be posted over the course of the trip. During the expedition Alex took me by surprise, posting some fairly sentimental writing on the site, but our most personal emails to each other remained relatively private. The technology at the time was such that all emails were relayed through base camp and crossed the desk of the project coordinator for Quokka, who forwarded them on. She also sorted email from fans and sent on questions for the climbers to answer.

One of Alex's first dispatches was from the village of Jhola:

June 20: It's a pretty special day for me. I woke up and . . . I had an email from home, which was very nice, and I opened up some images and there were pictures of my dear kids drawing a Happy Father's Day card in my backyard in Bozeman, Montana. Amazing world we live in. I was really, really touched. I have the most beautiful kids in the world. I think every father believes that on this day. It's always a struggle for me to figure out where the balance lies in pursuing my visions and my dreams here in the mountains and making sure that my kids are aware that they really are the most important thing in the world to me . . . it'll be interesting when they're all in their twenties and young adults, and we can sit down and reflect on whether they felt like I was fulfilling my obligations to them or not.

The site posted my first dispatch as well. Although I was happy to send it to Alex, I cringed to see it posted, suddenly worried over the loss of privacy. And though I knew he derived strength from his connection to his family, I was concerned about him being distracted from climbing. He needed to be completely present there on the mountain, with all of his mental and physical energy focused on the climb. But I loved getting his emails that took me right to his side.

> *June 23: We arrived in Base Camp yesterday and it is the kind of base camp you would love—sandy beach by a lovely pond nestled at the base of a perfect, unbroken sweep of granite rising into the sky. . . . My tent is surrounded by some of your favorite wildflowers: alpine forget-me-nots, buttercups, fireweed and a lovely little flower I recognize but can't identify that looks like a round cluster of pale pink phlox blossoms. I guess what I'm feeling is a desire to be here with you and the boys. It's a pretty romantic and peaceful place. I'm sure you'd agree.*

I watched as Max boarded the plane without looking back. "Bye, Mom," he said, walking through the gate. Jan and Murray had invited him to the annual Festival of American Fiddle Tunes in Port Townsend, Washington, where he would attend workshops with musicians from around the globe and camp on a beach with his doting aunt and uncle. At ten years old, he was flying alone for the first time, and I realized with pride and emotion that he was growing up quickly. I watched the back of his blond head round the corner, happy in the knowledge that my sister would treasure this time with him after her bout with cancer.

Meanwhile, I drove the minivan to Park City, Utah, for an art opening with Sam, Isaac, and my good friend Suzanne Hainsworth, a retired neighbor I'd met five years before. She had become one of my closest friends and was like a grandmother to the boys, who would disappear to her house for fresh cookies, root-beer floats, and the lure of a bucketful of vintage Hot Wheels cars. Suzanne brought Sam and Isaac to my show that evening in Park City, dressed in their best to meet the gallery staff, then whisked them away for a more fun-filled evening for little boys. I was grateful for Suzanne's company and admired her spunk.

Suzanne's daughter Pamela, a website designer, helped me to get up to speed on the new computer I'd bought for the Trango project, and assisted me in sending my dispatches. She worked at home on a wonderful piece of property along the Gallatin River, where stately cottonwoods rose from the riverbanks and a path wound its way through the woods to the rocky braided channels. Suzanne, Pamela, and I would share in the preparation of weekly picnics beneath the cottonwoods while Alex toiled away on Great Trango and we monitored his progress via the website.

> *June 24: We've got another beautiful day. . . . I elected to hang out here in base camp because I'm nursing a bit of a head cold and I figured the best thing to do is start off healthy, wait a few days and get over it, then get onto the mountain full-force. It's kind of interesting, there's great acoustics off the wall. We can hear Mark and Jared, can't quite understand what they're saying but you can hear them quite clearly from down here at base camp, and it looks like they're making good progress.*

> *June 26: . . . Current plans are to head off alone for a few days and convalesce away from mounting unsympathetic "get-off-your-ass-you-slacker" vibes (real or imagined). A group of dear friends and old climbing soul mates are camped at Paiju, according to a couple of Balti who came up to re-supply Spanish camp with fuel and fresh veggies today. I'll spend a night or two in the company of good friends. Hopefully the bugs will get bored with romping around in my bronchial tubes. I'm finding it awfully tough being sidelined. It's not my cup of tea.*

I read between the lines of Alex's emails and began to worry. Field producer Greg Thomas told me there were already grumbles from Mark and Jared about the site being "the Alex Lowe show," given the lengthy descriptive accounts that Alex was posting daily.

Alex was quite fond of the team's Balti cook, Ali Khan, a brother of Alex's old friend Rasool, and mentioned him often.

I woke this morning just prior to sunrise . . . went pattering as quietly as I could to the dining tent to scrape together the coffee kit. Good old Ali Khan woke as I tread softly past his tent and in his eternally caring, kind and peaceful way, he insisted on making me breakfast. I sometimes struggle with the amount he does for me. I want so badly to do for him in an equitable manner but he refuses to be waited on. He approaches saintliness. I have to say, I love the man dearly.

On June 30, Alex wrote on the site:

Awoke this morning at dawn and watched the sun usher in another day with Ali Khan. . . . I lobbied hard for an early start this morning in order to capitalize on the cool morning temperatures. Careful nudges toward a sunrise departure got pushed back to 6:00 am, but in the end, that gave us plenty of haul-time before the sun streamed over the shoulder of Great Trango, unleashing zillions of BTUs upon our sweaty efforts.

It was pleasant to get up high after being sick and out of commission for the first week of action. The slabs so far are pleasant but not terribly spectacular from a climbing perspective. The views however. . . . Oh what a horizon. Mountains marching off in stately splendor as far as the eye can see. If no other explanation can be offered for this climbing compulsion, the satisfaction of ascending and gaining a new perspective will always suffice.

Hauling inevitably elicits predictable groans and grunts from most climbers, but I actually find solace in the rhythmic cadence of throwing my weight against the resisting bag, over and over again until it grudgingly flops up onto the ledge like some great inanimate leviathan. I play mind games, of course. I chant the

complete names of my wife and sons in sync with each haul,
resting only once the entire family has been named. Kind of nice
really—meditation on a subject very dear.

While hauling the seventh bag to the top of the lines today, my
reverie was interrupted by a passing shadow. A huge raptor
with a wingspan easily reaching six feet was effortlessly gliding
past on the updrafts. I'm not sure what the Balti name is, but
no matter—such majestic creatures transcend encumbering
monikers. Goraks, raven-ish birds that are ubiquitous throughout
the Himalaya, are with us constantly. They dive and soar with
such seemingly joyful purposelessness, I can't help but conclude
that sheer mischievous fun is the motive.

It was obvious that Alex's mood had lifted. He was in his element—the vertical world, where his value to the team was obvious.
"Boy does it make a big difference to have Alex along," Mark wrote on
the site on June 30. As the expedition leader, he was the one who had
asked Alex to come, knowing that he was incredibly strong and that
his presence could help attract needed funding and sponsorship. The
Quokka executives were interested in the Trango expedition from
the start, when it was proposed by John Climaco, a college buddy of
Mark's who was director of programming for Quokka. But Alex was
a known climber and charismatic, as Greg Thomas pointed out. He
had a proven ability to communicate what it felt like to be climbing
in such a foreign place and wild environment. Greg said Alex was
instantly popular among their executives and their audience.

"I think Mark and Jared were a little proprietary about it being
their climb," filmmaker Michael Graber told me. "They were gifted
young climbers, and I sensed this insecurity about having to enlist
the service of the superstar. They were letting Alex into their club-
house but didn't want him to remodel it." The young climbers had
different views than Alex about what was OK, he felt. "If you wanted
to smoke a little pot, no big deal, or urinating on the ledge in the
night—so what. . . . But Alex had expectations of them—that they

would climb at a certain standard. He thought a leader should have qualities that he would respect."

"It's been kind of a crazy day," Mark wrote in one of his site dispatches. "I woke up this morning in a pretty foul mood. Alex and I had been doing some serious head butting yesterday. It carried over to this morning."

Writing for the site, Alex put it somewhat more philosophically:

July 2: Great day in the Karakoram. A bit of scuzzy weather kept us in camp watching sky and barometer. The clouds added much-needed depth to the almost monotonous bluebird skies of the past week, but taunted the weak of heart—me. Doesn't look like inclement weather will amount to anything dire, so we're up the ropes and on the wall tomorrow to push to the headwall. Storm clouds gave Mark and me some valuable time to explore each other's personalities, uncovering and appreciating the inevitable attributes and flaws in each other that make us all such unique and valuable gems. Climbing, after all is primarily a journey of self discovery.

The website posted the following:

Many matters, some smoldering for days, were at issue—the role of the expedition leader, Alex's high visibility in the climbing world, the virus that sent Alex down to Paiju for some R&R. Add to all that the enormous amount of work in setting up the Advanced Base Camp under the sheltered ledge and the added pressure of helping web viewers share their experience.

The climbers publicly aired their grievances on the site, with the strife increasing to such a level that it nearly caused them to abort the climb. Alex was despondent and wondered whether he should stay. "Alex, you are the only one who can answer that, but I will support you in your choice," I told him. Greg reminded the climbers that they had an agreement with Quokka, and they decided to stick with it. A solution was arrived at by consensus: "We have instituted a ban on looking at the website," Mark announced.

Behind the scenes, however, Alex continued to feel constrained:

> July 7: I'm definitely the driving energy in this group. I'm learn-
> ing, though, to tiptoe around Mark. I am learning a lot about
> giving up my need to move quickly. I am careful never to suggest
> Alex's better way and just rage up my pitches and let the rest go.
> All in all the social dynamics are cordial and I'm very aware of
> what I need to give up to keep it that way.

Mark had a different perspective. "Once Alex and I were off on the wrong foot, it was difficult to get back in his good graces," he said. "I tried, but Alex held a grudge and was disrespectful toward me. I think he was mad that I was the expedition leader.... Jared and I worked so hard on that climb. We were beat every night, but Alex was setting a superhuman pace. Nobody could have kept it." I knew that Alex's work ethic and drive were hard to match, and I also knew he could be a bear to communicate with if he was mad or put off.

Michael Graber felt Alex knew that Trango wasn't going to be his magnum opus. "He had nothing to prove," said Michael. "I think he was more committed to the Quokka website than anything—this early idea of a blog." Indeed, the website offered Alex a creative out-let that he felt strongly about. It was a way to share what he loved with an appreciative audience, and he was hopeful that if it was suc-cessful, it might lead to a new career.

A couple of weeks into the expedition, a Swiss and a Russian team arrived in the base-camp area. The Quokka website, perhaps seeking drama, suggested that a race to the Trango summit was in the offing, but Alex had a consistently different viewpoint, writing of the Russians, "We don't anticipate any sort of races or conflicts with them. They're just happy to do another line on this magnificent face that we're climbing on." At one point when the two teams were sharing a part of the wall, Alex even hauled loads for them. Their expedition leader, Alexander Odinstov, wrote that when he heard an American team was to be their neighbor on Trango Tower, he felt no elation. But, he said, "Alex met us with an open heart and such warmth that I felt ashamed of earlier thoughts."

> July 15: We are a thousand meters above base camp this evening, watching a silver moon creep above the horizon over an amazing silhouette of peaks that just look like black, cardboard cutouts. It's absolutely beautiful. We sat out and had dinner here on the front porch—our little bivi platforms here—and it was just an absolutely spectacular and soulful evening. . . . I for one am planning to just doze out under the stars again and fall asleep watching the Big Dipper spin across the sky.

The climbers at last seemed to have settled into a routine on the headwall, rotating leads and organizing, packing, and hauling food and gear for the days above. The filmmakers joined them for a time. I began to relax, thinking that Alex and his partners had worked out their differences, that the tremendous workload and shared hardship would bind them together. Then, on July 17, the computer that the climbers were using went down. As Alex wrote for the site:

> We had to solve a relatively minor but critical power issue for the small computer we use to transmit images down from the wall. . . . So after coffeeing up the team at sunrise, spending an hour replacing some ropes below the bivi, and organizing and packing all the food for the wall, I commuted down the ropes—a mere thousand meter descent. I delivered the stricken computer into the very capable hands of Darren Britto, our jovial rancorous and hilarious technical wizard.

I received a call from Alex at base camp, telling me that his partners had been a little mad about him bringing the computer down to be fixed. "They thought it would be fine to forget the computer and just do what they could over the radio," Alex said. "But I wouldn't feel right about that, knowing that the problem was likely a fixable one. Besides," he said, "it gives me a chance to talk to you."

A few days later I was surprised to receive another call from him, patched through from the radio by Greg at base camp. It was the middle of the night there, and Alex told me that he was having serious thoughts about bailing and coming home. "What now?" I asked.

Alex had been doing his usual emailing in the evening when he saw his name in the header of an email to Mark. Alex decided to read it. "You opened his email?" I asked, incredulous. "I did," he admitted. "I just had this feeling . . . and I was right," he told me. He was cut to the quick by the words within, which accused him of "rapping all the way to Base Camp . . . as a stunt" and suggested that his professions of love for his family were insincere. "Jenni, I just don't have the heart for this anymore," he said. I talked him through his worries, saying I was certain that his partners were solid and trustworthy. I encouraged him to talk to Mark, to trust his instincts, and to finish the climb if he could. Greg gave him the same advice after calling the office in San Francisco to consult.

On July 23, Alex wrote me a private email about life on the wall:

> Cheers my beloved wife! Sorry I haven't written more from the wall but I work all day and then late into the night sending images and writing Quokka dispatches. I'm always up until 10 or 11 doing the work while Jared and Mark sleep like babes. . . . I've accepted it as the work I have to do to make this whole internet thing a success. It will be worth it for us. Apologies for whining but I'm pretty alone spiritually up here and I need to vent a little.

It was normal for Alex to rely on me as a sounding board, although it usually happened after the expeditions. Knowing that he was still feeling defensive from the critical email, I encouraged him to hang in there. All seemed relatively well until July 28: "Woke up feeling pretty rough. I think I got some sort of bacterial infection. Lack of hygiene, probably. It's hard to keep everything clean living in such awkward quarters." I hated to think of him with a high fever and violently ill, in his portaledge thousands of feet from the ground. They were poised for a summit day, and if weather permitted, there would be no postponing.

But Alex rallied miraculously for a summit push the next day. In his voice dispatch he said, "I started leading, I guess probably because I've got lots of old-dog tricks up my sleeve and tend to climb pretty quickly—that sort of light, fast alpine-style climbing sort of designated me as the person to take over and punch on ahead."

Mark didn't see it that way. "He just came up and took over my lead without discussion," he told me later. "Alex was just flying up that climb." But they made it the top of the northwest face by three o'clock and then climbed on toward the West Summit, knowing they were racing darkness. As Alex led a difficult traversing section, he came to an impasse and tried to reverse his moves but fell forty feet, banging his head and arm. "I thought he was done, but the guy just raged back up and did the pitch," Mark said. "It was crazy." They made the first ascent of the West Summit of Great Trango Tower, and the weather window closed promptly as they descended through a storm.

On July 31 Alex gave the following voice-mail transmission:

This is Alex. We have landed back in Base Camp, and we're very happy to be here. We got the warmest reception I've ever experienced after a climb. It was just really, really moving. Tears were shed, and my dear friend, Ali Khan—basically here for us. We came in a little after dark and they had candles lighting the pathway to the mess tent, and oh, it was just so touching. Any amount of toil and struggle was easily justified. It was a culmination of several very hard days, and more importantly though, a really overwhelming challenge and the meeting of that challenge, and just all that entails—the relationships and the inner-searching and struggling, and it was just really, really wonderful to walk back into camp today.

On August 11 Alex came home from Trango Tower, to my great relief, although only four weeks later he would leave for Shishapangma. He arrived in time for Sam's seventh birthday, and we celebrated in the shade of our backyard with a passel of screeching little boys, a cake with a submarine sunk into its frosted top, and a piñata filled with goodies.

In Alex's absence Max had decided he wanted to climb the Grand Teton, and Alex was thrilled. Climbing was not something we wanted to push on the boys, but Alex was happy to indulge them if they initiated it. He invited Max's best friend, Jared Bozeman, and his father, Tom, a recreational climber and longtime friend, to make it a foursome. Arriving in the Tetons, the boys were delighted to be housed in our old cabin at the Climber's Ranch, in the familiar alpine meadows beneath the craggy peaks. They reached the Lower Saddle early and set up camp in perfect weather. Tom and Alex enjoyed a jovial evening with other guides, climbers, and park rangers while Max and Jared scurried about the talus, chasing marmots away from food stashes.

Arising early as he had countless times as a guide, Alex led the way up the Exum ridge the following day and proudly stood atop his favorite mountain with his oldest son and their friends. I herded Sam, Isaac, and Jared's little sister, Lauren, up the dusty switchbacks of Garnet Canyon to meet the triumphant team on their long descent, and we sat upon granite boulders to toast the summit with root beers and beers that I pulled from my pack. Alex was beaming. "It was the best climb I've ever done," he whispered to me.

Shishapangma Drops Her Veil

Security is mostly a superstition.
It does not exist in nature,
nor do the children of men as a whole experience it.
Avoiding danger is no safer in the long run
than outright exposure.
Life is either a daring adventure
or nothing at all.
—HELEN KELLER

I WASN'T KEEN ON THE SHISHAPANGMA TRIP from the beginning. Skiing an 8,000-meter peak is a dicey proposition, dependent on perfect conditions. Though Alex loved to ski steep backcountry, he defined himself as a climber, not as an extreme skier. I worried about his knees being weak after the surgeries he'd undergone in the past year.

In my presence, Alex had been on the fence about Shishapang-ma. His old friend Andrew McLean from Salt Lake City was the ex-pedition leader. Mark Holbrook, Hans Saari, and photographer Kris Erickson, all young extreme skiers, were eager to join the team. Alex and his friend Conrad Anker would bring the sponsorship of The North Face and American Adventure Productions, who would film the ascent of the south face and, if conditions permitted, the first ski descent of the same. Filmmakers Michael Brown, Kent Harvey, and David Bridges would wield the cameras, and MountainZone.com would host a website with daily updates.

Alex had signed on for the expedition months before, when he was restlessly rehabbing his knee. But when he came home from Trango, he was emotionally and physically exhausted. "I'm just not psyched to leave so soon for another dog-and-pony show," he told me.

"Great," I responded. "You could spend more time at home."

The news that he was to be given an award for alpinism in Europe prompted him to consider dropping out of Shishapangma, but in the end he stuck to his plan. "I can't get out of it," he apologized.

A few days before he was to leave, I got a panicky feeling that he was making a bad decision. I had awakened after a frightening dream of an avalanche, and I became convinced that it had some meaning and that Alex needed to stay home. I wasn't sure how to tell him. We stood talking in our backyard later that morning near the gate. "Alex," I said, taking his hand, "I have a bad feeling about this trip. I really don't want you to go. I had a dream and I'm afraid you will die in an avalanche."

He stared at me with a look of surprise. "Whoa, Jenni," he said, putting a hand on my shoulder and looking into my eyes. "You always worry that something will happen. It's just a dream. I'm not going to die. I'd like to get up this mountain, and if it's safe to ski it . . . fine. But this trip doesn't mean that much to me to risk anything for. My hope is to climb something with Rad after we're done on Shish. That'll make the whole thing worth it to me. Don't worry, I'll be OK," he said, knitting his eyebrows together for one last piercing look. And he went out the gate as I stood there staring blankly down at our yellow Lab Annie's brown eyes and wagging tail.

On September 11, Alex was up at four-thirty for a six o'clock flight. I awakened to the hiss of the coffee steamer but lay in bed, refusing to get up and say goodbye. Goodbyes were routine for us; normally I would rise to share coffee with Alex and perhaps help with some last-minute packing. But this one was different. In tears the night before, I had begged him one last time to stay home, and the resulting disappointment and anger threw me into a sulk. "I'm sorry, Jen. It's my job, and I can't let my friends down. I'll be back soon," he whispered. We had fallen asleep that way, silent, his arm gripping my ribs.

In the dark morning, he came to my bedside, sipping his coffee, sitting and stroking my hair.

"Goodbye, Bird. I have to go."

"It's time?" I asked, not getting up.

"Yeah, you know, I'm not taking my elephant hat this time. It's getting worn out and I don't want to ruin it. But it's kind of sad leaving it behind."

"I'll knit you another," I answered. Limp with resignation, I asked sadly, "Did you say goodbye to the boys?"

"I don't want to wake them."

"You need to say goodbye, Alex."

"OK, I will. I'll call you from Kathmandu. I love you. I'll be fine."

"I love you too," I called after him but still didn't rouse myself, choosing instead to lay there in self-pity and defeat.

I put my trust in Conrad, whose careful, contemplative nature complemented Alex's impulsive side. Conrad was not an extreme skier but a climber, which seemed more rational to me, and I knew Alex trusted his strength, skill, and mountain sense. I needed to feel that Alex's partners were solid and would be able to keep him safe. Conrad's presence was one aspect of the trip that gave me solace.

I had a questionable mammogram a few days after Alex left, and my doctor advised a needle biopsy because of my sister Jan's history of breast cancer. Though I knew it was mostly precautionary, I worried, and I wished that Alex were there. I was still trying to come to terms with the expedition and convince myself that Alex would be OK, and now I worried whether I would be OK too.

Through a chance encounter with the girlfriend of Kris Erickson, I learned that Alex and Kris had planned an extra climb at the end of the Shishapangma expedition—of Teng Kampoche, a peak in a distant region of Nepal, which would entail an extra two to three weeks of time away. I felt hurt and betrayed that Alex had told me nothing about this. When he called from Kathmandu, I confronted him and we had an argument that still haunts me.

"How could you be so selfish after all the time you've been away this year?" I asked.

"I told you I was going to get another little climb in," he backpedaled.

"Alex, that isn't a little climb."

"Jen, I'm a climber, and this trip isn't climbing—it's a work trip, a film trip. I have a strong desire to do something meaningful. It would only mean a couple more weeks."

"Fine, then do it, but don't think you're coming back here to a happy little family," I answered sarcastically. "Alex, I bent over backward for you on the Trango trip, and you were only home for a few weeks, and now you've left again on an expedition that I think is dangerous."

"Jen—"

"And now I'm looking at having a biopsy on my breast with my sister's cancer on my mind," I said emotionally, "and you won't be here—big surprise, because you're never here for anything."

"What? Jenni, I'm sorry I'm not there. If anything serious comes of it, I'll come right home. I am dedicated to you."

"You don't know what dedication is," I raged, in tears. "I wonder if you *are* just using your family for an image to promote yourself, because it sure doesn't feel like dedication to me."

"Oh God, Jen, how can you say that?" he asked. "Is that what you think?"

I knew he was crying. I had dealt him the lowest blow I could come up with.

"No, it's not what I think, but this isn't working for me, Alex. You're gone too much."

And while he caught his breath, I did something I'd never done before. I hung up on him, wishing in the same impulsive instant that I hadn't. It wasn't possible for me to call him back. "Damn it, Alex," I said to myself, "what happened to Saint Jennifer?" I burst into tears.

He called me right back, but the damage was done and we didn't talk long—just a couple of stiff apologies. "I'll come home right now if you want me there for the biopsy," he offered. I now think of that offer with anguish.

"No, you're there, so just do the trip and be careful. I'll let you know what they find out."

Conrad and Alex were sharing a room in Kathmandu, so Conrad knew of the phone call. "Alex came back to the room all sullen and shot down. I could tell he'd been called to the rug," he said.

"Jenni would be better off without me—maybe we should split," Alex said, "and I could just be focused on climbing."

"Alex, man, what do you expect—not even telling her before you plan a climb? Don't be a fool. I know how much your family means to you."

I received an email from Alex a day or so later, telling me that he had scrapped his plans for the extra trip. "I agree that I've been away far too much and need to be home with you and the boys," he wrote. "I'm writing from Nyalam, a wild dusty Tibetan village at 12,000 feet on the Tibetan Plateau where we'll begin our walk to base camp. I love these wild places, these wild people. Give the boys a hug, Love, Alex."

I checked the MountainZone website every couple of days, mostly to read Alex's dispatches. I was tired of the web hype and resentful that I even needed to look at the site to feel connected with my husband.

> *September 18: Seven thousand rejuvenating, invigorating, and life-giving feet of elevation gain today. We bade farewell to the humidity and heat of the lowlands and arrived on the high, dry and cool Tibetan Plateau. Proud, tough Tibetans, their coal black hair braided and wrapped on their heads, stroll resolute and aloof through the tacky streets of Nyalam. Grimy kids plague us for money, garrulous curs snap at each other and very high-mileage Dong Feng lorries growl inexorably through town. There's a visceral allure to these tough gritty plateau towns.*

From Nyalam the team made a fast push to base camp led by Alex, who was well acclimatized and racing at the helm, according to Conrad, who thought he still seemed distracted and moody about giving up the trip to Teng Kampoche. He was running the engine hot to blow off steam. "The first night out, he drank a bunch of scotch with Dave and got wrecked," Conrad said. Amazingly, it didn't slow him down, and the young skiers rose to the challenge. "It's like they were all measuring themselves against Alex. Can we keep up with the alpha dog? I was just hanging back, thinking we should go slow with so many who were inexperienced at altitude. I didn't need to compete with Alex; I already knew where I stood. He was top dog and we both knew it, but that made our partnership easier in a way."

I'm sure Alex was pushing, thinking he might burn them off, as he needed to feel in control somehow. The team went from 12,000 feet to 17,000 feet in two days. Not surprisingly, Andrew McLean, who had been fighting a stomach ailment, saw his condition deteriorate into pulmonary edema, a potentially life-threatening condition. When Andrew came to Alex on their first night at base camp with a gurgling in his chest, Alex was overwrought with guilt for having pushed too high too fast. He volunteered right away to take Andrew down. He also wanted another chance to talk with me on a real phone.

Having shifted his focus to someone other than himself, Alex came to terms right away with what was important.

> *September 27: I sensed a defining moment, an event that would clarify why I'm here. I jumped up, dressed hurriedly and rummaged around in six inches of new snow. . . . We set off into the snow, headlamps stabbing into the darkness, Andrew completely exhausted and needing to stop every few minutes. An hour before dawn, too exhausted to continue but a comforting 2000 feet lower, we lay out our sleeping bags in the snow and allowed Andrew a precious and much needed two hours of sleep. I lay beside him listening for any worsening of the audible gurgle in his lungs. Andrew and I continued down for the next ten hours, Andrew performing heroically.*

Alex called me from Nyalam, a surprise I didn't expect. The reception was scratchy but better than the satellite phone, and we talked for a long time. He told me of Andrew's illness and asked me to get a message to base camp through MountainZone to let them know he was improving. He pledged his devotion to me and the boys and apologized again for Teng Kampoche. I reassured him of my forgiveness and encouraged him to slip away and do a climb with Conrad in the area of their base camp, where countless 6,000-meter peaks exist. We talked about going to Costa Rica with the boys in November; Alex had arranged to do some work there for a friend, helping to set up a tree-top tour. "I can't wait to explore the jungle with the boys," he told me excitedly.

After the trip to Nyalam, Alex was much more at ease, and it was a close time for him and Conrad. They went for a hike together to 18,000 feet, and Conrad shared his own dilemma of uncertainty about his upcoming marriage. "Follow your heart. You'll figure it out," Alex advised.

Meanwhile, the presence of filmmakers had brought a unique atmosphere, as Alex wrote in a personal email to me:

> So—the trip so far—definitely a film trip. Everything is scripted, all dialogue gets repeated over and over—lots of very contrived and forced scenes. This is Hollywood at its finest. Nothing spontaneous gets recorded on film. . . . I'm having plenty of fun within the context of the trip—but the "film tail" is definitely wagging the "expedition dog" if you know what I mean.

He asked me how the website looked, calling it very different from the experience he had working with Quokka on Great Trango.

> I'm much less inspired and the writing is always done with half a dozen testosterone-laden skiers looking over my shoulder telling me what to write—which is not how I do my best writing. I think it's going well, in Mountain Zone's estimation—sort of shallow, razzle-dazzle stuff but pretty enjoyable for a broad audience. What's your read? I'd love to hear your thoughts on how I could add value to the site.

Alex's emails to me were more contemplative than the dispatches he wrote for the website, which were always upbeat and enthusiastic. He loved being in the mountains, but I think the atmosphere of the group made him realize he was the oldest by far, and in a different place in his life than his teammates. For instance, on October 3 he wrote to me:

> It's a pretty amusing trip. Penthouse pinups all over the group
> tent walls and massive bottles of scotch available at all hours.
> Not really the atmosphere I come looking for in the mountains,
> but—hey—it's a work trip. Makes me realize that what I really
> want to do is climb more with my sons and show them what
> I love in mountaineering. Life changes are in order to be there
> more often for you. I am very content in forgoing Teng Kampoche
> to be home with you and the boys. Much love, Alex

His writing for the site on that same day touched on some of the same themes, but in a more philosophical and general way:

> I appreciate why I come to the mountains: not to conquer them,
> but to immerse myself in their incomprehensible immensity—so
> much bigger than us; to better comprehend humanity and
> patience balanced in harmony with the desire to push hard; to
> share what the hills offer; and to share it in the long term with
> good friends and ultimately with my own sons.

On the morning of October 6, 1999, I had returned home from walking Max and Sam to school, pushing Isaac's stroller along the tree-lined streets. Isaac sat in the small world of his backyard sandbox warmed by a spot of autumn sun. I puttered mindlessly through my daily routine, cleaning the kitchen and picking up kid clutter between sips of coffee and glimpses of local news in the morning paper. When I answered my phone at 9:00 AM, I recognized the long pause and static of a satellite-phone call, but there was no voice.

"Hello? Hello, Alex? Is that you?" I heard only muted wind. "Hello?" Fear gripped me. I hung up quickly, not waiting for a reply. The phone rang again immediately, and this time I heard Andrew's voice.

"Jenni . . . this is Andrew."

"Andrew—is everything OK?" I asked, somehow knowing that it wasn't.

"There's been a terrible accident," I heard him say. "An enormous avalanche. Conrad, Alex, and David were crossing beneath the face this morning when it cut loose from way above. Conrad is injured but he's OK. We can't find David or Alex." His voice wavered. My heart leapt to my head, pounding wildly, as I felt my body sink heavily into a chair. For a long moment I couldn't speak, knowing all too well what Andrew's words meant. Suffocation beneath avalanche debris is usually immediate; survival depends on finding a victim within the first crucial minutes.

"Oh God . . . Andrew, are you sure? Is this really you?" I asked pitifully, wanting it not to be.

"I'm sorry, Jennifer," he said, his voice cracking.

Sorry—you can't be sorry, came to my mind, because this isn't real. It's part of a bad dream.

"Andrew . . . you need to keep looking," I stammered. "He could be in a crevasse, in a safe place. You can't give up . . . please?"

"OK, Jenni," he said flatly.

"Is Conrad there?"

"He's right here in the tent with me . . . he's pretty beat up, but he's doing great."

"Can he talk to me?" I gasped, still wanting to hear someone else's words—another reality.

"Hello?"

"Conrad, is this you?"

The injured Conrad's gentle voice came to me, and when he began to speak, I knew there wasn't another reality. He spoke haltingly, answering my frantic questions. When I finally understood that the avalanche had happened nearly twelve hours before, I knew how difficult it must have been for Andrew and Conrad. They both loved Alex fiercely. "Twelve hours!" I thought. "He has been dead for twelve hours and they didn't call me until now?"

Conrad said something about how much Alex loved us, how he had our picture in his breast pocket and how they had talked about Christmas the night before. I couldn't speak, and neither could he after that.

"I'll call you again this evening," Andrew promised.

I stared out the back door at Isaac, still crouched over his tiny trucks in the sand. "Oh my God," I thought. I knew this could happen, but it couldn't be true. He told me he wouldn't die. Didn't Alex have some uncanny ability to survive where others would not—and then lift an eyebrow and grin? How could Alex be crushed beneath tons of frozen snow?

With my head swimming and hot tears streaming, I gripped the phone with shaky hands and in succession dialed the numbers of my mother, my sister Jan, Alex's parents, his brothers, and my friend Suzanne. "Alex is dead," I told each of them between sobs, hearing the words I spoke as though they were someone else's.

"Oh Jenni, oh no . . . I'm so sorry," came my mother's voice to me. "And you with those three little boys . . . "

"Oh no—not Alex. Oh my God! Jenni, are you all right?" Jan asked.

"No—I'm not. It seems like a dream—a really bad dream."

"I'll be there as soon as I can, Jennifer," Jan said. "Murray and I will leave right away. I love you."

Dottie's familiar Southern accent asked, "Jennifer?"

"Dottie . . . is Jim there with you? It's Alex. He's been buried in an avalanche. I'm afraid they can't find him. I'm so sorry."

I heard a deep sigh and then resignation in her shaken voice. "Oh Jenni . . . we always worried . . . we expected it. How are you doing, dear?"

"I . . . I just can't believe it . . . I didn't want him to go, you know. It didn't feel right to me," I said, and I recounted all that I could from my conversation with Andrew about what had happened. "I'm so sorry."

Suzanne, who lived just around the corner, burst in the back door and hugged me hard as we both cried. "We need to get the boys home from school," I told her. "I have to tell them."

"I've already called Pamela. She can take you to get them while I stay with Isaac," Suzanne said.

I walked over to little Isaac and crouched next to his make-believe world in the sand, wishing I could join him there and forget the terrible reality. "Honey, I have to go get the boys, so Suzanne is here with you," I said, deciding not to disrupt his play until I returned.

Sam was seven and Max was ten. They looked frightened and confused as I pulled them from their classrooms and quietly took them to the car, where Suzanne's daughter, Pamela, sat waiting to drive us home. I can imagine that I looked awful, my face white with shock and eyes red from crying, but I said nothing to their teachers other than "There's a family emergency. They need to go." Once in the car, I sat between them with my arms around each and told them as gently as I could, "Dad has been in an avalanche and they think he is dead. He is buried under the snow and they can't find him." They stared at me, eyes wide and faces serious, as I robbed them of their childhood innocence.

"Could he still be alive, under the snow?" asked Max, blinking away tears.

"I wish he could, honey, but I don't think so. I'm so sorry. Dad's gone—he won't be coming back to us this time." When I said the words to them, I felt a terrible knot in my stomach grow tighter and more painful, making me catch my breath. But saying the words helped me to believe them myself, and I struggled hard not to lose control completely.

At home, I picked up Isaac and held him, sitting him down with Sam and Max to explain that he no longer had a dad. I told him about a big mountain where Dad had gone and how snow had fallen down the mountain and covered Dad up. He looked confused and sad, watching each of our faces, but didn't cry. His weeping brothers became angry. "What's wrong with him?" they asked, and I tried to explain that he was too young to understand.

"He's only three," I said. "We need to be kind. I love all of you more than anything, and you are my first priority. I know this is the saddest and hardest thing for us to face, but I will be here for you boys no matter what, and we are here for each other."

I barely had time to notify our family and close friends before news of the accident went out over the MountainZone website. It seemed that within a few hours the entire world knew Alex had died, before I had even begun to process what had happened.

That same day, I opened an email to Max from Alex, with an attachment, a photograph of a watercolor painting:

Happy Birthday, Max my dear friend! I borrowed Conrad's watercolor paints to send you a birthday yak. Yakitty-Yak-Yak! I hope you have a wonderful birthday party at home. We'll have a party here in your honor beneath the south face of Shishapangma. I'm sorry I won't be with you in Bozeman on your eleventh big day but you are in my thoughts and in my heart every day and every step I take! I can't wait to be home with you in a few short weeks. You're great! I love you with all my heart. Dad

The painting featured a yak in front of snowy mountains with the words "Happy Birthday Max" and "Love Dad." It was an early greeting for Max's birthday, and it was as though Alex himself had flown into our home to be close to us. "Dad's still alive?!" exclaimed Max in excitement when I showed him the email.

"No, honey," I said, fighting back tears, but felt the same confused sense of hope. Words written before but only read now, the last "letter" we would ever have from Alex—his last words of love.

Max crawled out the window and sat on the porch roof overlooking our backyard and the Bridger Mountains. It was the place he chose to go for quiet grieving.

The doorbell began to ring as one after another of our friends came to wrap their arms around us and cry. A few close friends were sucked into answering the phone, politely screening out everyone except the people I needed or wanted to talk with. Mostly I sat staring in a dreamlike daze, an observer of some other person's life. "This can't be real," I kept thinking.

People came and went all day long with hugs and tears and food and flowers in a surreal procession that would continue for many days. As our home filled with people, Suzanne whisked the boys to the quiet comfort of her house for macaroni, movies, and root-beer floats.

In the late afternoon, my friend Maddy steered me out the door to the sun-dappled sidewalk to clear my head and get an idea of how she and the sisterhood of my book club could help me through the difficult days and weeks that stretched out before me. As we navigated the sidewalks of our neighborhood, it seemed remarkable but reassuring that the world around me was going on as usual, people driving by, riding bikes, and walking their dogs as though nothing had changed.

When Jan and Murray arrived, I fell apart in my sister's arms and told them everything that had happened that day. I also told them about the conversation that had been haunting me since Andrew called. "I had a premonition that Alex would be caught in an avalanche—that he would die. I tried to talk him out of going," I said. "Why didn't I insist?"

"Jenni, don't. It's not your fault," she consoled, rubbing my back. Together we drank beer and cried.

In bed that night, my chest felt as though a very heavy weight was pressing down on it, and I wondered whether I might be having a heart attack. It couldn't be, I reasoned, feeling no numbness in my arms. I sat up and breathed deeply, then paced in the darkness of my home, staring at the dim vases of colorless flowers on every table, staring into the sleeping faces of the children, wondering what our future would be. Sleep would not come, even as exhaustion consumed me. "Why Alex?" I kept thinking selfishly. He was the only one on the expedition who had children and the only one who was married. I lay down and sobbed until my pillow was damp with salt, feeling the emptiness of despair.

Morning was almost as shocking as the previous day, as I awoke and momentarily thought that it really had been a bad dream. I now know that the unconscious mind can take up to several months to process a tragedy of such magnitude. When we sleep, our unconscious mind takes over and the conscious mind rests. So for many weeks, each time I awoke I had the same experience of confused panic. I heard Jan stirring in the kitchen and remembered my grim reality. I didn't want to get up. I was not prepared to see the story of Alex's death as a headline in our local paper, his face staring up at me from the planks of my front porch.

I closed the door on the world, hiding my grief. The media felt like wolves at my door. There were requests for interviews from television, newspapers, and magazines. I quietly refused them all. Hundreds of well-wishers also called to offer us their love, condolences, and support. The ringing phone pierced the silence like a crying child that couldn't be comforted, and Jan began her job of managing the nonstop cacophony for weeks to come.

As I sipped coffee in my kitchen, I heard the NPR announcer say, "The man who was called the world's best mountain climber has been lost in an avalanche on a mountain in Tibet. Alex Lowe was forty years old. He leaves a wife and three young children in Bozeman, Montana." I sat frozen listening to the story, which included taped interviews with Alex from Trango and interviews with Gordon from the day before. "There's a magic to the mountains that's addictive to the human spirit," said Alex's familiar voice, giving me a sick feeling. Gordon answered questions with sad reverence for Alex, saying, "The reaction around the world is disbelief that someone with Alex's strength and ability could succumb." To the last question posed, "Will you climb again?" Gordon replied, "I'll climb again, but . . . I can't imagine putting my family through the kind of experience that I've witnessed with Jennifer Lowe's family today."

Jan stood over me, rubbing my shoulders. Like a lioness, she seemed to have arrived to protect me from unnecessary pain, efficiently ushering me through the steps I needed to take. It felt natural to have her at my side, as she had been the first member of my family to meet Alex and embrace him because of the mere fact that I loved him. And she had loved him too. Now she took calls and helped me make decisions. So many things had to be done: legal matters, service arrangements, on and on. Just getting a death certificate from China was challenging in light of the fact that there was no body.

It became apparent that our service would have to be private, as I did not want it to become too large or attract the media. This led to agonizing decisions over whom to invite. There were hundreds in the climbing community and the outdoor retail community who considered Alex a close friend. There were many family members, some close but others distant. There were the people of our local community, whose help we needed to survive the tragedy and who I knew would see us through it. And there was a public who adored Alex and wanted to say their goodbyes.

Jan helped me through the entire ordeal. We decided to hold a second memorial at the University Fieldhouse in Bozeman later in November, which would have room for everyone who wanted to attend. Planning the two services was a mind-boggling effort to undertake amid the craziness of our household, where more relatives and friends arrived each day, but Jan carried it off with aplomb and the help of many friends.

Sadly, Andrew later told me that he assumed I hated him for being the expedition leader. When I had asked to speak to Conrad during Andrew's first call, I had inadvertently given him the impression that I didn't want to talk with him. It was not the case, but it was Conrad who called each day to update me on what the team was doing. I looked forward to his calls from the "other world," which somehow made me feel closer to Alex. They had given up hope of finding the bodies; the amount and depth of debris was too massive. They built rock chortens to honor their dead friends and held a ceremony at the base camp while they waited for yaks to come for their gear and begin the sad trek home.

I felt anger for the first time when Conrad told me of their service—not at any one of them in particular, but at all of them for having the last days with Alex. For having twelve hours to come to terms with his death, while I had only one before it was public knowledge. For having that ceremony as though they had ownership of Alex. For thinking that would make anything better.

I hadn't known David, but I'm sure he looked to Alex as a mentor and perhaps followed him to his death in that autonomic moment of fate. For that I felt guilt. The image of Alex, David, and Conrad walking across the slope and then running frantically beneath the billow of roaring snow was a waking nightmare, repeating itself relentlessly through the day to teach me the new reality of my life. At night I dreamed of Alex crawling through crevasses, looking for a way out.

I wanted to know every detail of what happened, so I grilled Conrad during our brief phone conversations. "What was Alex wearing?" "Why did you cross the slope?" "In what order were you walking?" "What did you say when you heard the avalanche and saw it?" With patience and sadness he answered each question, and the picture in my head became more vivid.

The one question that haunted me most was "Why did Alex run down instead of across the slope?" How did all his knowledge of avalanche safety and years of practical experience in the mountains escape him in that most crucial moment of decision making? Conrad couldn't say, except to note that Alex and Dave had both been wearing plastic boots, while Conrad had been wearing lighter leather boots. "Perhaps Alex thought that his stiff boots would hinder his ability to run across the slope," he offered.

Whatever the thought process, there was no discussion, only the moment of realization and then reaction coupled with fear. Hundreds of times, the scenario played out in my head in the days, weeks, and months after Alex died. "If only Conrad had been in front," I thought, "then Alex and Dave might have followed him, and perhaps they all would have lived. If only they had crossed the slope five minutes later. If only they had gone down the ridge." There were an infinite number of "if onlys," but none of them mattered now. What mattered now was the acceptance of that grand finale of life, which was death. Alex had lived his life, and the living part was over in the physical sense.

One question I will never know the answer to is "What were Alex's thoughts?" But I had a pretty good idea. I remembered a dispatch Alex had posted from Trango base camp in June, and I read it again with horror.

> I was startled by a cataclysmic roar emanating from Great Trango.
> I spun around to face a billowing wall of cascading ice, thundering 4,000 feet from the hanging glacier beside our wall. There's something visceral and mesmerizing about avalanches of this magnitude rumbling ominously upon you. The fear wells from the groin. I suspect the emotion is akin to that felt by a deer paralyzed

by the scream of a panther, coiled to spring in the final fatal instant.
I realized immediately that I was in no danger; that the lethal
debris would stop far from where I stood gaping. As the pulverized
ice settled serenely about me five minutes later, my heart still raced.

The morning of October 5 had been sunny and leisurely, with everyone enjoying coffee, when Alex began to rally the troops for a look at the Swiss-Polish Route that they hoped to climb and ski. Conrad had been building the outhouse and returned to camp, finding Alex and Dave ready to go. At 8:05 he joined them to hike up a ridge to the right of the south face and the glacier. They hiked with Alex in front, then David and Conrad at the rear. David was talking about paragliding for most of the time. They came to a knoll and saw Andrew and the rest of the team waving from across the glacier below. "Let's go meet them," Alex said simply, and without question they started across the glacier beneath the massive face. It was 9:10. At 9:18 to 9:20, Alex noticed the fracture far above them. "Fuck!" he exclaimed, and they all began to run. Alex and David ran down the slope, but Conrad ran across. In a letter to me, he tried to put the experience on paper:

> *We were walking along the glacier when . . . time changed*
> *from a sunny morning to 30 seconds of fate. We ran in different*
> *directions—I looked over my shoulder two times and saw Alex*
> *and David, and then laid down the third time just before the*
> *wall of wind and mass of debris hit us. I saw Alex and was*
> *unable to help him. And then we were hit by the tons of snow.*
> *Being dragged down the glacier, I thought this was it, that death*
> *was meeting me. It stopped, and the huge cloud began to settle.*
> *I realized that I was alive, by some miracle. I immediately stood*
> *up and began looking for Alex and David. The surface I had*
> *just run across was now a landscape with huge blocks of ice and*
> *what appeared as large moguls. I began with a grid back and*
> *forth looking for my two companions. I searched for twenty-four*

*minutes with my watch, which I had found ripped off of my arm.
I was calling their names, but to no avail. They were not there.*

*Alex was struck by a forceful amount of moving snow. He may
have been instantly killed by the initial wave of snow. Perhaps he
was thrown some distance and knocked out by the fall. Ultimately, he was buried and if he was still conscious, he would have
been aware for only minutes before he suffocated. This is what
happened. Sorry, so sorry.*

I was consumed with thoughts of Alex, to the point of exhaustion. The fragmented conversation in my head seemed relentless. If
he had remained alive for a few minutes beneath the snow, was he in
pain? Did he know he was about to die? Were his thoughts of me and
the boys? Was he at peace? What if he thought of our conversation
at the gate about my premonition of an avalanche? Oh God, why did
I ever say that? Maybe I made the avalanche happen by dreaming
it, by worrying about it or even thinking it could happen. Maybe
it's my punishment because I didn't get out of bed to say goodbye to
him. "Oh Alex," I thought, "I'm so sorry. If only this could be a dream
and I could wake up now."

The boys and I needed time alone, so one day we walked to the
top of Story Hill, where Alex often had taken them on outings to fly
kites, look at wildflowers, or hike to the radio tower. Overlooking
the valley is a grassy windswept hill with coulees of brush where
migrating birds ride updrafts above the backs of grazing cattle. We
walked, feeling the wind on our faces and peering out at splashes of
yellow aspen, red dogwood, and orange willow dotting the outskirts
of Bozeman below us. The Hyalite Range and Spanish Peaks rose
up beyond. So much of our history lay within the boundaries of the
mountains and streams that it was like looking out at the map of
our lives. I hoisted Isaac to my hip as I hiked the ridge toward the
hilltop, listening to Max and Sam reminisce. "Remember when Dad
brought us up here to see the comet?" Sam said.

"Yeah, that was so cool," answered Max.

"Mom, do you think if we found Dad's body, we could clone him?" Max asked, taking me by surprise.

"Well, I don't think so. It wouldn't be Dad anyway. It would just be a baby that looks like Dad," I answered.

"Well, I guess we already have Isaac, so we don't need another baby that looks like Dad," Sam reasoned. "Maybe if he's frozen under the snow, we could bring him back to life."

"I think that only happens in movies, Sam. When someone dies, they're gone, and they can't come back no matter how badly we want them to. Except in our memories, and we have lots of good memories."

"Mom, are angels real?" Max asked.

"Well, no one knows for sure," I began. "We know that the body just deteriorates and goes back to the earth over time. Some people think the spirit of a person becomes an angel."

"Do you believe in heaven, Mom?" Max pressed me further.

"I believe that heaven is right here on earth and we just have to look for it," I said. Suddenly an enormous bird took flight from a hummock before us, so close that we were startled by its beating wings. A golden eagle rose above, gliding in wide circles, and we stood speechless. Coincidence or not, I had an overwhelming feeling that Alex was there with us too. "I think angels are really birds," I whispered, "and maybe Dad's spirit is right here with us in that beautiful eagle." And the eagle swooped overhead, riding its updraft on a migratory path that had been the same for thousands of years, maybe longer. "What could be more perfect?" I thought as we watched it sail beyond the ridge and Sam quietly said, "Goodbye, Dad. We love you."

Max's eleventh birthday party was arranged for the Saturday before his father's memorial service in an attempt to keep the children distracted and out from underfoot on that busy day of last-minute details. Tom Bozeman and his wife, Pam, were joined by Sandy Hill Pittman; together they took a few carloads of kids to the local go-kart park, where Max was showered with gifts from sympathetic friends and relatives. I did not go but waited at home with nervous anticipation. Ten days had passed since the avalanche, and Conrad was due to arrive in Bozeman that day. I knew he would be bringing Alex's things and, more importantly, perhaps some insight into what had gone wrong.

At last the doorbell rang. I have a vivid memory of the four of them standing there on my front porch, looking somber and awkward as I opened the door: Conrad, his fiancée, and Jon Krakauer and his wife, Linda Moore. Conrad had made the long journey from one world to another, but he was hardly the guy I remembered from Alex's previous climbs. His wild blond hair had been shaved close, and wounds were visible on his head. He was too thin—gaunt, with shoulders hunched forward. His blue eyes looked sad and red. He had suffered a cracked skull, a sublocated shoulder, and a broken rib. That much I had known, but until that moment I hadn't realized just how much he had suffered. "My God!" I thought. "This man is broken, and I need to be strong for his sake." And then it occurred to me, "He is alive and Alex is dead. He didn't keep him safe after all." I thanked them for coming, invited them into my home, and did not cry.

Conrad carried the precious yak painting that Alex had done for Max's birthday, along with some of Alex's belongings from the expedition. He presented them with tearful ceremony and I whisked them away, trying hard to contain my emotions as I thought of Alex carefully packing his things one month before. Everyone was quiet but Conrad seemed dazed, staring around the house. I remember that we looked at the Shishapangma website, which featured tributes to Alex and Dave, and suddenly Conrad broke down and began to sob. Tears stung my own eyes but I turned away, fighting for control. Their visit was brief—after the long drive, they went to their hotel to check in and rest.

That evening the five of us went to dinner in downtown Bozeman. Both Conrad and Jon had been so kind, answering my questions and offering support. I wanted to thank them with dinner out, to spend this one evening together. When they came to pick me up, the boys were there and Conrad greeted each of them. I remember that Sam was sitting on the floor in his room, and Conrad joined him. Seven-year-old Sam put his hands on either side of Conrad's face and looked into his eyes.

"Why couldn't you save my dad?" he asked, and I sucked in my breath and bit my lip. It was the one question I had so wanted to ask but hadn't dared.

"I would have if I could," said Conrad. "I loved your dad. He was my best friend."

It was a long, sad evening for me. The moment we arrived in the restaurant, I realized that I had been there with Alex recently. I stared at the table where we'd sat together, seeing a ghost of my past. Once seated, I was painfully aware that I was alone and no longer part of a couple. With Conrad and his fiancée across from me and Jon and Linda next to me, my lost love seemed unbearable. Adrift in time and confused, grappling to hold myself together, I wanted to be there, but I also wanted to run away.

Four hundred people attended the memorial service on October 17 honoring the life of Alex Lowe, the maximum capacity for Bozeman's beautiful Springhill Pavilion. Craggy Ross Peak rose behind the lovely old farm nestled against the forested hills. Shaggy Scottish Highlander cattle stood in pastures, and Burmese mountain dogs trotted to greet us from a farmhouse flanked by apple orchards and a big red barn. To me it seemed as much like heaven as any place I could imagine us gathering.

Tom Bozeman conducted the service. Only six weeks had passed since he had stood atop the Grand Teton with Alex, sharing the proud moment with Max and his own son, Jared. He ministered elegantly, but not without tears.

The open-air pavilion was strung with prayer flags. The women of my book club busied themselves like bees attending their queen. Silky white prayer shawls called *katas*, brought by Conrad from Nepal, were draped over the shoulders of every guest as they arrived. Pictures of Alex in the mountains and Alex with family adorned walls and tables. Classical guitarist Stuart Weber opened the service with a song composed in Alex's honor. Max played "Ashokan Farewell" soulfully on his violin, and evoking a tearful ovation. Alex's brothers, Ted and Andy, stood singing with guitars in hand, two brothers who had been three. Bluegrass ballads were performed, and everyone joined to sing "Wildflowers" by Tom Petty, Alex's favorite song. A string of mountaineers came forward, along with family, friends, and a favored math professor, to tell their stories of Alex. One by one we walked to the front of the crowded room and tried to make words do what they could not do: bring Alex back.

As Halloween approached, I remembered that it was the day that Alex was to have arrived home. "Leave my truck at the airport so I can catch up with you and the boys trick-or-treating," he had written.

"How ironic," I said sadly to Jan. "Should I be a black widow for Halloween?"

"Oh, Jennifer!" she replied, knitting her brow.

When Jan went home after Halloween, the first days without her were the loneliest I had ever experienced, but she had put her own life on hold to tend to mine for weeks. She left with a promise to be back in late November for the public service. By day I was stoic, but I was still consumed with memories of Alex. I went through the motions of routine activities such as caring for the kids, but I was distracted by the ever-present feeling that life was now different. Alex wasn't just gone—he was gone forever.

"Mom . . . don't cry, Mom," Isaac would say. So my bedroom became my haven of grief. Letters kept coming from everywhere, from relatives, friends, and acquaintances and from total strangers in distant places. Reading them was for me a tremendous emotional release, so I piled them on my bedside table. Each night after the boys were asleep, I leaned against my pillows in the loneliness of my bed and ripped open envelopes to read. Words of sympathy spilled out, stories of meeting Alex, of climbing with Alex, of seeing him speak. Some had never met him but were great admirers. There were writers who knew nothing of climbing but much of grief and loss, writers from the White House and the New York Times; from Russia, Pakistan, Baffin, and Nepal. There were letters from kids for the kids of their hero, and there were poetic pages of sorrow, inspiration, and thanks for sharing the man who was my husband. "Alex inspired me," they said, "to live larger—to dream bigger and to pursue my dreams. He set high standards for us all."

The Passion of Grief

But the love will have been enough:
All of those impulses of love return to the love that made them.
Even memory is not necessary for love.
There is a land of the living and a land of the dead,
And the bridge is love, the only survival,
The only meaning.
—THORNTON WILDER

ONE EVENING IN THE WEEKS AFTER Alex had died, I slipped out my front door, sank to the worn wooden steps of the porch, and turned my tired eyes to the stars. With the children in bed, I wanted a moment outside to clear my mind and reflect on how time was progressing. It seemed that each passing day left Alex a bit farther behind us. "Oh Alex," I whispered, "how can I keep going?"

The sound began as an almost inaudible melody—a high faint note, then low. It grew louder quickly as I focused on a rhythm from the dark sky, searching for shapes. And they appeared like ghosts in the night, crying their calls of flight. With their voices they let each other know their position, the patterns and speed of their airborne caravan. Snow geese, elegant as angels in their southbound journey, were winging their way directly overhead. I caught my breath at the sense of Alex's presence in their timely appearance. Could it be a sign from him?

I remembered then, the two of us young and newly in love, heading north into Montana as the sun was setting. Alex was driving and abruptly pulled over, turned off the engine, and looked at me. "What?" I asked in surprise. "Listen," he had said and smiled. We hopped out and found ourselves beneath a storm of snow geese high overhead, fluidly pulsing north, with evening sun glinting from outstretched wings tipped in black. Neither of us spoke. We stood and watched the sprinkling of white confetti float across the sky until their calls were quiet and their forms had faded into the blue.

I shivered at the plaintive cries that came to me now like a persistent voice of life itself, saying that this ritual, this migration, this coming and going is nature's pattern. It is one we cannot expect to interrupt or change. It is a ritual filled with hope, like the changing of seasons, and there is no choice but to keep flying, just as the snow geese have spread their wings and flown for many thousands of years.

After a month of receiving meals and gifts of food from my loyal book club, friends, and community, I began to go out in public. Earlier it had been too painful to go to the grocery store, where everyone seemed to know of my loss, offering sad stares and awkward hugs. But now the simple routines of shopping for food, picking up around the house, and cooking became comforting and easy to accomplish. I baked batch after batch of chocolate chip cookies, presenting them warm with cold glasses of milk to the boys. I baked banana bread and biscuits and I roasted meatloaf, chicken, and pot roast to help fill the empty hole that Alex had left. I ate very little myself, growing thinner and thinner, but at least I could cook for the boys.

My old friend Holly Tarlow, whom I had known since high school, came to my house each week to help sort the massive amount of mail, pay bills, and keep track of appointments. We took some of Alex's things and put them into boxes to be sorted later.

I removed his jackets and shoes from the places they occupied by the door, but I could not pull his clothes from our closet. I listened to certain songs over and again, their lyrics repeating and blending together, enmeshed in images of Alex, my tears flowing: "Now I heard the owl calling . . . And I'm wondering where the lions are, wondering where the lions are . . . "

I fled to the outdoors each day for exercise, pedaling my bike, walking nearby trails, or trudging to the M, a giant letter of white-washed rocks on the hillside at the base of Bridger Canyon that stands for MSU. "I thought the M was for mountains," Sam once said to me as we hiked the trail. "It should be," I answered.

Walking the footpath that I had traveled so many times with Alex, where he had run routinely and where we had ambled with our children over the years, felt comforting. I breathed easier in the fresh air and stretched my legs to climb the rocky path while Annie bounded up and down the hill, sniffing about and returning to check on me every few minutes with wagging tail.

I found the yellow grasses of autumn, the chokecherries and flowers gone to seed, marking the calendar of time ongoing. I knew that they would soon be covered in snow and that green shoots would follow the dormant time of winter. Buttercups and shooting stars would adorn this path in the months ahead, followed by wild iris, lupine, and balsam root. I remembered Alex bringing me tiny bouquets of wildflowers from his runs. "I got them way up where no one goes," he'd say. "They are the wildest of wildflowers."

With the boys to care for, I was far from alone, but I couldn't burden them with my thoughts and grief. My dear friend Maddy checked on me daily, and some of Alex's best friends continued to reach out to me by calling and stopping by. Doug Chabot, who'd been an Exum guide with Alex, came every few days to have a cup of coffee, and his laughter instantly lifted my spirit. I spoke by phone with my mother and Jan nearly every day, and Conrad called most days to say hello and share feelings of sadness or despair, joy or hope, or just events of the day. He wrote to me in November while promoting his new book, *The Lost Explorer: Finding Mallory on Mount Everest*, which told the story of his May 1999 discovery of the legendary British climber's body:

May this letter find you in good spirits. I'm on a packed airplane en route to New York. The past couple of days have been a blur, as I expect the next ten to be. At one point I was so excited about this, the opportunity to have written a book. Now, well, it's just another month in my life.

The people along the way have been very supportive and understanding. They reach out with a kind smile and offer a meaningful word or two. This is very special. It must be very difficult for you and the boys. There is hardly a moment that the four of you are not in my thoughts. At times it is difficult for me—I cry myself to sleep, waking up long before the roosters and tossing and turning, grinding my teeth with very dark thoughts. This is the last thing I had ever expected and I am so unprepared.

I gather strength from the four of you. Knowing that you are there and that I can talk with you openly and honestly is a great source of strength. Caring for and helping people has long been a part of my life and now it is even so much more. You and the boys are the ones I want to help and care for. To be there for the boys is something I hope to do, an action that will bring a sense of fulfillment to my person.

People ask what is up next in my life. A simple question. A deep sense of responsibility rests with me, as Alex shared his love for you and your children with me. He trusted me, knew my appreciation for his life and was confident that I was sincere in my respect for him. After all this, my sense of caring for you four has increased. I ask myself why my life was spared in this tragedy. I can answer that by saying I ran in a different direction. But that isn't the answer to the question I am asking. In many ways I wonder, waking up in the middle of the night with why, why, why running about my mind.

I was surprised but deeply touched by his letter. Though I had felt great comfort from the frequent phone conversations we shared, I still felt unsure of how Conrad would fit into our lives as time went on, especially since he did not live near Bozeman. This is something he needs now, I told myself, but in time he will lose interest and go on with his own life. He was still part of a couple, and I asked him gently one day, "Is it awkward—you calling here so much and me calling you?"

"No," he answered, "It's what I need as long as you do. A few moments out of my day."

But I worried about him when he spoke of dark thoughts.

A terrific guilt is upon my soul, one that rears its head when I am tired, after a long day. Perhaps it is karma related. . . . Is there some karmic connection between finding the body of George Mallory and losing our beloved Alex? This sounds wild, no doubt but it causes me a good deal of turmoil within.

My heart went out to him instantly for the guilt that weighed on his soul, but oddly enough, similar thoughts had crossed my mind. Conrad had given me a copy of his book, and I had read bits and pieces when I could not sleep. One of the first coincidences I had noticed was that Mallory's funeral service decades ago had been on the same day as Alex's service at Springhill, October 17. Mallory's handsome face, his intellectual leanings, and his propensity for writing long, descriptive love letters to his wife, Ruth, all had striking parallels in Alex. Mallory had pondered life's meaning and wrestled with the classic question about why he wanted to climb the highest mountain, ultimately answering with the oft-quoted "Because it is there."

"We're not looking for the risks, we're looking for the rewards," Alex had said in response to similar questions. "The appreciation of life that comes from putting yourself in a risky situation, but with the tools and rationale and the desire to live and love life. I think we live much richer, fuller lives because of it. . . . I always climb with the ultimate goal of returning home to hold my kids in my arms and love and support my wife."

I wondered how to hold on to that love and feeling of support that Alex had given me, to raise my children and be strong enough to give them everything I wanted them to have and everything I knew Alex had wanted for them. I knew I would not forget Alex, but I didn't want the boys to forget him either. I wanted them to know his character and passions through the people and the places he had loved—his dearest friends and the wild places.

I drove my van toward Great Falls to meet Mother and Papa in early November, for a weekend of fishing with my stepbrother, Bruce. The kids needed an adventure, and Mother knew I needed to get away. "Come meet us at the ranch," she said. "It will be good to see you."

I loved the drive along the winding rivers through the little community of Wolf Point and on toward Augusta. Out there on the plains at the edge of the Rockies was a small lake that Bruce and Papa liked to fish at this time of year. The land was private and the trout were enormous—big rainbows that thrive on freshwater shrimp.

We met them at a turnoff in the road with smiles and waves. Bruce and his wife, Caroline, hosted us from their house near the Sun River, and Mother brought lots of extra food. We got right at the fishing, driving over winding dirt roads and hills to arrive at the lakeshore. White birds covered the water. Snow geese and a few swans floated in groups that numbered in the thousands. As we stepped from the car, hundreds burst from the water in startled flight to alight closer to the opposite shore, and I burst into tears.

"Jennifer," my mother said to me, quietly steering me away from the others, "I know it is hard for you, but you need to get on with your life. You have these little boys, and I won't be around for a whole lot longer."

"What do you mean?" I asked as she looked at me with purpose.

"I'm ill," she said. "They don't know how serious yet, but it's a blood disease. Multiple myeloma—it can lead to leukemia."

"Oh, Mom!"

"I need more tests," she said, amazingly calm, though I saw tears in her eyes. "They don't know how far it's progressed, but it's going to be serious. And I'm worried about you."

"Me!" I said. "What about you?"

"I'm old," she said, jutting out her lower jaw and pursing her lips. "I've had a good life, but you're young and those little boys need you. You were always the most sensitive, Jennifer, but you have to be strong now."

"Oh God," I thought, but I quickly stuffed my feelings into a closet of denial. "Mom, you're going to be OK," I said, staring at her for signs of decay. I saw none. "You're not old, and I think you're just worrying too much."

She wasn't, though. Six weeks later, just after the New Year, my mother would be given the news: she had terminal cancer in her bones. "I might have a year," she would tell me.

⸻

One of my dearest friends during that difficult time was Greg Mortenson, who appeared at my door frequently to give me a hug and offer a bit of support. He is a bear of a man but as shy and gentle as anyone I know. His quiet demeanor belies the storm of energy and ideas that emerge from his heart to manifest in acts of kindness. Greg is the founder and president of the Central Asia Institute, a nonprofit organization that has now built and sustained, in a grass-roots capacity, more than seventy schools for children in Pakistan and Afghanistan, with an emphasis on educating girls. His recent memoir, *Three Cups of Tea*, tells his amazing story.

Alex had visited one of Greg's schools in the village of Korphe and was greatly inspired by his mission. On the approach to Trango in Pakistan, Alex hiked up to the tiny village and took time to have tea with Haji Ali, the elder who oversaw the mountain community. He later wrote to me, "Many thousands of *Angrezi* [white men] pass my village every year. But none stop. Alex did. He asked for permission to visit our land in our old Balti tradition. I gave him tea. I gave him goat meat. May Allah almighty bless his family. They have refuge in my home forever."

Overwhelmed by the number of donations that had already been made in Alex's memory, I discussed with Greg the possibility of creating a charity. He told me of his own experience—that his mission for the Balti people had been in part inspired by his desire to honor the life of his late sister. It was a wise bit of advice, as it encouraged me to focus my energy on something other than Alex's death—specifically, founding the nonprofit Alex Lowe Charitable Foundation.

It felt good and right to think that I could reach out and help the indigenous cultures of the remote places where Alex had traveled. I knew he had loved the Sherpas, the Inuit, the Tibetans, and the Baltis. He had lived and laughed with them, felt their kindness and their pride, accepted and admired their simple and ancient ways and the hardships that they faced with dignity in their daily lives.

His friend Ali Khan wrote, "He was not a sahib, he was a Balti brother." Indeed, it seemed that Alex had found a closeness with his Balti cook beyond any brotherhood he had with many of his climbing partners. As I reread Alex's letters from Trango, I felt sure that this was a way for me to go forward and honor his memory, to keep his spirit alive in the hearts of many.

On December 3, we held a public memorial service for Alex at the University Fieldhouse in Bozeman. Several thousand attended. Conrad and Jon Krakauer drove up from Boulder together to appear as guest speakers for the evening along with a handful of other friends. Jan and Murray returned for a few days, my father came from nearby Butte, and many friends and relatives came from out of town. I stood beneath the bleachers with Jon, shaking as people filed in. "I'm nervous," I admitted, pulling a beer from the pocket of my down coat. "I'm not too good at this."

"Neither am I," Jon said emphatically, opening his own beer. "I usually avoid crowds." Then he added as an afterthought, "Alex was a great speaker."

Gordon Wiltsie generously put together a beautiful slide presentation, and Chris Naumann, our friend who managed a local climbing shop, arranged the entire evening. Looking out at the large gathering of people who had come, I was reminded once more how lucky my children and I were to live in this caring community. My oldest son inspired me with his strength as he bravely climbed to the podium to play his fiddle. The program was a beautiful tribute but evoked in me the same mixture of panicky loss and drained emotion that I had experienced two months before. As I walked home from the large gymnasium, I was ready to be finished with memorials.

Most of the climbers who had come from other places took advantage of the good ice conditions in Hyalite Canyon over the next few days, and Conrad and Jon were among them. Jan and I drove to meet them after their ice climb, for a most important tradition—cutting our tree and gathering firewood. We always got a permit to cut a Christmas tree, and aside from the one December that Alex was in Antarctica, we had done this as a family for nearly a decade, following the tradition of both of our Montana families. Trudging into the woods with a flask of hot cocoa, we would drag sleds with bundled children aboard while Annie leaped about, rolling and digging in the snow.

This year I dreaded the task, knowing the private anguish I would feel, but Jan and Murray brought a positive note (and a thermos of chili) to the expedition, as did the climbers. Conrad was immediately "in the spirit," scooping Isaac to his shoulders and tossing snowballs about with the other boys. "Oh yeah—we always go out and cut a tree at Priest," he sang out. "This is awesome!" I could feel his joy and see the happiness he brought to the boys as we inspected spruce and fir. He and Jon wielded the chainsaw and gathered a suitable amount of firewood to keep the occasional fires burning in our fireplace through the winter.

Afterward Jan and Murray went home with the promise of returning for Christmas, and Jon said goodbye as well. Conrad spent his last day with us in Yellowstone, where we hiked the boardwalks of Mammoth, then soaked in the steamy water of Chico Hot Springs. I sat against the edge of the pool watching Conrad play with the boys, tossing them into the air and cheering their antics as they sang, "Watch me, watch me." Steam drifted over the pool, and I felt as though I were suspended in a dream. Tears mixed with mineral water as I grieved Alex's greatest loss—that he would not watch his children grow up and would never know them as men.

We had dinner after swimming, and I sketched out a drawing while waiting for burgers and fries. It was the first drawing I had done since September. In my small journal, I drew a mother bear walking out across a field, with three cubs before her and a starry sky above. I scrawled out a poem, then tucked it into my purse for a later time. When I dropped Conrad at the airport to continue on his book tour, I felt a pang of sadness and confusion at his parting.

I knew that Conrad wanted to end his engagement. He had told me so in one of our many long conversations, but I still sensed that his path led elsewhere, and although I appreciated his kindness, I thought of my own future and that of the boys as separate from his. I saw myself as stoic and alone, leading them forward through life, consulting them like little men: "Well, boys, what shall we do for dinner, for Christmas, for spring break? What shall we do this evening?" We were used to this life, as Alex had been away so often, but I realized how very much I had relied on Alex's love for my strength. And corresponding with Conrad had been a great solace, a continuation of sorts.

I was surprised when he asked to come for Christmas, telling me that it would be very meaningful to him. Alex had spoken of the coming holiday on the night before the avalanche. He had told Conrad how much he was looking forward to Christmas and being home with the kids this year, sharing their excitement. "I guess so, sure . . . ," I said, but wondered whether it might be a bit awkward. "We'll have Jan and Murray with us too."

Near Christmas, he arrived alone and quietly walked in the back door while Jan cooked, Murray played violin with Max, and Sam and I danced about, swinging Isaac into the air. When I looked up to see Conrad watching us, my heart quickened. Was this man becoming more meaningful to me than perhaps was right?

The next day was Max and Sam's Christmas program and Conrad came, along with Suzanne, Jan, and Murray. He sat on one side of me and Suzanne sat on the other with Isaac in her lap. As soon as the children filed to the stage, I fell apart. Suzanne handed me a tissue and patted my leg while Conrad gently placed his arm around my shoulder.

Back home, he settled in to watch our Christmas chaos as the boys were showered with gifts. Aside from the usual holiday feasting, skiing, sledding, and movies, we rented the Hyalite cabin for a night in the woods. In the evenings, Jan and Murray and Alex's brother Ted filled our house with the sweet sound of bluegrass, playing on fiddle, mandolin, and guitars, singing songs of love and loss.

I remembered Alex telling me about Conrad with great excitement after their first trip together, to Russia in 1993. I eventually met him and was struck by his soft-spoken demeanor. He had visited us a couple of times in Bozeman to climb with Alex and kindly offered to babysit the boys, giving Alex and me a night out alone. I never had an opportunity to really know Conrad, except through Alex's eyes.

In the year before Alex died, he wrote the following words about his favored partner for some review. I found the text on his computer:

> If true soul-mates are the gold bullion of the climbing experience, Conrad Anker is the mother lode. To extol his matchless technical and athletic climbing genius and dwell on his boundless résumé of climbing adventures misses the most remarkable and profound aspects of this unique person. Conrad's motivation for climbing is altruistic and endearingly simple—he reveres the mountains. Being in the mountains, for Conrad, is as natural and essential as breathing. . . . It's where his heart beats, where his soul abides.
>
> Conrad is also the most gentle and caring person I know. . . . He has a clear grasp of the purpose of life—to experience happiness. Happiness that stems not from dogged pursuit of personal ambitions, but from sharing other people's burdens and giving of himself, his time, possessions, and illimitable energy. When the time comes to climb, Conrad's strength and enthusiasm literally explode upon the project at hand, but along the way, his unflagging energy cultivates kindness and good will. No one who

*comes in contact with Conrad will walk away unaffected. When
I dream of a climb that scares me and tugs at my heart, I pick
up the phone and call Conrad. I know that the adventure that
follows will be life changing. He's just that kind of partner.*

When I read Alex's words, I was touched by the sincere admiration he'd had for his friend—but more than that, I was a bit spooked. I was beginning to have strong feelings for Conrad, and it seemed as though Alex was speaking to me. I was getting to know his partner through my own eyes now, but the letter gave me pause. I wondered, was I falling in love with Conrad or hanging on to Alex—or both?

By the end of the year, Conrad was back in Boulder and I called him. "Conrad," I said, "I don't know if I should see you again, and I don't think we should call each other for a bit. I'm just too vulnerable and confused . . . and so are you. I know you mean well, and I so appreciate your support through these last months, but until you sort out your own life, we need to say goodbye."

"I'm sorry," I said sadly, thinking that I would not see him for some time. I knew he was depressed, and I also knew that he had grown dependent on the boys and me for a sense of purpose. I needed to break away and let him choose his path.

"I understand," he said. "Goodbye, Jenni."

The next day he ended his engagement, packed up his car, and drove away to his parents' home at Priest Ranch in Big Oak Flat, California. Meanwhile, I opened my journal and read the poem that I had hurriedly written next to the sketch of the bears I'd drawn at Chico:

> *One autumn night a mother bear ambles forth in cool night air.
> Three cubs around her dance along, listening to the night's still song
> While overhead in darkened sky, the big bear also travels by,
> Always there to lead them on quietly into the dawn.*

I began to create a painting for the first time since Alex had died. I made the sky deep purple speckled with stars, and among them drew the shape of a bear walking forward. The purple then turned into the yellow of a dawn horizon over mountains of blue. The forms of a grizzly bear sow with cubs emerged against the morning mist. They walked upon blood-red grass, their blue shadows falling across the earth, that undeniable place of life and death.

I named the finished piece *Into the Dawn*, intending to create a limited-edition print whose proceeds would benefit the Alex Lowe Charitable Foundation. And with its completion I returned once again to my studio and the recesses of my imagination, making images of the birds and animals that I loved. They appeared in twos and in threes: bears in fields of white lilies, and howling wolves singing the blues; mother hens on piles of eggs; swallows, chickadees, nighthawks, and magpies swooping, and big yellow moons.

In mid-January, I agreed to allow *Dateline* NBC to come to Bozeman for an interview that they had requested since October. "Tom Brokaw will be the correspondent for this story," they had written to my lawyer. "As a member of the climbing community, he is exceptionally able to guide the viewer through Alex's world and has a personal interest in the story. Mr. Brokaw would like to interview Jennifer Lowe and Conrad Anker." Yvon Chouinard and Rick Ridgeway had both assured me of Brokaw's intent to portray Alex with honor. Three months had passed, so I agreed to do the interview, thinking that I would be more able to remain composed.

Conrad flew back to Bozeman for two days, and I was thankful to have him at my side as I faced the camera crew and the well-known newsman in my living room. Both of us were nervous, but somehow Conrad's fragile mental state gave me the impetus to be strong.

The interview gave me an opportunity to honor Alex, to speak of the foundation, and to thank the many people who had offered their love and support over the previous months. At one point Brokaw asked Conrad, "What was it like for you and Andrew to make that phone call?"

"Probably the most difficult, worst phone call ever," Conrad answered quietly. I knew he was near the breaking point, and I instinctively reached out to take his hand.

The *Dateline* story was aired on January 21. It triggered another wave of mail from people across the country, extending their sympathy, admiration, and support. I did not know most of the writers but read every letter and was filled with gratitude. "I have somehow followed Alex's climbing adventures and your career as an artist," said one of the letters. "Alex's death has affected me deeply—I wish I could offer some words of comfort for you and your family. Oddly, you have comforted me and showed me how to be a better person."

Most of the writers said they were not climbers, and many spoke with reverence of the love that Alex and I shared. "I cannot begin to imagine the strength you possess allowing you to inspire and support the man whom you loved, sometimes a world away. . . . I only hope to find a relationship in which love is so selfless."

Their words were comforting, but they also made me keenly aware of my lonely status. A widow. A widow. I wondered if I would ever again feel the enduring love that I had shared with Alex for so many years.

But Conrad continued to write to me lovingly:

Dearest Jenni, May this find you in happy spirits. I think of you every day, with awe and admiration for your strength. Being with you is wonderful. Your presence, however far, is comforting in this period of grief. May I bring to you comfort and happiness? Love, Conrad

I wrote back, thanking him for the gift of his compassion and love. But privately, bewildered by my swirl of emotions, I reached out to others for guidance. "I think I am falling in love with Conrad," I told my friends and relatives. "What should I do?"

"He is so wonderful, I don't blame you," my sister Jan said, "but be careful."

"Jenni, I trust your instincts completely," said my friend Maddy. "You have made every decision over the last few months with such clarity."

"Life can be short," said my great-aunt Margie, who was nearly one hundred. "Alex is gone now—but you aren't. Live your life."

I searched within myself. I knew I would grieve for Alex for many months, perhaps years, but sharing that grief with Conrad had eased my burden. And it seemed that Conrad's presence in my life was a good thing for me and for my children. I had never felt so needy in my entire life, and though the cautious side of me said "Wait," my heart was filled with love for Conrad. I knew what Alex would have told me: "Follow your heart."

Then, in early spring, another friend reached out to us: Dr. Gil Roberts, a member of the first successful American Everest expedition in 1963. He knew the pain of survivor's guilt, having lost his own climbing partner, Jake Breitenbach, in the treacherous Khumbu Icefall years before. Now his own time was short—he had been diagnosed with cancer—and he wrote frankly:

> *Dear Conrad and Jennifer, Normally I would be more discreet but we all know the climbing grapevine. I seem to be off on my own expedition so I'll be presumptuous and say this. I really don't know either of you well but I sure like you both and I think it's great you are getting together. A very brave and honorable thing. I'm very impressed and it makes me happy. . . . Alex had big shoes but Conrad may be one of the few dudes who can fit into them, and I don't mean just as a super climber. Love to you both. You are good people. Gil*

The letter took both Conrad and me by surprise. Although we had grown close through our phone calls and letters, we had spent less than three weeks in each other's company since Alex had died. But it encouraged us to see where the love and compassion that we felt for each other might lead. I now feel indebted to Gil for the confidence he gave us.

"Go to Antarctica," I suggested to Conrad.

Before his death, Alex had agreed to participate, together with noted climbers Reinhold Messner and Stephen Venables, in an expedition to cross South Georgia Island in the footsteps of the great polar explorer Sir Ernest Shackleton. The journey was to be filmed by the respected documentarian George Butler, in a venture coproduced by White Mountain Films and Nova/WGBH Boston. Alex had looked forward to it with excitement.

Following Alex's death, Butler had written to me from South Georgia on October 29:

> Yesterday, about twenty of us gathered around Sir Ernest Shackleton's grave overlooking Grytviken Harbor. We spoke briefly, remembering two souls who were much a part of this filmmaking enterprise: Shackleton and Lowe.
>
> It was an azure spring day; sunny and a very clear blue. Some wind. Above us in grass tussocks, sooty albatross nested. From time to time, one flew by. Beneath us a loud colony of elephant seals grunted at the harbor's edge.
>
> Shackleton and his admirer, Alex—and all of us, together for you. We send greetings and remembrances from the Antarctic perimeter.
>
> Onward, George Butler

Now Butler was offering Conrad a place on the expedition. "Who do you think Alex would wish to take his place?" George had asked me. It seemed a perfect way for Conrad to move forward in his life. It was an opportunity to honor both Shackleton, whom Alex had held in the highest esteem, and Alex himself. Even more importantly, it would give Conrad the chance to regain faith in the life he had chosen for himself, that of a mountaineer and explorer. He accepted, and planned to leave at the end of March.

Mom was not happy when I told her of my feelings for Conrad. "It's too soon, Jenni," she said, "and another climber!"

"Mother, he is a great comfort and very kind to all of us. Don't worry," I told her. But my fear of losing her drove me to lean even more on Conrad. It was terrible to think of my mother not being there for me, especially now, as I struggled to find my footing. I spoke to her nearly every day, and she told me of the treatments she was undertaking, hoping to prolong her life. She became tired and sick. She lost her hair. Even so, it was difficult for me to see her as anything but strong and busy. I sent her letters, pictures, and gifts from the boys, and she sent them loving letters in return.

I planned a spring break for the kids and me in California, an escape from the long Montana winter. Alex and I had long talked of a trip to Disneyland—oddly, it was his idea—and the boys had looked forward to it. "Can we still go?" they asked now, and I decided to take a chance: I invited Conrad to join us. "This is a test," I told myself, thinking that any bachelor climber in his right mind would avoid amusement parks. But he accepted instantly, and we stood beneath the tiny Matterhorn in Disneyland as I thought of Alex soloing the real thing long ago. Isaac perched on Conrad's shoulders in the endless long lines, and we flung ourselves about on lots of rides.

Our minivan was packed with gear and littered with toys, books, and empty juice boxes. As Conrad drove along the sunny coast, Max asked out of the blue, "Are you going to marry my mom?" I cringed, glancing over at the man who had just extracted himself from an engagement. "I would love to marry your mom," he said, "but these things take time." I sighed thankfully, but Max did not stop there. "What would you do if my dad came back?" he asked. I caught my breath and Conrad paused, then answered, "I would be the happiest guy in the world . . . I loved your dad, but I was there when he died, and I know that he can't come back. I'm sorry, Max," he said, and reached to touch my son's hand.

Staying in the homes of friends, we traveled the coastline to run on sandy beaches and play in salty surf. We visited Legoland, which was the boys' idea of heaven, and the Getty Museum, which was mine. In Joshua Tree National Monument, we camped among the granite spikes and domes scattered between cactus and desert sands. The boys chased lizards and climbed on boulders, and we slept beneath the stars with coyotes singing.

And joy returned to our hearts.

Then the boys and I went back to Montana, and Conrad returned to Big Oak Flat. Early in April, Max received a letter from Montevideo, Uruguay, where Conrad was preparing to set sail to South Georgia Island with the Shackleton film crew:

March 31: Greetings Max, I hope this letter finds you in good spirits. Thanks for accepting me into your life. I love your mother greatly as she is a wonderful person. Your father was undoubtedly my best friend. Given the turn of events, the way we are together is quite good. My outlook on life is most joyous—I cherish each and every day. Your mother, aunt and uncles, grandparents and myself are immensely proud of you. Your enthusiasm for life is a wonderful gift, one you share with many. I look forward with excitement to a shared adventure of your choosing—a raft trip, backpacking, a journey to the museums, a boat journey—whatever your heart desires. You are a most amazing young man, one who I would always like to help. You are most dear to my heart. Love, Conrad

Conrad emailed me from the ship, describing his daily routine:

Today I will grease my leather boots to make them more water resistant. I've been debating whether to use the leather or plastic boots, and my final choice is leather. Sir Ernest had worn-out leather boots and was a month closer to winter. If he did it, well then, so can I. After lunch I will be showing an abridged selection of Everest slides. Reinhold is keen on watching them. I feel honored just knowing he is on this journey.

As I pictured Conrad greasing his boots, I wondered if he had worn them since Shishapangma. I thought of him in his leather boots, running across the glacier, and Alex in his plastics—the painful memories that I knew would always be with him.

It seemed impossible that only a year before, I had been ready to send Alex off to Trango and I had been so engrossed in my work, not realizing the treasure of each day we had together. My heart still ached for Alex and I worried for my mother, but I was full of thanks for Conrad and the possibility of a new beginning. He brought us laughter and a sense of connection to faraway places, just as Alex had. He brought us a feeling of security and hope.

We planned for a trip to Boston to see the Shackleton exhibit when Conrad returned in late spring, and he was eager to bring us to Yosemite and his parents' ranch at Big Oak Flat. We would travel to Mongolia in late July, launching the first project of the Alex Lowe Charitable Foundation, a climbing wall in Ulan Bataar. Conrad also spoke with excitement of traveling together to Nepal, Antarctica, Pakistan, and Baffin in years to come.

"It sounds wonderful," I said, "but I don't know if I can afford all that."

"We can make it happen," he answered with confidence. It seemed that Conrad once again believed that each day needed to be lived with purpose. As he wrote while on the Shackleton expedition:

> The story of the Endurance is without question one of the most riveting tales of adventure ever. Although the goal Shackleton set out to do was never attained, something far greater than crossing the Antarctic continent resulted from the tribulations of twenty-eight men. The ability to persevere, to keep trying in the face of insurmountable odds, and the tenacity of the human body and spirit are vital lessons that supersede time. May the will and determination of Shackleton motivate our own actions.

Leap of Faith

May you live all the days of your life.
—JONATHAN SWIFT

I BEGAN LIVING LIFE URGENTLY AND INTENSELY that spring, as though I had been woken from a long hibernation. I was not sure whether my state of heightened awareness and determined energy came from a growing sense of new love or the realization that time was precious and fleeting. I prepared our breakfast each morning with children crouched over the heat vent at my feet and public radio telling me the news of the day. In a mad scramble I hunted for jackets, shoes, and packs and walked the kids to school, then returned to my day's work.

Methodically, I finished enough paintings for one show and provided work in smaller amounts to my galleries. One large painting, titled Leap of Faith, featured a cowgirl leaping from the back of one running horse to another, suspended in that moment of time where nothing is sure. Frames were spread on the workbench and floor of my garage. I pounded them with hammers and scraped them with the edge of a crescent wrench, sanding off sharp corners, then rubbed black paint into their scars to create a distressed finish. They surrounded my colorful works with a final touch before I sent them away to find new homes.

My neighbor Suzanne often joined me as I walked to meet the boys in the afternoon, pulling Isaac in his red wagon. We viewed the emerging gardens of our neighborhood with eager joy as the valley turned green beneath snow-covered peaks. The robins had announced their punctual arrival with crisp voices and a sense of elation, reminding me that seven months without Alex had already passed and my mother's life was like sand slipping through an hourglass.

I traveled the familiar road to Missoula to see Mom, but the children were too much for her fragile condition. "I don't want them to remember me this way," she said, so I left them with Suzanne and made the trip alone. Jan came to join us and Mother was filled with resolve. "I'm giving these things away—do you want them?" she asked. She sorted through clothing, dishes and jewelry, pictures, and memorabilia that Jan and I delivered to her from one closet after another. She scrawled notes to attach to items of importance, bringing order to her life and the lives of those she loved. With care, she divided the soft green mound of her shamrock plant to give a section to each of her daughters. I helped her pack and label the boxes, reminded of all of Alex's things, still not sorted, at my home.

"Mom, would you like to go somewhere . . . on a trip?" I asked her.

"Are you crazy?" she said.

"Yes," I answered, and we looked at each other and laughed.

"When I'm gone, I want you to stay close to your sisters," she told me.

"Mom!" I began to protest, not wanting to contemplate her absence, but finished sadly, "I will, I promise." My youngest sister, Camilla, joined us there with her beautiful baby daughter, Haley, who was born in the spring of 1999, and I was reminded that Haley's life had begun the same year that Alex's ended.

Gardening filled me with satisfaction as I dug a larger plot in my small backyard to remember Alex. I planted it with fistfuls of forget-me-not seeds and dozens of varieties of perennials, favoring those that also grew in the wild: lupine and larkspur, penstemon and phlox, coneflower and columbine. With Suzanne, I searched the local greenhouses for monkey flower, fleabane, and western pasqueflower, placing them gently into the ground. My neighbor Kerrie brought me tiny forget-me-not plants from her own garden, and I dug black dirt from my fingernails each night before bed.

Projects that Alex and I had begun seemed imperative to finish, and I ticked them off on a list in my head. The Disneyland trip had been one. Remodeling the kitchen and adding a laundry room was another, so I pulled the sketches that Alex and I had doodled from a drawer to show to our architect friend. Our house had been a work in progress ever since we had taken its hundred-year-old structure into our care. We had rented apartments upstairs and down until we could afford to occupy the entire place; we had painted and pulled up carpet, restored stairways to where they had once been, and slowly turned the old house back into one home. The kitchen was the final step in the process, and the one that I had most looked forward to. Construction began.

Conrad arrived from California and we traveled together to Boston, where he met with producers of the Shackleton film and we viewed the traveling exhibit at the nearby Peabody Essex Museum, looking in awe at the replica of the *James Caird*, the lifeboat that delivered Shackleton over 750 miles of treacherous open ocean to South Georgia Island.

Each evening in March when Conrad was sailing toward South Georgia, I had read to the children from Alex's tattered copy of *Endurance* by Alfred Lansing. "Does Raddy have to ride all that way in that little boat?" they asked with concern. "No, no. He is on a big ship," I explained. Even little Isaac knew of the hardship that Shackleton and his men had faced. We peered into the cramped hull of the *Caird*, trying to imagine riding for weeks within while wet, frozen, hungry, and exhausted, and being tossed about by the Antarctic sea.

We also visited the Boston Museum of Science, where Brad Washburn, a founding director and a distinguished early-day mountaineer, welcomed us with an extensive tour. Although nearly ninety, he was sprightly and sharp, full of enthusiasm, and fit and handsome. He and Conrad stood beside a model of Everest discussing Mallory's route for over an hour, and the intensity of his curiosity and passion was inspiring. "I want to be just like Brad," Conrad whispered to me. "Isn't he great?"

We stopped to see my friend Maddy and her family on Martha's Vineyard for a few nights, baptizing ourselves with Atlantic surf and breaking bread over seafood chowder. In double kayaks, our families paddled across a bay and walked gingerly among live horseshoe crabs, whose prehistoric forms littered a sandy shore. The children were fascinated with the creatures' hard curved shells and spiky tails that predate most life on earth. Meanwhile, Conrad and I walked the beach hand in hand in a dreamlike trance of love while waves rushed to shore.

Conrad's place in our lives was clear. He had been there for us emotionally from the day Alex had left us, and his presence had eased our suffering, as we had eased his. I knew that a life shared with Conrad would be similar to the one that I had shared with Alex in some respects. I also knew it could end in a similar way, even if he did choose climbs with less objective danger, as he professed he would.

But I was not deterred. I had a strong feeling that with Conrad I could continue to follow the path I had chosen with Alex, of adventure and passion and determination to live our dreams.

Our next visit was to Conrad's sister Kim, who lived in nearby Mystic, Connecticut, with her husband, Dick, and their three teenage daughters. They welcomed us warmly with barbecued chicken and cold beer and arranged for a local submarine tour, a big hit with the boys, and fishing and sailing on the nearby bay. As we sprawled on the sailboat of a family friend, hair blowing in a briny breeze and the bow slapping waves, I thought of Alex saying long ago, "We'll sail around the world with our family." "We didn't," I thought sadly, as I watched Conrad cradling Isaac in his arms and laughing with the boys. "We didn't have time to do that." I squinted into the wind, looking out at a horizon where faraway sails dotted the swell.

It had been four years since the boys and I had visited Priest Ranch, the home of Conrad's parents; Isaac had been a tiny baby. Going there now evoked a mix of emotions and memories, just like every place we'd revisited since Alex's death. But Wally and Helga welcomed us with open hearts to their home amid towering pine and gnarly oaks. The numerous lizards were instantly popular with the boys, who spent hours creeping about trying to catch the streaking creatures. Legos were pulled out of storage boxes that had rarely been opened since Conrad and his brother, Steven, had played with them. Conrad sat on the floor of the breezy guesthouse with the boys, sorting through the tiny plastic bricks and memories of his childhood with Steve and his sisters, Kim and Denise.

With pride and enthusiasm, Conrad ushered me from one corner of the ranch to another, both on foot and on the backs of two buckskin horses that came from his father's herd of roans, buckskins, and bays. It had been years since I'd held the reins of a horse and felt the powerful animal beneath me; racing back to the house along a road overgrown with grass left me giddy with a rediscovered joy. Conrad recounted the history of his grandparents' hard lives on this land and took me to the tiny local cemetery to view the gravestones that marked them in time. He took us all to his swimming hole, Rainbow Pool, where we swam in the swirling water of a cascading stream and watched Conrad dive from the cliff above.

When Albert, the great horned owl who had learned to eat from Conrad's hand, appeared on the deck our first evening there, fluffing his feathers and turning his head to stare about, we were riveted. His blinking eyes seemed to hold answers. Wild yet tamed, he was a contradiction of sorts, a curious example of holding on and letting go. In his coming, the boys and I found magic—and he found the juicy leg of chicken that Helga and Conrad offered. He spread his magnificent wings and flew off into the night as we watched, knowing that he might not come back the following day.

I remembered previous visits as we drove into Yosemite Valley in early morning and my tears flowed. Conrad seemed doubtful as I herded the whining children toward the trail, tying shoes, adjusting pack straps, and stopping for drinks before we had even reached the trailhead to set off toward the top of Half Dome.

"It's too far, I don't want to go up there," Sam cried.

"This is stupid," Max groused and kicked at the ground.

"Jenni, we don't have to go," Conrad began, but I persisted.

"They can do it," I said with resolve.

"OK. Come on, you guys!" he said quietly but firmly. "This is going to be fun—now quit acting like a bunch of fluff-kittens."

Max and Sam carried light packs and Isaac scampered along the trail behind them over rocks and up steps, around boulders and across bridges. We peered over railings at roaring rapids and stopped to look at bugs, chipmunks, rocks, sticks, little birds, and of course, lizards. We hiked the familiar trail to Nevada Falls and beyond with sun warming us after the cold shower of the Mist Trail. In late afternoon, Isaac rode on my back and fell instantly asleep before we arrived at the much-anticipated Little Yosemite campground in evening sun.

Once all of us had piled into a small tent to sleep, Conrad told stories of his youth, spent camping in the Sierra backcountry with his parents and siblings. The boys interjected with the usual rude boyhood noises that occur in a crowded tent, followed by peals of laughter. Much to their delight, Conrad joined their chorus of "Fire at will!" punctuated by flatulence. "My sisters were always trying to teach us manners," Conrad told the boys, as if it had been hopeless.

"You guys are all gross!" I informed them. They all grinned in a moment of silence, broken by Isaac, who giggled madly.

Morning arrived as we followed a trail in the soft duff of decaying cedars and pines whose offspring towered above us, winding our way upward to the base of Half Dome's cable route. With the boys in harnesses and tied to Conrad and me, we donned gloves, grabbed cables, and carefully climbed the granite dome. Half Dome's wide summit was a celebration of sorts, the first we had attained together. We built a small chorten for Alex, stacking loose rocks and arranging small pebbles to form his name, and Conrad sprawled out on sunny granite with the boys piled over him in tired bliss.

I looked about and recalled my first time on this plateau of granite, with Alex years before. I remembered, too, sleeping here beneath a full moon with my sister Jan and a friend after climbing a route called Snake Dike. We had wandered about and read various messages written in pebbles that would eventually be dispersed by wind and rain. One came to mind: "E.T., phone home," it had said. I surveyed the landscape that stretched out below, looking at all of the places I had explored with Alex over the years, and felt deep sadness. But when I looked at the heap of men before me, I couldn't help smiling.

Back at the ranch, we sat on the deck to share a summer meal with Conrad's parents. Conrad recounted our journey with pride while Wally and Helga dispensed endless praise for the boys' successful ascent of Half Dome. I was filled with a peaceful sense of belonging. A young black foal had been born at the ranch that spring while Conrad was in Antarctica, and she ran and bucked in the field below us as we picnicked. "Do you boys want to name her?" Wally proposed. Max was reading the story of Miss Chippy, the cat that been aboard the *Endurance* with Shackleton and his men. "How about Miss Chippy?" he asked. "Wonderful!" Wally proclaimed.

En route home, Conrad was a guest speaker at an annual festival of mountain films held in Telluride, Colorado. We arrived at the scenic alpine town for Memorial Day Weekend.

I had been in Telluride the year before with Alex; now I walked the streets with Conrad and the boys, remembering.

While attending one of the films there, Conrad received another piece of tragic news: his friend Seth Shaw had died while climbing in Alaska, buried by a toppled tower of glacial ice. Roommates through college, Conrad and Seth had been close and climbed together for years. The news was whispered to Conrad as we sat in a crowded auditorium, and he struggled to maintain his composure until we were alone. Then he sobbed with anguish: "It's fucked—this life is fucked!" Helpless to console him, I took the children for a walk.

"What's wrong with Raddy?" Sam asked.

"His friend died," I told him as we walked on a nearby trail.

"Everyone is dying," he said. "Poor Raddy."

In July Conrad came to Bozeman and drove south with us to Sun Valley, Idaho, for my latest art opening. I stood before my work as usual, greeting guests as they strolled through the Kneeland Gallery on the evening art walk. Conrad wandered in and out of the gallery with pride, watching after Isaac, while Max and Sam played their repertoire of fiddle tunes in the gallery courtyard. Conrad took the helm of my minivan the following day, and we traveled over Lost Trail Pass and through the Bitterroot Valley to Missoula, the place of my beginnings. We passed the place where Alex had lost the canoe in the Bitterroot River, and we passed the ranch where I had once ridden bareback across hay fields and through sandy-bottomed groves of cottonwoods with my sisters.

My mother was well enough for all of us to visit after a stretch of difficult treatments in early summer that had left her frail and exhausted. I kept abreast of her condition with Papa, who helped to soften her view of Conrad, asserting that the boys and I were lucky to have found someone so caring. "Jennifer needs to live her life, Tots," he told her gently. Papa was warm and kind, but Mother was weak and stiffly polite to Conrad at their first meeting since Alex's funeral service. At the first opportunity, she took him aside and asked him bluntly, "What are your intentions toward my daughter?"

"I intend to marry her as soon as a respectable amount of time has passed. I love her and I love her sons," he answered after a moment of surprise.

She was relieved to hear that, but gave him one last request, "Don't do to my daughter what some men do when they have tired of new love," she lectured. "I don't want her to suffer any more pain." Shocked by her boldness, he answered quietly, "I won't."

I apologized when Conrad told me of their conversation, but as always, he said he understood. He wrote and spoke kindly of Mother:

How is your mother doing? I think of her daily and how close
you are and have been to her. Visiting, calling, availing yourself

and loving her, you have made her proud to have you as a
daughter. She also receives from you affirmation that she has
done well as a mother. May we be so fortunate in our future
years. I do hope she is doing well. Her acceptance and support of
us as a family is tremendous.

Late July found us flying into the capital of Mongolia, Ulan Bataar, to launch our foundation's first project, a climbing wall. Conrad, the children, and I looked down upon clusters of round white *ghers*, the Mongolian tents that a majority of the traditionally nomadic culture still call home. They dotted the outskirts of town, with the center dominated by bleak modern structures, blocky cement relics of Soviet occupation.

Greg Mortenson had visited the city of Ulan Bataar as a guest of the Altai Club, a small local group of mountaineers from the region, and had suggested the climbing wall to me as a project. The club wanted to promote climbing as a way for the predominantly young urban population to connect to their outdoor heritage. An indoor climbing wall would provide a refuge and physical activity for city-bound youth during long dark winters, when temperatures can dip to sixty degrees below zero and alcoholism is like a plague.

Alex and I had dreamed of visiting Mongolia, so the project seemed perfect, combining an adventure that we had envisioned for our family with the first charitable nod to Alex's spirit. With the help of Greg and my lawyer, Buzz Tarlow, and with focused effort over the past eight months, we had created the foundation, nominating a board of directors, filing for tax-exempt status, raising money, and soliciting supplies from vendors. At my urging, Jonathon Knight, a veteran builder of climbing walls, volunteered his time. He orchestrated the construction of a state-of-the-art indoor wall with the help of Altai Club members and Kent Madin and Linda Svendsen, friends from Bozeman whose company, Boojum Expeditions, arranged our travels and stay.

Rick Ridgeway and his son Connor joined us to put the finishing touches of paint and plastic holds on the structure. We sorted harnesses, shoes, and ropes for the grand opening in the university gymnasium where the climbing wall was erected. We were welcomed with pomp and celebration by kind and gracious members of the Altai Club. At the ceremony were fine musicians and throat singers, mighty wrestlers and skilled archers. I wiped away tears as stories were told and songs sung about Alex, and a large portrait of him was unveiled on the wall adjacent to the climbing structure. I had never felt so honored or deeply appreciated. I looked upon the portrait of Alex's smiling face and thought of him, one year before, near the summit on Great Trango. It was surreal to think of all that had happened since then.

Conrad and Rick taught a course on safety and technique to eager students while the children and I explored the city. The mix of poverty amid modern amenities was more shocking to them than I had anticipated. We came upon Mongolian children their own age begging for food while caring for a tiny baby at the street's edge, and watched others dig through garbage. "Where is their mom?" Sam asked with concern. "I don't know," I answered, but bought loaves of bread from a nearby vendor to give them while my own children and Connor stared in sad wonder. Max, at eleven, recorded his impressions in his journal:

> The city was largely grey, dirty and crowded. Some of the people were dressed in suits and fashionable clothing while others were dressed in rags. While walking down the streets, I saw small children begging for food and money while older kids sold little trinkets. We took a cab to the only monastary to survive the Russian invasion. I went and saw the hundred foot tall golden Buddha figure and watched the monks chanting their prayers.

In the northern regions where Mongolia borders Russia, nomadic descendants of Genghis Khan still migrate with herds of yak and sheep and the Tsaatan people still travel with their reindeer. To get there after the climbing class ended, Conrad, the boys, and I traveled first by plane to the tiny settlement of Muren, by jeep to Lake Hovsgol, and then by boat to a remote shore, where we camped overnight.

In his journal, Max recorded the next day's adventure:

I awoke to the thundering of horses' hooves running into camp.
They were driven by Kent's herdsmen and they became our steeds
for the ride up over a high mountain pass. The sturdy little horses
seemed to know the trail by heart. We arrived at the camp late at
night where I crawled into bed.

Each of us rode our own small horse, aside from Isaac, who rode
in the lap of an experienced Mongolian horseman named Mishig.
"Mishig, like Michigan," he said with a wide smile. The second
day of the ride stands as one of the most memorable and magical
experiences of my life. The herdsmen, three handsome Mongolian
brothers, sang in perfect harmony as they accompanied our small
caravan. We rode through a winding river valley, flanked by mountains that reminded me of nowhere so much as my native Montana.
Their voices echoed from cliff walls as hooves splashed through
gentle currents of a winding river and we raced for mile after mile
through endless meadows where edelweiss and forget-me-nots grew
in profusion. During a welcome rest in forest shade, we found wild
blueberry bushes heavy with fruit and gorged before riding on to arrive at the vast Darhad Valley and the tiny village of Rinchinlhumbe
as the sun dropped from the sky.

Our final destination was the Boojum lodge, built at the conflu-
ence of the Tengis and Shishgid rivers. Max wrote of our time there:

Today, the local herdsman was asked to butcher a sheep for our
meals. My brothers and Connor and I came out and watched.
First he cut a hole in the live sheep's stomach then reached in and
grabbed one of its vital arteries until the animal died. Then they
carefully skinned the sheep, gutted it and proceeded to clean all
the meat off the bones. We were treated to a rodeo when several
of the herdsmen brought a wild horse to break in front of us. The
Mongolian cowboys dressed in tall black boots to their knees and
the traditional del, a robe-like jacket with a sash wrapped several

*times around the waist. They saddled the horse and took turns
riding the bucking beast until it finally walked.*

By the end of this journey, I had faith that Conrad and I would remain together. He had professed his love and desire to be there for us long before, but I had been unsure how he would handle the strain of a relationship that involved five people instead of two. I knew that traveling abroad would test his commitment. But the long flights and jeep rides with all of our gear, the tired boys being boys, and the emotional ride of our own grief did not affect his resolve. "I am the happiest I've been in my life," he told me. Our friend Rick Ridgeway, a father of three, was amazed by the tender and consistent care offered by Conrad, whose patience rarely wore thin.

And so at the end of summer, when the boys prepared to return to school, Conrad moved his belongings from Big Oak Flat to Bozeman. Stepping into my life in Bozeman was not easy for him, and I had great admiration for his bold grace in meeting teachers, friends, and members of the community who had known and loved Alex as he settled into the home where Alex had lived. But Conrad loved the cohesive chaos of our everyday life. He was instantly immersed in the foreign tasks of rousing kids in the morning, preparing their breakfasts and lunches, and delivering them to schools with books, homework, permission slips, and money for various activities. After school came violin lessons, soccer, and gymnastics; he helped with these and with the many chores of maintaining our house as he set up his office and continued the work that The North Face and his life as a professional climber demanded.

As the anniversary of Alex's death approached, I grieved for the year that Alex did not spend with us but was thankful for the love and hope that Conrad had brought. On the day, October 5, it didn't seem possible to me that a year had passed. But for Conrad, the avalanche that had changed the course of his life still haunted his dreams, and the anniversary date loomed large. We kept the children home from school to spend the day together, driving the winding roads of Yellowstone and into the Norris Geyser Basin. As steam from the earth spewed forth over yellow grasses of autumn that were dotted with bison, we walked to peer into ancient turquoise pools.

Rounding a corner in the road, I spotted a brown form emerging from red willows that lined a stream. A lone grizzly ambled along, swinging its great head slowly about and lifting its nose to the sky. "A grizzly bear!" cried the boys, who all knew that laying eyes on one of the great predators is a rare gift. We stopped to watch in awe as the beautiful animal made its way across the meadow, seemingly oblivious to the people who stared with hushed excitement. "Wow—I've never seen one!" Conrad exclaimed. Our mood lifted then, and we were filled with a sense of gratitude for each other and the life we shared in Montana, where such wonders of nature still abound.

Our closest friends were supportive of our union, although some other individuals surprised us with insensitive comments such as "Wow, that was fast" or "Did you have something going on before?" In November, Conrad scheduled a slide presentation to benefit the Gallatin National Forest Avalanche Center and was slated to tell his story of finding the body of George Mallory on Everest. Once he was introduced, I listened with a mix of shock and admiration as he began to address the crowded auditorium on a quite different topic.

"As I'm sure some of you already know," he began, "Alex Lowe died in an avalanche last year. I survived, and I don't know why. But by some miracle I'm here, and in the memory of Alex, and of carrying on what he began with his family, Jenni and Max, Sam and Isaac . . . we're together." I sucked in my breath as he paused. "And that's the best way I can honor Alex, and I just thought I'd say that and get that out there."

"Well, that was a surprise," I told him gently, later in the evening. "It was very brave. Just one thing, though . . . I know you loved Alex and want to honor him . . . and I appreciate that, but the reason you are here with the boys and me . . . is because we love each other. Right?"

He took my hands and looked at me with seriousness. "I love you dearly and genuinely. You know that," he said. "There is no way we could be together if that wasn't the case."

In November, Conrad invited me to accompany him on a week-long business trip to Japan. Alex's mother, Dottie, generously agreed to stay with the boys while we were away, and conveyed her and Jim's blessings to the two of us. We flew to Tokyo, where Conrad had lived as a child between 1970 and 1973. We visited the school he had attended and he told me about his life there as a ten-year-old. "Oh, I used to love dried squid," he announced, bringing a package to the counter of a small shop one evening. We saw the beautiful sights of Fuji and Kyoto between meetings and presentations, visiting gardens and museums and dining on sushi and noodles and green tea ice cream.

Among his other activities, Conrad was surprised to have been scheduled to appear at the opening of a movie that I dreaded seeing: *Vertical Limit*, a Hollywood film about climbers. I had watched the trailer with horror, as it showed dramatic scenes of avalanches sweeping tumbling bodies down mountainsides. Now, we learned, he was to climb on a wall erected outside of the theater at the movie's premiere, then sign posters for the crowds. "He can't do that," I told his hosts at the meeting where we saw his schedule for the first time. "The movie is too close to the tragedy that he lived just one year ago." But Conrad looked at me in surprise and said quietly but tersely, "It will be OK."

"How can you do that?" I asked him once we were in private. "It is so insensitive! They didn't even ask you. And I'm not going to that hideous film."

"You don't have to come," he said gently, "but they've made the plans . . . and it's my job. I'm sorry, Jenni, I didn't know." Despite my feelings, I ended up at the theater with him the following day as we were shuttled from place to place in Tokyo. "I'll wait outside," I told him, but ultimately could not stand the thought of him promoting a film that seemed to prey on the tragedy that had befallen us. After a few minutes, I walked off in anger into the city of Tokyo, telling no one where I was going because I did not know.

I found a traditional Kabuki theater within a mile or so, bought a ticket, and went inside. Among an audience of Japanese families, I watched the elaborately costumed actors float on and off the stage as if in a dream. Tears streamed down my face as I listened to the foreign music and words that had no meaning to my ear. Afterward, I found my way back to the movie theater and watched from across the street as Conrad climbed the wall next to giant images of the film. "Where is his dignity?" I thought in disgust.

That evening, Conrad and I had our first painful argument as I accused him of disregarding my feelings and the memory of Alex. He was equally angry with me for my rudeness to his hosts, who had been anxious and concerned about my whereabouts. "You don't understand this culture or my commitment to my job!" he raged and stomped out of our hotel into the night, while I cried myself to sleep. "I don't really know Conrad," I thought. "What am I doing here?" As morning sun streamed into the room, I awoke to a strong arm around me. "I'm sorry, Jenni," Conrad whispered. "I'm sorry too," I said, feeling terrible about the hurt and embarrassment I had caused him.

In December, Jon Krakauer, Andrew McLean, renowned mountain guide Dave Hahn, and glaciologist Dan Stone joined Conrad for an expedition to Antarctica that he had proposed. They would ski-traverse the Vinson Massif and climb a new route on the highest summit in Antarctica. Filmmakers Liesl Clark and Rob Raker would document the expedition for *Nova*, incorporating a scientist's perspective on climate change. While en route to Antarctica, Conrad wrote me an appreciative letter about the time we had spent together:

> *Greetings my dear loved ones, May this letter find you in good spirits and fine health. The time we spend together is with me always. Thinking of the highlights is very wonderful. . . . Do you recall when the boys chased the goat about? A lesson for myself in how boys are. Better to accept and redirect their energy. . . .*
>
> *Each day I think about how lucky we are to have each other and the family we have created. I think of the various things we have done. The climb up Half Dome was a highlight last spring. Remember when Isy ran up the steps on the Mist Trail? I think of being here in Antarctica together. A peninsula trip with the boys in a boat is one option.*

To be more understanding and forgiving—this is my goal with you and the boys. Smiles, love and compassion. Conrad

As Christmas approached, my mind filled with memories of past holidays. I drove to see Mom and Papa, persuading them to erect a real tree even though they hadn't had one in years. Mother had once told me that she missed the smell of evergreen needles. I brought her gifts and letters from each of the boys and gave her a tiny heart-shaped locket with her picture in one side and mine in the other. I wrote her a long letter to tell her all of the things that I wanted her to know, the kinds of things that I did not get the chance to tell Alex.

I wrote of my earliest memories of her: Mom with red-gold hair, bright blue eyes, and a laughing smile, singing funny old songs like "Get Out o' the Way, Old Dan Tucker" while going about her work. I thanked her for the images I held of her waxing our wood floors with broad swirling strokes and spading the earthy gardens in our yard. I thanked her for showing me how to plant marigolds and pansies and how to bake pies, for making jam and sewing curtains and doll clothes and dresses. I thanked her for the love and generosity she had shown my own family and for accepting Conrad, and for showing me that she could love again and life could be good after her marriage to my father ended.

The next months were a continuing mix of sorrow and joy as Mother's condition deteriorated and Conrad officially proposed marriage in a carefully orchestrated and endearing scenario that took place in our living room. Having enlisted the help of each of the boys, he knelt before me in the company of our friends Doug Chabot and Molly Merica, who had come for dinner. Max played a waltz on his violin and Conrad wore a paper hat made by Sam that said "merry me jenni," while Isaac came forth with the ring on a pillow. Doug popped the champagne after Conrad popped the question, and we all toasted our future with great joy.

We decided to wed in Italy, early in April. "Elope!" Mother

encouraged. "Go on a trip and enjoy yourselves." She was filled with relief to know that Conrad and I would be married. In the last weeks of her life, Jan and I went to Missoula to help care for her along with Papa, his daughter Linda, and the local hospice. "I'm going to die at home," Mother said. "I don't want to be in a hospital." She lay sleeping in the metal bed that had been delivered and set up in the living room, where morning sun streamed through picture windows. We listened to her labored breathing and ministered to her needs until late each night. In a nearby guest room, Jan and I slept in twin beds next to each other, just as we had in childhood, and talked late into the night of our lives and the twists of fate that had befallen us since we were children. And we waited, just as children might have waited, for some fearful thing to happen in the night. With Jan there, I felt braver, for she was a pillar of strength and caring, acceptance and grace, just as she had been when Alex died.

"Remember when we were in Yosemite that time, waiting for a shuttle on that bench?" Jan said one night.

"No," I said.

"There were these three guys who sat in front of us on the curb," she said, giggling. "You leaned over and whispered to me, 'I think they bought a package of Fruit of the Looms and divided them up.' It was the funniest thing!"

Then I remembered. We were sitting in the hot sun, looking at the bare backs of these three ratty climbers on the curb before us—and each had a stripe of brilliant clean white underwear sticking out above their filthy shorts.

"Oh God, I do remember that!" I said, and we began to laugh at that goofy memory until tears soaked our pillows and we fell asleep.

One morning, Mother slept in a morphine fog while Jan and I stood beside her to give Papa a rest. He was tireless in his vigil, sleeping beside her at night to hold her hand. Mom had not been coherent for a couple of days, and Jan and I stood on either side of her sleeping form, rubbing lotion on the hands that had cared for us since birth. Jan began to sing very quietly, "Some bright morning when this life is over, I'll fly away." I joined her for the chorus, "I'll fly away, oh Lordy, I'll fly away."

Suddenly, Mom stirred and opened her blue eyes. "What are you singing for?" she asked, seemingly annoyed.

"Hi Mom. No reason—just for fun," I told her, as though caught in a naughty deed.

"Oh," she said, then squinted at the window and asked, "What's that light?"

"The sun," I told her. She smiled, squeezed our hands, and closed her eyes.

Jan and I looked at each other with surprise.

It was the last thing I would hear my mother say. Conrad was caring for the boys and due home from camping. It was St. Patrick's Day, and I had been away for a week, so I decided to drive home and have dinner waiting for them. "I'll be back," I told Jan and Papa and kissed my mother's cheek as she slept. During the three-hour drive, I sang over and over, "When I die, hallelujah by and by, I'll fly away!" and tears washed over my cheeks.

Moments after I stepped in the back door of my kitchen, the phone rang. "Mother died," Jan told me.

The house was silent. I walked to my kitchen sink, filled a pitcher, and watered the wispy shamrock that Mom had carefully divided. Then I wept.

"I'll postpone our wedding," I said to Papa the next day.

"No, Jennifer . . . your mother looked forward to that so much. Go on your trip, and know that your mom is happy for you."

Within weeks, Conrad and I flew to Rome with Max, Sam, and Isaac, where we toured the relics of temples and ruins, walking through the history of ancient time. We stared up at the mythical ceiling of Michelangelo's Sistine Chapel, something I had always dreamed of seeing, and with great celebration I told the children of its importance to art historians and people throughout time.

Sam and Isaac amused themselves by clomping noisily on the marble floors, and I shushed them with exasperation every few minutes. They were more fascinated with the thought that the pope lived on the other side of the enormous wooden door than with anything else. I remember Conrad, Max, and I turning our eyes from the angels above to see Sam and Isaac on hands and knees, trying to peer beneath the door. "Sam!" I chastised, dragging him away, while Conrad swung Isaac to his shoulders.

"Who's the pope?" asked Isaac.

"He's like a king," Sam explained.

"No he's not, you dummy," Max chimed in. About that time, Conrad gallantly offered to take them outside so I could enjoy the masterwork of Michelangelo in peace.

We traveled by train to the coastal city of Naples, where our friends Topher and Kim Gaylord met us to help plan our wedding. Conrad and I did not want a large gathering, for fear it would remind us of funerals. That evening over pizza and wine we paged through guidebooks, with Kim calling potential venues to check on last-minute availability. The next day, Conrad's parents arrived on the *Queen Elizabeth* II, on a cruise to celebrate their fiftieth anniversary. Conrad, the boys, and I helped carry their overnight bags to a rental car, and we all drove south to the place we had chosen, the Villa Maria in the tiny town of Ravello.

Perched above the Amalfi Coast on a hillside of lemon orchards and vineyards, the Villa Maria was reachable only via switchbacks of narrow cobbled streets that climbed steeply up and up. An entrance of wisteria-covered arbors welcomed us, and we were shown to our simple rooms. A few hours later, Conrad donned his tuxedo and I my ivory dress, and all of the boys were spiffed up in jackets and ties. I carefully hooked my mother's pearl necklace about my throat and walked to the patio, shedding some tears along the way. A bouquet of orange roses was delivered into my hands, and we stood in our finery beneath a lone pine with Wally and Helga, Topher and Kim.

Topher ministered our wedding with feeling, celebrating the strength of our love, while Kim captured the memories on film. Then we strolled arm in arm across the garden to a wall that overlooked the sea far below. "A lizard!" Isaac cried as he spied the creature soaking up the last vestige of sun. The moon rose full in the pink glow of evening, and in that moment life could not have felt any sweeter or more beautiful.

The Endless Knot

The best way to predict the future is to create it.
—Peter Drucker

Alex spoke often of his passion for the mountains and his desire that his three sons might one day understand. "I hope they see in me the ability to believe in yourself and follow your passions," he said. "Be passionate about something. That's my fundamental desire for them."

I determined to take the boys to the faraway places that Alex had loved. By journeying to that wild, I thought they would come to know the man he had been and learn something of themselves and of life as well. And what better way for us to go than in the company of Alex's best friend, now my husband and their father. As Conrad and I began our life together, we shared a goal of raising the children to be caring and good citizens. We hoped to show them the wonders of wild places and to impart awareness and compassion for our planet, its many species of life, and its many cultures of men, in hopes that they would find their own passions along the way.

Conrad's life and livelihood were the mountains, and he continued to pursue his calling. His discovery of Mallory on Everest had a lasting impact on the course of his career, launching him into the limelight on a wave of media coverage, and it helped to assure his employment as a professional athlete and speaker. His job security increased after the Vanity Fair Corporation, another apparel maker, purchased the floundering North Face. He went on with his work, planning for an expedition to Pakistan.

His objective was a peak in the Karakoram of Pakistan called K7. I felt very connected to the high villages and the indigenous people I had come to know through Alex's letters and the stories of my dear friend Greg Mortenson. I was prepared to send Conrad off at the end of May with confidence that he would have a safe and meaningful journey, bearing gifts for some of the families that we had corresponded with, including Ali Khan.

May was a time to tend gardens and clear their beds of winter debris and emerging weeds, turning black soil to add compost for a new season of growth. Conrad had joined me in the garden on a warm day in the first week of May when we received a call telling us the terrible news of another accident. Hans Saari, a gifted Bozeman skier and climber and a member of the Shishapangma team, had died while skiing the Gervasutti Couloir on Mont Blanc du Tacul. He was thirty, a graduate of Yale, a cellist, and a good friend. After Alex's death Hans had stopped by often, bringing us cookies and small gifts. His death sent Conrad and me spiraling backward to the losses of Alex and Seth as we grieved the passing of yet another bright young soul. I fought feelings of fear and anxiety as Conrad departed for K7.

Summer began, and our house filled with boys of every age. I worked in my studio, and the boys came and went to nearby parks and the pool. One morning I rallied the kids for a hike to nearby Sacajawea Peak, high in the Bridgers. As we plodded up the skirt of moraine, a shaggy white goat stood backlit against the sky on the craggy summit, watching our progress. But the animal was nowhere to be seen when we climbed the last steps to the summit. I surveyed the alpine basin below and the long spine of the Bridgers as hawks circled above us, gliding on updrafts. Springhill Pavilion was visible in the valley to the north and I looked upon it, thinking of Alex's service there and how much time had passed. The boys were visibly changed already. "Let's go, Mom," Max said, bringing me back to the present. He started off down the trail at a fast clip, racing for the promise of a visit to Dairy Queen.

Conrad called me twice weekly to report on his progress, but storms had pinned him and his partners, Jimmy Chin and Brady Robinson, on the mountain. As they used up their food and fuel, their chances of reaching the summit decreased. I was greatly relieved when they descended to the safety of base camp and reported that they were on their way out. It was only when I saw Conrad's slides that I questioned the seriousness of the route in regard to objective danger, and I confronted him.

"You said you wouldn't take those risks," I said. "I trusted you."

"I didn't," he said. "It was unsafe, and I came down."

"But you were lucky to get a break in the weather, right? What if you hadn't?" I asked pointedly.

"It's fine, Jenni. I'm fine. And I get your point. Do you want me to quit climbing?"

"No," I said. I knew that he was aware of the anguish that Alex's death had caused all of us. I knew that he weighed the risks he took with every decision he made. And I knew that trust was the basis of our love and that ultimately, I had no control of his life or mine—or the boys'. Our lives would end when they ended.

The tragedy of Shishapangma shaped the course of Conrad's life beyond his commitment to the boys and me. With the avalanche had come an acute awareness that there was more to life than climbing and that the time we each have to make a difference is short. The loss strengthened his already benevolent spirit. In Conrad, I was surprised to find one of the more charitable individuals I had met.

Although he had been a single and fairly transient climber for the entirety of his adult years, his parents had instilled in him the desire to do good, and he had given both money and time to many good causes while possessing little more than his clothes and his climbing rack and an ancient Toyota sedan that he fondly referred to as the Silver Bullet. Alex had dubbed Conrad's apartment the "Zen den" for its sparseness, and when Conrad arrived in our old home, with all of its amenities and entrapments, toys and clutter, it was most certainly a big adjustment. There was a lawn to mow and gardens to tend, walks to shovel and gutters to clean, along with the care of kids, pets, and a hundred-year-old house that requires attentive maintenance. It was a far cry from the Zen den, but he adapted admirably.

As autumn arrived, more tragedy befell our family when Conrad's sister Kim lost her husband, Dick, to cancer quite suddenly in October. They had driven through Montana and stayed with us just weeks before, having no inkling of his illness. Dick and I had fished a stream beneath the Spanish Peaks, where he cast his fly to cutthroat trout, and we all picnicked in the tall grasses of late summer, poking at a campfire until dark.

Conrad traveled to be with his family in Big Oak Flat during Dick's final days and grieved deeply with his sister and her daughters, as we were reminded once again that life has no guarantees. Conrad and I clung to each other as death kept calling for people who were part of the fabric of our lives. In our two years with each other, grief was the most prevalent force in our relationship. Indeed, loss was arriving with such regularity that it seemed difficult to do anything but go forth with purpose, giving the boys and each other as much of ourselves as we could.

Conrad was a regular visitor to the boys' classrooms and schools, finding solace in helping them with homework, sharing his adventures in class presentations, and accompanying them on field trips and class outings. I was continually aware of the gift of his being there as I adjusted to the quirks and habits that accompany any new person who comes into one's daily life. And I knew that his adjustment was far greater than mine, having gone from bachelor to husband and father of three.

Conrad's job provided him with plenty of opportunities to explore the globe, but the growing demand for his services as a lecturer gave him the chance to bring his new family with him, to show us some of the places we had long dreamed of going. A wilderness-travel symposium and trek in Kathmandu was the first such opportunity that Conrad and I took. He was invited to be a guest speaker at the symposium, called "Perspectives on the Himalayas," which was to benefit the

American Himalayan Foundation and honor the fiftieth anniversary of the first ascent of Everest by Sir Edmund Hillary and Tenzing Norgay. Afterward, we would trek with a group to Everest base camp, over the Cho La pass to Gokyo, and back down to Lukla. We would hike up the renowned and beautiful Khumbu valley, a region so precipitous, rugged, and remote that only foot travel is possible there.

The trip would be our honeymoon, and Dottie would stay with the boys. We would go to this high place to celebrate the happiness of sharing our lives, but also to share a pilgrimage of healing. Conrad would be going to the Himalaya for the first time since the tragic Shishapangma trip, and I for the first time ever. We would not go to Shishapangma herself, but we would walk among our memories, among her sister peaks, and along a rugged, winding trail in the most celebrated mountains on earth.

Going out into the greater world together brought us the intrigue and excitement of exploring and the hope of putting our own life's tragedies into perspective. Jan and Murrray spoke excitedly of joining us, and with great anticipation we planned for Nepal the following spring.

But plans changed. Early in 2002, Jan's breast cancer returned, in the form of a tiny spot in her sternum. I despaired, despising the insidious disease, but tried to take heart from Jan's positive outlook as she faced another round of treatment. "Today is another beautiful sunny day," she wrote me. "My thoughts are turning to gardening. Another sign of spring—a small flock of Canada geese landed in the back pond. We wondered if they were some of the babies that have hatched on the little island over the last few years."

While Conrad and I departed for Nepal, Jan was relegated to treatments and rest. I would think of her often from the villages high in the Khumbu as I trekked with Conrad, and I would spin prayer wheels and light many candles with her in my heart as we carried on toward the south face of Everest.

Our flight was dropping into the Kathmandu valley, and I peered from the window in wonder that I had finally come here. Alex had traveled to the Himalaya on nine expeditions, but for one reason or another, I had never joined him. A morning mist separated the low emerald hills and waking villages from the jagged peaks that crowned the horizon. The landscape of the Kathmandu valley is a patchwork of terraced paddies and fields, producing everything from rice, corn, and wheat to chili peppers and brightly colored flowers. The city itself seemed a patchwork of history, culture, and mystery as we descended over temples, markets, and crowded streets to land. I was filled with excitement to be here, but I was keenly aware that I was walking in Alex's footsteps, some of the last that he took before climbing to the flanks of Shishapangma.

Immersed in the sensual surroundings of Kathmandu, Conrad and I attended presentations by an impressive list of Himalayan experts including Sir Edmund Hillary, legendary field biologist George Schaller, and renowned photographer Galen Rowell. We visited temples that were beautifully restored, and artisans' workshops where craftsmen plied their trades of woodcarving, weaving, and bronze casting. In our free time we poked around the shops and restaurants of Thamel, the tourist center of the city, and explored Pilgrims Book House, which had been one of Alex's favorite haunts.

We visited the Baudhanath, an enormous Buddhist shrine on the outskirts of the city, circumambulating its magnificent form to spin prayer wheels as we walked. Alex had sent me many postcards of this beautiful stupa over the years, with its wise eyes and thousands of prayer flags flying from its gilded pinnacle. His last visit here was with Conrad in 1999, and the remaining members of the Shishapangma team all made a pilgrimage to this spiritual place after the tragic end to their expedition. They lit a thousand butter lamps to honor their lost friends and stared into the fragile, flickering flames as they thought of the two lives that had burned brightly but were now extinguished.

On the day that Conrad and I flew from Kathmandu to Lukla, I thought of Alex describing the same flight to me when he had taken it years before. I could see his one lifted eyebrow and wide grin as he told me how the plane dropped from the sky toward the tiny uphill runway with a mountain rising like a great wall behind it. He loved being delivered in such a fashion to this magical Himalaya, this highest place on earth. "You've got to see it," he said. "We've got to get over there together, Jen!"

Now, two and a half years later, I was coming to see the earthly giants. It was odd how significant they were in my life, how often I'd pictured them or seen Alex's beautiful photos of them. He had brought the Himalaya to life for me with his eloquent descriptions and complete love. His intense enthusiasm for the telling of an experience always sucked me in and gave me the feeling that I too had lived it in part.

Conrad and I sat in the tiny Twin Otter jammed with other trekkers and piles of gear, the smell of fuel and the roar of the engines making it an adventure in and of itself. We rose like a tiny bug over the spectacular roof of the world.

I felt overcome with emotion as we gained our first view of Everest. Chomalungma, Mother Goddess of the Earth, stood regally with a distinct plume of spindrift flying like a flag from her summit. I felt great pride knowing that both Alex and Conrad had stood atop her glorious mass, even though neither of them thought of the climb as their finest achievement. I thought of Alex on his first trip to her summit, taking baby Max's hat that he had received from the hospital in Bozeman at his birth. I could picture that tiny blue hat with a white stripe, lovingly knit and donated to the hospital by a kindly grandmother, perched on Max's fuzzy head and then transported halfway around the world and up to the summit of this planet, placed there among rock and snow by Alex's large mitted hand. Maybe it had blown away into Tibet by now or been carried off to soften the nest of a lammergeier, those magnificent bearded vultures that soar on the highest Himalayan thermals, dipping and diving with their nearly ten-foot wingspans.

I thought of Conrad traversing Everest's high north slope to find the body of George Mallory after seventy-five years, frozen in time, just as Alex is now frozen in time on Shishapangma. I wondered if someone would find Alex's body one day. I remembered hearing the NPR broadcast about Conrad's discovery. "Alex, Alex!" I had screamed in excitement. "Conrad is on NPR. He found Mallory!"

"Ha!" Alex had laughed, bounding up the stairs, "He did it! Hot damn! He did it! The Rad found Mallory." Alex was the first person to send Conrad an email of congratulations at Everest base camp.

Our plane dropped into Lukla's precipitous airstrip, now paved, where hundreds of tourists and climbers are delivered each year for expeditions. This is a walking society, one of the few left in the world where an automobile would have nowhere to go. As we shuffled off the airport tarmac, I looked around. Feeling a mix of déjà vu and anticipation, I breathed deeply of the cool mountain air and walked hand in hand with Conrad into the colorful village of Lukla.

Our gear was sorted by porters and loaded onto the backs of fuzzy yaks, which groaned and continued to chew their cud as ropes were pulled tight around their girths. Once they were securely loaded with duffels that appeared to double their size, the animals were herded off up the trail with whistles, yelps, and bells ringing as little clouds of dust rose from their hooves.

We soon followed, and I felt glorious in the long shadows of morning light, stretching my legs to begin our journey. I thought of the boys as we passed the many children in villages along the way. This would be the first time I had left them for longer than a week, and I missed their energy and presence. Being a mother of boys sometimes feels like being at the center of an ever-present tornado, and the unaccustomed quiet made me feel as though I'd forgotten something important.

The age-old trail meandered up the valley through beautiful back-lit fields of wheat, winding stone walls, and stone buildings flanking the dusty path, some perched high on terraced hillsides with colorful prayer flags flapping everywhere. Flocks of small birds rose and fell in swarms, dancing across the landscape in an orchestrated drift. The Dudh Kosi, or Milk River, carved this deep valley over centuries, cascading meltwater from glaciers and snowfields far above to valleys and villages far below. The flow of water is a constant here, and there is a comfort in the sound of its cascade.

We arrived in the village of Namche Bazaar after an exhilarating climb up the steep final switchbacks, and were drawn into a teahouse by the irresistible scent of fresh-baked cinnamon rolls wafting through the open windows. As we sat at a table sipping tea and taking in the spectacular views, I wondered if Alex had sat in this very place putting pen to paper. He'd written me about the village many years before, in 1989:

> April 4: We arrived in Namche Bazaar today. It is an amazing little village perched tenuously on the hillside some three thousand feet above the valley. Gaily painted buildings cling to the slope under snapping prayer flags, all capped by the towering snowy peaks. Truly breathtaking!

> April 5: It's another clear blue morning in Namche. Steve and I strolled up above town for the sunrise. Kwangde catches first light while Everest is outlined in silver. Stunning! We're now sitting in Khumbu Lodge having cinnamon rolls and cheese omelets and listening to Radio Nepal. It freezes at night here but days are warm. Human backs are the major mode of transport, although porters are in short supply, and we used three yaks to carry our gear here. Actually, they are dzokios—half cow, half yak. They have particularly lethal-looking horns but their temperaments are quite benign. They all wear bells and the clanging is heard all over the hillsides. I miss you an awful lot and wish like mad you were both with me.

Conrad and I spent two nights in Namche, just as Alex and Steve had. A traditional spot for acclimatization, it hosts the thousands of tourists who come to trek or climb in Sagarmatha National Park.

As the gateway village into the park, Namche had seen vast growth in the last forty years. The Sherpa people, who once herded yaks and planted potatoes for a living, had become largely dependent on the tourist industry. But there had been a lull in tourism since the attacks of September 11, 2001, and the rise of

Maoist guerilla activity and violence in Nepal. Although foreigners had not been targeted by the rebels, the tourist economy saw a sharp downturn. The royal army had taken over the museum above Namche as a base from which to guard the Khumbu from Maoist insurgents.

Not surprisingly, we found the streets relatively quiet, and we were warmly welcomed by locals eager to sell their wares. Our sirdar, the Nepali trek leader Sherup, owned the comfortable Panorama Lodge, where we stayed. Built on the hill just below the museum, it afforded a bird's-eye view.

We joined a few others from our trekking group to hike up the hill and take in the sunrise. From the vantage of the hilltop where the museum is perched, we could watch the first rays of sun come reaching around the world to touch its very top with a silver halo. The museum had been cordoned off with barbed wire and was housing the military.

Walking to a point just below the museum on a well-worn path, we tried to position ourselves for a good view of the southwest face. "Let's drop down this ridge just a bit," suggested Conrad, but I was reluctant to leave the path with armed guards standing about in the grey light. My fears were confirmed in a few moments when two young soldiers sauntered toward us and continued some twenty feet down the ridge, where they stopped to disarm a pipe bomb, pulling it from beneath a juniper clump. We stared in amazement as they wandered back to their compound with hardly a glance our way.

A few barking dogs and crowing roosters pierced the quiet dawn as yak bells clanged on shaggy necks here and there in the village below. The rooftops and timbers of buildings turned from grey-black to bright blue, crimson, and kelly green against the stark white of carved stone as the mountain village came to life. In the juniper bushes and grasses nearby, tiny wrens and finches flitted about, beginning their daily rituals, oblivious to the endless sea of snow-capped, craggy peaks that surrounded us. We were silent, observing the extraordinary beauty of this world above the clouds. When the first streak of sun glinted off the summit of Chomalungma and her dark silhouette was lit by a silver glow, warm tears spilled off my cold face. They were tears of sadness for Alex not being here and tears of grateful relief that Conrad was. They were tears for the boys being so far away at this moment, when life felt fragile yet miraculous, and tears of jubilation for being a humble visitor on our amazing planet and having the gift of another day.

Our next night found us at Tengboche, where we camped on a precipitous knoll that afforded an incredible view of this famous Buddhist monastery, with the mountain called Ama Dablam rising gloriously behind. The monastery had been beautifully restored after a devastating fire in 1989. Tengboche is a destination for many trekkers, who visit the richly adorned sanctuary to witness the daily prayers of resident monks in flowing maroon-colored robes. Wooden altars are intricately carved and brightly painted, and incredibly detailed murals of goddesses, deities, and sacred realms grace the walls. An enormous gilded Buddha sits cross-legged in the lotus position at the head of the hall, as if orchestrating the prayers of the monks who emulate his pose. I learned that he is Sakyamuni, the Buddha of the Present. "Fitting," I thought, as I listened to the deep, resonating voices of monks chanting their prayers in the dimly lit room while streaks of sunlight filtered through a haze of burning incense.

Wherever we walked in the villages lining the pathway into the Khumbu, we saw the endless knot, decorating windows and doorways, adorning rugs and blankets, even on the headstalls of burros. A sacred emblem of Tibetan Buddhism, its intertwined lines overlap and continue with no beginning or end. It is said to represent many things: the intertwining of wisdom and compassion, death and rebirth and the infinite nature of life ongoing. Alex and I had chosen wedding rings that bore the symbol to represent infinite love.

The stunningly beautiful Ama Dablam rises to dominate the eastern sky as one treks toward Everest. Before we had children, Alex and I talked of climbing it together. I was a confident alpine climber at the time, and upon seeing pictures of this exquisite peak, I was eager to stand on her summit.

"Alex, do you think I could climb Ama Dablam?" I asked.

"Of course—with me as your guide," he teased. He later soloed the peak on one of his trips and enthused, "Jen, it's easy. We could still do it." And as I camped beneath her towering form with Conrad, I felt sadness for that lost opportunity. I looked up at the route we would have taken, and envisioned myself climbing the high snowy ridge with Alex as Conrad told me of his own ascent eleven years before in winter.

We scrambled up the moraine for a lunch on the scree-covered mound. A blustery wind whipped stratus clouds across the cobalt skies overhead. I laid my head on my pack and watched them flying by like the years of my life. "If you still want to climb it, I would love to do it with you," offered Conrad.

"Thank you," I answered, touched, but knowing that my desire to climb such peaks had diminished more with the birth of each of my children and had perhaps vanished altogether with the snows of Shishapangma that took Alex.

Throughout this land one encounters chortens, pyramid-shaped cairns built from gathered stones to mark a holy place or remember a person, usually gaily adorned by prayer flags. Conrad and I hiked the steep ridge above the village of Dingboche, where several chortens occupied a lofty perch overlooking the surrounding mountainous region. Goraks, the large black ravens of the Himalaya, called to each other as they playfully rode the winds. I watched one carry off a bit of tattered prayer flag and imagined its colorful nest, like an archaeological site, with bits of humanity gathered over years of time. These birds seem wise to me, resigned to their role of scavenger, comical, clever, and ever present among the scattered disbursement of mankind.

From Dingboche, Conrad and I hiked the steep knoll past a small temple, or *ghompa*, and along the eastern side of the ravine. A pair of lammergeier were soaring on updrafts high above our heads, and we stopped to watch them whirl down in lazy spirals, then speed toward the heavens, swept away by an invisible gust. I was riveted by their presence. Conrad told me that two of these magnificent birds had appeared just minutes after the avalanche settled on Shishapangma, gliding silently over his head. It had seemed as though Dave and Alex had vanished and the birds were their spirits, soaring into the welkin above.

I walked fast to warm myself in the frosty morning, finding a rhythm. I loved this place, this day-to-day life of straining my legs and lungs to carry me ever higher, to another village, another breathtaking vantage graced by majestic peaks. I walked, watching the ground, and noting colorful splashes of flowers that were becoming familiar. I walked behind Conrad, watching his long stride and thinking how similar it was to Alex's. Alex had rarely had a partner who could keep his pace, but Conrad came close. In the first week after Alex died, when Conrad called me from Tibet and Nepal, I had a sense that a little part of Alex was still alive in this gentle voice from afar.

Walking in the clouds, we talked about each of the boys, then shared stories of our own childhoods. And of course we talked of the man we shared. Alex had lived two lives, one at home and another in the mountains. In sharing our memories, Conrad and I have come to know more fully the man we both loved.

As I looked at Conrad's fine blond hair sticking out wildly, like the cartoon character Calvin of *Calvin and Hobbes*, I mused silently over the turn that my life had taken. He is gentle, kind, and full of compassion; and he is now the only "Dad" Isaac remembers. Conrad carried him on his shoulders so much over the last year that Max and Sam accused Isaac of causing Conrad's bald spot by holding onto his wild hair like reins. "Isaac pulled your hair out!" Sam announced one day. "Don't put him on your shoulders anymore, Raddy!"

I felt the altitude as we ascended the switchbacks above the tiny settlement of Dugla, breathing hard and sweating up the steep moraine that is at the toe of the Khumbu Glacier. I pushed myself, moving steadily ahead of Conrad and alone, feeling my lungs burn and my thighs ache. The pain of pushing my body seemed to take away the pain in my soul.

At the crest of the moraine, I was greeted by a sobering but beautiful sight. Dozens upon dozens of stone chortens had been erected over the years. Each one was a monument honoring the life of a Sherpa or a climber who had died on the slopes or in the jumbled ice fields of Mount Everest, or on one of her sister peaks. They stood in regiment like miniature pyramids on the ground or rested on large boulders, with thousands of bright prayer flags and gauzy white prayer scarves fluttering in the breezes around them. It was overwhelming to think of so much life lost, all for the desire to climb a mountain or, in the case of the Sherpas, to help someone else climb a mountain. I thought of the many families who grieved as I did, whose lives had been forever changed.

When Conrad arrived, we walked among the chortens while the beautiful mountain of Tawoche loomed behind. Quietly we read the names and years that were carved into stone. Some were names we recognized; some were friends. Conrad wandered off toward a large boulder with a small cairn of stones on top and a few tattered prayer flags. He stopped abruptly and called, "Jenni, come here."

As I reached his side he began to weep, and I instinctively knew why, before I even read the words carved into the boulder: "ALEX LOWE, FRIEND," beneath the Buddhist mantra "OM MANI PADME HUM" in Tibetan script. Though it can be interpreted in many ways, it translates roughly to "follow the path of wisdom and compassion to gain purity of mind and body." We stood before the chorten and wept as all of the memories of Alex came flooding back.

As the rest of our group hiked on to our lodgings at Lobuche, Conrad and I stayed behind to restack the little cairn, retie the prayer flags, and hold each other in the buffeting wind. By the time we trudged to Lobuche, the day had disappeared with the sun. The temperature had grown cold, but the lodge provided a warm refuge as mountains turned pink in the glow of evening light and yaks bedded down beneath the stars. That night I held tight to Conrad, pulling him near me, for it is love that seems to soothe the anguish wrought by love lost. Thomas Moore wrote in *Care of the Soul*: "Our love of love and our high expectations that it will somehow make life complete seem to be an integral part of the experience. Love seems to promise that life's gaping wounds will close up and heal."

There in the dark chill air of Lobuche, with Conrad's arm around me and Everest rising above us, I had a clear understanding of the passion that Alex had felt for these high places. I had admired the bright flame of his spirit the first time I laid eyes on him. That spirit made him different from anyone I'd known, and it drew me to him like a magnetic force. Now, with Conrad, a similar spirit, I felt a sense of calm to be in the magic of the highest mountains, the place where Alex had thrived and where his soul abides.

In the days that followed, Conrad and I rejoined our group to trek down the moraine. We traversed the snowy glaciers of the Cho La pass, gingerly making our way on icy switchbacks where our porters preferred to remove their shoes, trusting more in the grip of their callused feet.

Conrad spied a frozen waterfall in one high valley, and we dug our ice climbing gear from duffels to climb it. Our Sherpa trekking guides were fascinated and followed us to the base, watching as we ascended. Then we shared our gear with fellow trekkers and offered one eager young guide, Rinji Sherpa, a chance to try. He had never held an ice ax or strapped on crampons, but he climbed with ease and a little coaching while Conrad belayed and his Nepali companions went wild with cheers of enthusiasm.

Our return took us through the lovely and serene village of Phortse, where Rinji proudly introduced his wife and baby. At 13,000 feet of elevation, their one-room stone home had a dirt floor with a fireplace in the corner. The room was filled with a dim haze of yak-dung smoke, but their hospitality was heartfelt. Conrad had worked with several other Sherpas in the village when he climbed the north side of Everest; we visited each, sharing food and drink in modest homes.

I could see that life in these high villages had many hardships, but I was particularly struck by the realization of how difficult the death of a husband, son, or father would be for those left behind. Given their generations of work as high-altitude porters, this community has been profoundly affected by the deaths on Everest, of which nearly one-third have been Sherpas.

Flakes of snow laced the air as Conrad and I left the village and trod the muddy trail from Phortse to Namche Bazaar. "I want to do something here with the foundation," I proposed to Conrad.

"Let's do it," he enthused. "We can do a climbing school. The ice climbs here are a perfect way for them to learn the skills they need. And in winter, they aren't busy with work or their crops."

Farther down the trail, near the village of Lukla, Conrad and I had created our plan, and with great excitement we began to dream of a climbing school for the people of the Khumbu as we departed the Himalaya and traveled home.

Conrad began preparing for an expedition to Tibet. Rick Ridgeway, Jimmy Chin, and renowned adventure photographer Galen Rowell would be his partners. They hoped to traverse the Tibetan plateau known as the Chang Tang in search of the calving grounds of an endangered and elusive species, the chiru, or Tibetan antelope. If they could pinpoint the area, then safeguards could be put into place by the Chinese government to create a sanctuary and protect the threatened animals. Rick and Galen had garnered sponsorship from *National Geographic* for an article and film, but their biggest challenge would be to carry enough food and water to survive the uncharted crossing. A high-tech rickshaw had been specially designed using bicycle parts to carry their heavy loads, which far exceeded what was possible to carry on their backs. The journey would begin in Lhasa, crossing the vast high-altitude Chang Tang plateau over two mountain ranges and ending in the Taklimakan Desert: a three-hundred-mile trek with no points of resupply. They would carry a satellite phone but would have limited reception; Conrad would be largely out of touch for seven weeks.

When he departed in May, I fell into a rhythm of finishing my work for galleries, planting the garden, and ferrying the boys to soccer games and swim lessons. In late June we drove across Idaho and Washington to the tiny seaside town of Port Townsend for the music camp held in conjunction with its annual Festival of American Fiddle Tunes. At the edge of the Olympic Peninsula, Port Townsend's

Victorian seaport is an artists' community where music is celebrated through the summer. Jan and Murray had taken Max there when Alex was on Trango, and I decided to enroll all of the boys for an enriching week. Jan drove down from Bowen Island to join us for the many workshops with musicians as diverse as the many places they hailed from. We walked the sandy beach with the sounds of bluegrass, Cajun, Celtic, and Cape Breton fiddle music not far from our ears. Jan's cancer was once more in a state of remission, and with tears of joy I watched her accompany Max and Sam in their performance of "Red Haired Boy" on Talent Night.

Conrad arrived home from the Chang Tang exhausted beyond any other expedition he had undertaken, having hauled the heavy carts to a point of physical collapse on many days, operating with a minimum of calories and the additional strain of altitude. But their team had witnessed the migration and successfully pinpointed the birthing grounds of the chiru, providing crucial information for the protection of the species. "It was one of the most difficult things I've done," Conrad told me, "but one of the most rewarding."

For some time I had been thinking that a journey through Darwin's paradise would be the perfect way to celebrate life and my sister's birthday. "Jan," I asked sometime that summer, "would you like to go to the Galápagos Islands with me?"

Conrad and his sister Kim graciously cared for the boys for two weeks that autumn so Jan and I could make our journey. We witnessed nature's diversity in iguanas that swim and birds that don't fly, in finches with beaks of all sizes, tiny brilliant red crabs, and leggy pink flamingos. We crouched before enormous tortoises, snorkeled over the backs of giant elegant sea turtles, and dipped our kayak paddles into waves that lapped at the roots of mangroves. "This is so amazing!" Jan exclaimed on each unique landing, and I tried hard to hold on to her joy and the joy of our time together. The small schooner that carried us from island to island each day also lulled us to sleep by night on the rhythmic swell of the Pacific.

The following February, Conrad, the boys, and I set out on another stretch of ocean to realize one of our wildest dreams. Conrad would be a guest lecturer for Fathom Expeditions, and the children and I would be able to join him aboard an ice-rated ship with reinforced hull to tour the Antarctic Peninsula. Sailing to the southern continent, we would then follow in the footsteps of Shackleton to visit Point Wild on Elephant Island. Among the black zodiacs on our vessel was a small wooden boat, new and freshly painted, a replica of Shackleton's *James Caird*. Departing the southern tip of the continent was thrilling, setting out across the Drake Passage on an adventure that honored the great explorer. But it was especially poignant to be in the wilds that both Alex and Conrad had explored and cherished beyond anywhere they had been.

Alex was so enamored with Antarctica that he declared it his favorite place on the planet. He once told me that there are no words to adequately describe its pristine beauty and vastness. Just knowing that such a place exists on earth was solace to a wild soul like Alex. But to feel the bite of the katabatic wind and look upon an endless horizon of white, or to see a glacier as old as time march into the sea, calving great bergs with a crack and a roar—that was his heart's desire, and now it had become mine.

In 1995, Alex had written to Sam as he departed on the *Pelagic*:

> Hi Sam, there are lots of right whales in the ocean down here and we will most likely see a number of them on our crossing to Antarctica. We sail today—just a short way. Tomorrow we'll round Cape Horn and, if the weather cooperates, begin the 500-mile crossing of the Drake Passage. We can make the crossing in as little as four days, but if we must hove to and wait out strong wind, it can take seven to ten days. We will make our first landfall at Deception Island, an old volcanic island. I've seen several of the wandering albatross; their wingspan is the largest of any bird. I love you, Dad

When I spied my first wandering albatross, with great elegant wings reaching over the waves, I watched it with tearful reverence, knowing that the birds are dwindling in number and may disappear one day. When the children stood amid thousands of king penguins trumpeting their cries into the Antarctic wind, they grinned with glee; and when a pod of great fin whales rose from the sea to blow, all of us gasped in awe. Max wrote in his journal:

February 28: We steamed through the night to Deception Island and entered through Neptune's Bellows and into Whaler's Bay. We landed on a black volcanic sand beach near the old whaler's station and British Antarctic Survey station. The base was abandoned in 1964 when the volcano erupted. While there, I saw fur seals lying on the beach and gentoo penguins.

March 5: Today we were in King Haakon Bay, our first landing was at Cape Rosa where Shackleton landed after his long crossing of the Scotia Sea. It was amazing thinking of how overwhelmed with happiness these men would have been to see protected land after a week of nothing but huge seas. While ashore, I saw giant petrel chicks, nesting albatross and three light mantled sooty albatross. In the small, protected cove, there were also sea-lion pups playing in the clear water.

On Elephant Island, our small group went ashore at Point Wild to that bight of land where Shackleton's men had wintered over, living on chinstrap penguins. We stood among penguins and seals and stared out at hulking icebergs in the protected bay. "Look," Conrad said pointing to a small sailboat that was moored among them. Pelagic was written on the bow of the small boat which, from this distance, looked as fragile as the James Caird herself.

There we were in the vast southern ocean, and our path had fallen upon Alex's footstep. I stood where Shackleton and his men once stood, a marvel in and of itself, and stared out at the Pelagic, quietly bobbing on the swell. I had never laid eyes on her, but I knew of her retractable keel and her many voyages in these waters, and I knew that Alex had once stood upon her deck and lived within. As I stared across the bay

I saw people standing on deck, and for a moment I imagined one to be Alex, watching us from afar—knowing that Conrad and I were there, and happy in the knowledge that his sons were playing among seal pups in the shadow of great turquoise blue bergs and great men.

In the spring of 2005, Conrad and I sat in the worn wooden seats of Willson Auditorium to watch Max perform with his high-school symphony. I remembered Max as a wide-eyed six-year-old standing on the same stage. Alex and I had watched with lumps in our throats and cameras flashing as he sawed out "Boil the Cabbage" on his violin. I thought of all the times I made him practice when he didn't want to and the tears he cried, saying, "I don't want to be a musician. I'm going to fly jets." Alex practiced with him often. Bows gliding across strings in unison, they would play all of Max's simple tunes, and Alex would end by playing a favorite Bach sonata while Max looked on. And I thought of Max, brave and eloquent at age eleven, playing "Ashokan Farewell" at Alex's memorial service. He accepted the unknown with quiet resignation. Now at sixteen and six foot three, he was playing Mendelssohn's Symphony no. 5, "The Reformation." I thought of the transformation of boy to young man and all that had transpired in the course of his life, in the course of my own. How time slips by.

Alex had played viola in high school and joined the civic symphony in Missoula. He spoke of it as his fondest experience during high school. Music came easily so he didn't practice much, according to Dottie, but preferred to strum away on a guitar in his room. Sam, our middle son, does the same thing of late.

"Mom, I want an electric guitar," Sam announced at twelve.

"But Sam, you already play violin, and I want you to continue with that. We've put a lot of time and energy into it," I lectured while imagining the noise of a teenage rock band.

"I can play two instruments," he argued. "I'll pay for it myself and practice my violin more if you let me. Please, Mom." I finally agreed. Eventually I found a great deal of joy and pride in his twelve-year-old rendition of "Stairway to Heaven." When he learned Neil Young's "Old

Man," I was moved to tears; I remembered Alex playing the song for me years before. Jan was thrilled that Sam had taken up guitar.

That spring, cancer had reappeared in my sister Jan's chest cavity, constricting her esophagus. My entire family was consumed with worry as we kept tabs on the progression of her illness. Over the next nine months, she battled its grasp as cancer spread to her brain, lungs, and liver. With quiet dignity, Jan and Murray welcomed the alternating visits of concerned family and friends to their island sanctuary. Paula and I each left our families and traveled to her side on four occasions, and Camilla joined us there with Dad and Carol in the last week of Jan's life. I am ever grateful to Jan and Murray for sharing those precious weeks with all of us.

Losing my sister was every bit as painful as losing Alex had been. The grief was amplified by my mother's recent death, as I became the matriarch of my own family and felt a cumulative loneliness from each of their losses.

In Jan I had known a best friend and sister, a soul mate who was there from the very beginning of my life, and losing her in the autumn of 2005 was like losing a part of myself. Murray and I planned a memorial in Bozeman at the Springhill Pavilion, where Alex's service had been. A patchwork of family, friends, and musicians gathered there to remember Jan, in a room graced with her exquisitely sewn quilts and beautifully knit sweaters on that sad October day.

Death is ever present if we just take notice, I have realized. It happens each autumn as frost hits the garden. Lush tomato plants thick with fruit are transformed overnight into limp black tangles. The reds and yellows of autumn celebrate this cycle of life and death in a glorious last hurrah. With changing seasons I had always welcomed a coming and going of living things, knowing that with all birth comes death. I knew the equation from a young age. It seems an easy equation until love is robbed from your heart and nothing that unfolds before you is what you had planned. Max had arrived with the colors of fall, and Alex had departed with them. And now . . . Jan. As autumn slipped away and turned to winter, I knew that for me the season would always be an ominous reminder of life's bittersweet bargain.

In January 2006, Conrad, Isaac, and I returned to the village of Phortse to host the third year of the Khumbu Climbing School, accompanied by our Sherpa friends Chhongba and Dawa as well as a group of Western guides who were there to volunteer their time and expertise. When Conrad and Jon Krakauer had launched the first Khumbu school in the winter of 2004, thirty students had attended. The boys and I had hiked in to Phortse for a joyful graduation ceremony, celebrating our dreams of bringing the family to the Himalaya and launching the school.

Each year since the first had seen growth as word spread and more students applied. This year seventy-three enthusiastic students were arriving from villages near and far for instruction in technical climbing on rock and ice, wilderness survival, rescue and medical training, and classes in English and environmental ethics. Some of the original students now work as teachers and translators, their skills having improved each year.

Our hope is to empower our students with knowledge that will make their chosen vocation safer and more lucrative. To reduce the high mortality rate of these mountain people is our ultimate goal.

The plateau of Phortse rises above a birch forest where tiny musk deer and the colorful Danfe pheasant are abundant in thick underbrush. As we climbed dusty switchbacks through the forest, excited chattering could be heard from above. We arrived to greetings of "Namaste" and "Tashi delek" from an assemblage of residents dressed in their finest traditional garb, who had gathered at the edge of the village to receive our entourage. Smiling toothless elders and wide-eyed children peered from the crowd. Kata scarves were draped about our shoulders, and ceremonial chang, the local brew, was offered.

Isaac led the way into the pastoral village, whose residents we had come to know in these last years: Panuru, Danuru, Mingma and Pasang; Phunuru, Pemba, Rinji and Lhakpa, and all of their families. They felt like our own family now as we walked to the familiar lodge. The people we have come to know in this high village and those who have attended the school have given us so much more than we could hope to give them: a sense of purpose and belonging, a humility about how we live our own lives, and a deep appreciation for all that we have. Knowing of the hardships they face has diminished my own sense of loss by their example of fortitude. And we cannot help but think of Alex each time we come, of how much pride and joy he would have derived from this special project and place.

Several days later, Isaac and I hiked with a few good friends to visit Alex's chorten at Dugla. Isaac stomped on the frozen puddles along the way, and I remembered when I too loved to stomp on the ice that formed in winter puddles in Montana. Watching Isaac, I thought how strange it is that ice has assumed such a prominent place in my life. Ice in one form or another has always had a presence.

Isaac kept my pace, climbing steadily, skirting a scattering of enormous boulders as he moved up the last steep hill toward the chortens of Dugla. He looked to the sky and counted ten Himalayan griffons that soared above us. We sat in a breeze at the same place where Conrad and I had trekked four years before, and looked upon the letters that were carved into the rock: "ALEX LOWE, FRIEND." The black had worn from their forms. Isaac took a piece of charred wood in his fingers and whispered to me, "Can I color his name with this?"

"That's a great idea," I whispered back.

As I sat before the stone marker watching Isaac darken the letters, I thought of my last visit here. How raw the loss of Alex had been, and how I had ached for him. Now I thought of Mom and Dick and all the friends we had lost since Alex's death. I squinted, juniper smoke stinging my eyes, when I thought of my sister Jan, who had died just months before.

I pictured Jan in her hospital bed, reclining in the powder blue pajamas that accentuated her serene blue eyes, her tired eyes, weary of the struggle. I missed her desperately. I had looked into the blue eyes of my mother and, long before that, my grandmother as cancer consumed each of them. It did not seem fair. But death rarely seems fair, I suppose.

I remembered when my mother had tried to explain it to me as a child. "What?" I had protested. "Life ends? Everyone's going to die?

How can that be possible? That isn't fair." And she'd tried to explain heaven—that place that I could never quite conceive of. "I would rather just stay here," I told her. "I like it here."

When Isaac finished coloring the chorten, I hugged him to my chest. His life has been so different from mine, with death at his door as a three-year-old. Grief has become a familiar companion to all of our family. Once death arrived to take Alex, it always seemed to lurk nearby. Conrad and I have not lost sight of the urgency that we felt at his parting to live each day since, and I believe that our children also feel that urgency.

"Mom," Isaac said to me, "I like climbing, but I'm not going to be a mountain climber. It's too dangerous."

"You're right," I answered. "It is dangerous."

"I'm going to live in the rain forest and be a naturalist. I need to stay alive to try and save some of this planet for all of the other species that live on it," he told me.

"That's good—the world needs people like you," I replied, and hugged him tighter.

"Alex will melt out of the glacier one day," Reinhold Messner told me one evening at a dinner we shared, recounting the experience of his own brother, whose body had been yielded up from a glacier in Pakistan many years after he was swept away by an avalanche on the mountain. The thought had occurred to me, and I do not look forward to it. Conrad and I still plan to take a pilgrimage to Shishapangma to look upon the mountain where Alex lost his life, but for now I have grown used to knowing that he is part of the ice beneath that mountain far away.

I know now that his death was just the death of a man, but his life pushed me forward to live my own more fully. It pushed Conrad and me to live our lives together. And Alex is a part of each of the boys, just as Conrad and I have made our impact on who they are as they go forth into the world to live their own lives and the adventures that await them.

coda

"Mom, when are you going to be done with that book?" Isaac has asked with exasperation on more than one occasion, and I am ready to return to tending the garden of my life in the present. Isak Dinesen wrote that "all sorrows can be borne if you put them into a story," and it rings true. For me, the writing of *Forget Me Not* has delivered catharsis—perhaps in part because it has taken so long to write, and in the writing, life's joy has been recalled and rediscovered along with its sorrow. It has been my own summit of sorts. On a summit the entire world is beneath us, horizons are expanded, and clarity envelops our senses. It is this feeling that the mountaineer seeks, and perhaps it is the feeling that we all seek as we search for love and purpose in our own measured lives. In reaching for the summits of the heart and holding on to them, love and hope transcend the tragedy of our ultimate end.

I look forward to being more attentive to Isaac's needs and those of Sam, Max, Conrad, and the rest of my precious and extended family. And to my own needs. A certain black horse named Miss Chippy awaits my attention in her pasture overlooking this valley beneath the Bridger Mountains, where autumn has once again arrived in all of its glory.

acknowledgments

THIS BOOK WOULD NOT HAVE BEEN POSSIBLE without the unending love, encouragement, understanding, tolerance, and shared memories of my husband Conrad Anker and my sons Max Lowe, Sam Lowe-Anker, and Isaac Lowe-Anker.

For reading or listening to drafts over the last five years and providing valuable feedback and encouragement, I am extremely grateful to Dottie Lowe, Jim Lowe, Andy Lowe, Ted Lowe, Marie Lowe, Elise Lowe, Alex W. Lowe, Paul Daly, Carol Daly, Jan Daly, Murray Journeay, Paula Daly, Camilla Daly Haynes, Lester Madsen, Trish Madsen, Wally Anker, Helga Anker, Kim Anker Padden, Denise Anker, Steven Anker, Pamela Hainsworth, Suzanne Hainsworth, Maddy Pope, Chris Pope, Martha Collins, Joanne Dornan, Molly Merica, Emily Stifler, Krista Wright, Luanne Freer, Lila Bishop, Tara Bishop, Anne Sherwood, Tami Knight, Alice Phinney, and Rebecca Martin.

Special thanks to Hooman Aprin, Ken Kamler, George Lowe, Steve Swenson, Eric Winkelman, Michael Graber, Gordon Wiltsie, Doug Chabot, Jack Tackle, Mark Synnott, Greg Child, Greg Thomas, Kim Johnson, Lynn Hill, Pat Callis, Andrew McLean, Kris Erickson, and Steve Gipe for sharing their unique memories and views.

For their encouragement, companionship, and shared interest in reading, I'm also grateful to my book club members Martha Kauffman,

Sue Higgins, Carmen McSpadden, Melissa Blessing, Deidre Combs, Sunny Mavor, Louise Forrest, and Rienne McElyea.

I would like to thank all of my Bozeman community as well as the climbing and outdoor communities who stepped forward in the wake of Alex's loss, including John Tarlow, Holly Tarlow, Tom Bozeman, Pam Hiebert, Bill Belcourt, Meredith Wiltsie, Bill Simon, and Topher Gaylord. Unending thanks to each of the hundreds of people who took time to write messages of hope and condolence and to all of those who have given so generously. A special thanks to Terry Cunningham, Aaron Shuerr, and the U.S. Forest Service for their efforts in bestowing the honor of naming Alex Lowe Peak.

My sincere thanks to all of the individuals and companies who have supported and given generously to the Alex Lowe Charitable Foundation. A special thanks to Boojum Expeditions, Kent Madin, Linda Svendsen, Jonathon Knight, and the Mongolian Altai Club. Ongoing thanks to Chhongba Sherpa, Dawa Sherpa, Ang Tsering Sherpa, Adam Knoff, Karl Swingle, Per Saari, and all of the dedicated instructors who have made the Khumbu Climbing School possible. I offer my heartfelt thanks to all of the inspirational students and all of the people of the village of Phortse, Khumbu, in Nepal, with special thanks to all of the fine strong women.

For their immeasurable inspiration, advice, and encouragement, I thank Jon Krakauer, Greg Mortenson, Rick Ridgeway, David Quammen, Yvon and Malinda Chouinard, Tom Brokaw, Meredith Brokaw, Reinhold Messner, Caroline Alexander, George Butler, and Michael Brown.

I am grateful to the Banff Centre for the Arts and the Mountain Writing program, including Bernadette McDonald, Tony Whittome, Marni Jackson, Jon Bowermaster, Maria Coffey, Kim Csizmazia, Colin Wells, and Katie Ives, for promoting mountain writing and sharing their valuable insights.

This book came to be through the expert attention and devotion of the fine staff at Mountaineers Books. I am especially grateful to editor Kate Rogers, designer Mayumi Thompson, and project editor

Mary Metz. I'm enormously indebted to copy editor Sherri Shultz for her graceful insights and expert editing.

Thanks to John Paine for his initial edits of my proposal, to Susan Golomb for her initial encouragement and support as my literary agent, to Jon Mozes and Casey Panell and the rest of the staff at the Susan Golomb Agency.

In memory of Florence E. Daly, Dick Paddon, Seth Shaw, Hans Saari, Galen Rowell, Barbara Cushman Rowell, Charlie Fowler, Natalie Phillips, Marjorie Finch, Julie Culberson, and David Bridges—with thanks for their ongoing inspiration.

Reading Group Guide

FORGET ME NOT

A MEMOIR BY JENNIFER LOWE-ANKER

A Conversation with Jenni Lowe-Anker

Your husband, Alex Lowe, died in 1999; your memoir was published almost 10 years later. Why did the process take so long? Was it a struggle or cathartic to dig through these memories?

Forget Me Not was published in May of 2008, eight and a half years after Alex died. Although I kept some journals immediately after his death, I didn't actually begin to write the book for several years. I needed time to grieve, first for Alex and then for my mother who became ill and died eighteen months after Alex. I also felt protective of the boys in those first few years as they were very young and I was not ready to share our life with the public.

At first, I thought I would have a co-writer or ghostwriter but in investigating that possibility, I realized that I wanted more ownership of the story. I chose to use my own voice and began to write. Then my sister Jan became ill with recurring breast cancer in 2005 and lost her battle in September. Jan had been so supportive of my writing that I felt compelled to finish *Forget Me Not* for her; a writing residency at Banff Centre for the Arts helped me to get there. When I was able to concentrate on writing, I was immersed in recounting and reliving the life that Alex and I had shared, which was emotional. Certainly, it was both difficult and cathartic. It was painful but also wonderful. And, being a novice writer, it took me awhile to get the job done. I had to fit writing in around mothering, painting, and launching the Alex Lowe Charitable Foundation. There was also a healthy amount of travel and recreation mixed in.

As a visual artist by trade, how did you make the transition from using paints to using words to express yourself?

I think that visual artists have the ability to truly see the world in detail; I carry vivid images of places, people, and past events in my life. That has always helped me to imagine and create my artwork, and, as I began to write, it helped me to write descriptively about experiences that I had lived many years before. I often have a vision for a finished work of art before I begin to draw and paint. In writing my book, it was similar in that I had a vision for the story as a whole. I wanted it to do more than tell of my life with Alex—I wanted to take the reader on an adventure into our lives and I hoped readers might find in my vivid descriptions of experiences and places some similarities to their own lives.

On the surface, this book is about the life and death of a great mountaineer, Alex, but in it you also describe losing your mother and sister. What are the cumulative effects of death and grief, and how can your story help others?

My sister's death was no easier to process and accept than my mother's or Alex's had been. Each was painful in a unique way but I did learn how precious my own life was. I like to think that my story is about living life, and ultimately, death is part of life. We will all die and we will all experience loss and grief if we live long enough and risk loving someone. I think love is truly the biggest risk we can take. This is the sad and seemingly unfair truth about life. But at the same time, that painful reality is what makes each day precious. I feel more compelled to live each day to the fullest.

How has Conrad Anker—your husband, Alex's former climbing partner and close friend, and a renowned mountaineer in his own right—responded to your desire to write this book and remember Alex? A lot of emotions from all three of you are laid bare in these pages; what was that like for him?

Conrad was very loving and supportive as I delved into documenting my life with Alex. He encouraged me all along and offered his help in reading and editing, taking on household chores, and giving more of his time to the boys. I know I was not always easy to live with during the years that it took me to write *Forget Me Not* but Conrad was always understanding. The challenges of writing something so emotional were not easy to shake when I turned off the computer. It was hard on the boys and Conrad in that it took a chunk of my time that might have been spent with them. In the last months, Isaac routinely asked me, "Mom, when are you going to be done with that book?" That got to me. When writing, I was focused on my past life, so I wasn't always living fully in the present.

Conrad was Alex's best friend and climbing partner for seven years. In some ways that set them up as competitors and Conrad felt that Alex had been the alpha in their partnership. "He was top dog and I knew it," was how Conrad put it. But he had loved Alex too and he respected my desire to tell our story. For Conrad and me, love had grown out of the shared burden of grief for Alex and the challenge of going forward. Conrad's love arrived in my life like an incredible gift and he gracefully took the role of husband and father all at once. He cooked dinner and fed the kids many nights while I struggled to write one or two more pages and, after the book was published, he held down the fort while I traveled on book tour. I am deeply grateful to have him as my husband and partner.

Tell us about your personal connection to mountains and climbing. How has that connection evolved over time for you, during your life with Alex, in the wake of his death, and now married again to a climber?

I was born and raised in Missoula, Montana where rivers wind their way through mountain valleys to spill off of the continental divide. The Rockies were a fine place to grow up and I can't imagine living where I could not see mountains around me. In addition to year-round beauty in changing seasons, mountains are always there to remind you of which direction you are facing or traveling. They are comforting in their wildness and their solid and stately being just as the waves of the ocean are comforting in their rhythmic ride to shore. Growing up in Montana, I realized at an early age that standing on a mountain or high hill afforded a view that was better and more far reaching. My early association with mountains was always fun. They hosted summer picnics, visits to hot springs, horseback rides, camping trips, sledding, and skiing. We took family vacations to Yellowstone and Glacier National Parks and I developed a deep appreciation for our rugged Rocky Mountains and their diversity of life. When I was in high school, my friends and I liked to venture into the wild places around our city. We hiked to high pristine lakes and scrambled to the tops of local peaks. When introduced to rock climbing, I found it exhilarating; it seemed a natural step to feeling confident and skilled at navigating through the wild places that I loved.

Wanting to climb and travel to climb was something Alex and I shared during our courtship and in the early years of our life together. We were eager to explore faraway places and see the world. It was adventure and solace that both of us sought and found in the mountains, whether scaling warm golden granite or hacking our way up a frozen ice face. We shared sunsets in serene camps, toiled together up and down rocky trails and through deep snow to find summits of peaks and rock walls and frozen waterfalls.

I loved being in the mountains with Alex but as time went by, I found myself less interested in pursuing the summits that continued to be Alex's focus. When our oldest son was born, I felt a sort of self-preservation instinct kick in that I had not experienced before and the tops of mountains held even less appeal for me.

When Alex died, I was consumed with hate for the mountain that had lured him to her dangerous flanks but that was short-lived. I knew in my heart that mountains such as Shishapangma had played a huge role in shaping the character of the man I had loved.

Certainly, my decision to marry Conrad was one that required careful thought—it's risky to love but I decided it was worth the risk. Conrad vowed that he was finished with climbing mountains such as Shishapangma but he is still an avid climber and both of us live with the knowledge that life is precious and fleeting. Do I worry when Conrad goes on an expedition? Of course. But one thing I have learned is that we never know what is around a corner in life and we can't live very well if we are living in fear. Conrad and I share a common history of venturing out into wild places and the intensely rewarding feelings of meeting the challenges that mountains have posed.

A lot of this book is about passion—for your lover, for climbing, for painting, for your kids, for travel. How is it that you can maintain such passions at a high level?

I love and appreciate my life but I am not always on "high." I just plug away all the time and I dream big! I juggle lots of balls at once but I drop one every now and again. And that's okay.

Can you tell us what each of your three sons—Max, Sam, and Isaac—is up to these days? What qualities of Alex or Conrad do you now see in each of them? Which of your qualities do they share?

Max is attending Westminster University in Salt Lake City and traveled with his school to China last spring semester. He loves to ski, enjoys photography, and plays fiddle. He works part time teaching skiing and in the outdoor industry. As of this moment, I believe he plans to major in environmental studies or business or both. He is outgoing and has Alex's gift for engaging people. Max has followed Conrad's path in business and adopted his concern for the environment. He has my stubbornness and calm.

Sam is 16 and attending Bozeman High School. He is very focused on filmmaking and has won two awards for his short film, *Antarctica The End*, which traveled to over three hundred cities across the United States and abroad. He loves music and plays guitar in two bands and violin in his high school symphony. Sam also loves to ski and made a film called *Stay Alive* for our local ski area, Bridger Bowl, to earn his season pass this year. He documented the dangers of skiing out of bounds in cooperation with the Gallatin Valley Avalanche Center. Sam is very strong like Alex, and sensitive and caring like both Alex and Conrad. Like Conrad he is understated and quiet. He has tons of creativity like Conrad and me.

Isaac is 12, a seventh grader, and still very interested in being a naturalist. He loves every animal and is especially fond of wild birds. He keeps a lovely journal with sketches of his favorite wild birds. Isaac fills our backyard feeders and also tends to our cockatiel and three Barred Rock laying hens. In his room, he has a 48-gallon fish tank and a tarantula. He is learning to tie flies for fishing. He works for Montana Outdoor Science School, helping to care for their animals. Isaac also plays violin and piano and, like his brothers, he loves to ski. He is a cross-country runner and made it to nationals for the past two years. Isaac has lots of energy like Alex and is physically very similar to him. He has Conrad's silly streak and, like Conrad, he is very detail oriented. He shares my love for drawing and my soft spot for all creatures.

Do you plan to write another book? If so, what will it be?

Although I'm in no hurry, I have been thinking about the next book I will write. I grew up with three sisters in an extraordinary place called Montana and have lots of wonderful memories of that. My grandmother lived with three of her sisters in her later years and I cherish the time I spent with them, listening to the stories of their childhoods and their lives. I hope to juxtapose the two skipped generations of sisters in a way that shows the strength, competition, love, and mentorship of women in families and their relationships with the places that bind them together.

At the graduation ceremony of the Khumbu Climbing School in 2007, I shared the joy of the women and children of Phortse village. (Lowe collection)

Alex Lowe was one of the finest alpinists of his time, and he was a man who had remarkable rapport with the inhabitants of the lands where he ventured in order to climb. His compassion for the difficult lives led by these indigenous peoples is a continuing inspiration for those who knew and admired Alex.

The **Alex Lowe Charitable Foundation** (ALCF), founded by Jennifer Lowe-Anker in 1999, is dedicated to preserving Alex's legacy by providing direction and financial support to sustainable, community-based humanitarian programs in the world's remote regions.

Recognizing a need for increased technical competence among Sherpas and other Nepalis who work in mountain regions, the ALCF established the Khumbu Climbing School in 2003. The school offers the more than 50 men and women who attend annually, classes in climbing as well as English, leadership, mountain rescue, and wilderness medicine. The school's mission is to increase the safety margin of Nepali climbers and high altitude workers through encouraging responsible climbing and wilderness practices in a supportive community environment.

The ALCF has recently partnered with Room to Read and, under the direction of Liesl Clark, has launched the Magic Yeti Children's Libraries, bringing books and improved education to remote villages in Nepal.

Please visit www.AlexLowe.org to learn more.

Alex Lowe's love for a strong cup of coffee was legendary among fellow climbers. It is in this spirit that a partnership with Summit Coffee was born. The ALCF receives $1.00 for each bag of Climbers' Series coffee sold. Visit www.summitcoffee.com to learn more.

About the Author

JENNIFER LOWE-ANKER WAS BORN Jennifer Daly in Missoula, Montana. She spent parts of her childhood riding horseback around the Missoula Valley and across the fields of her great grandparent's homestead in Grasshopper Valley. A well-known artist, her paintings are rendered in the vivid color and rich texture of livestock markers, depicting whimsical images of a Western upbringing. Lowe-Anker began using the oily paintsticks while a student at Montana State University in 1984. Her work has been featured in gallery shows and exhibits throughout the West and hangs in private and corporate collections worldwide.

Lowe-Anker is founder of the Alex Lowe Charitable Foundation and resides in Montana with her husband Conrad Anker and their sons, Max, Sam, and Isaac. This is her first book.